THE COMFORT OF GOD

THE COMFORT OF GOD

Preaching in Second Corinthians

By

HAROLD J. OCKENGA, Ph.D.

Minister, Park Street Church, Boston
Author of "Every One That Believeth"

WIPF & STOCK · Eugene, Oregon

Wipf and Stock Publishers
199 W 8th Ave, Suite 3
Eugene, OR 97401

The Comfort of God
Preaching in Second Corinthians
By Ockenga, Harold John and Rosell, Garth M.
Copyright©1944 by Ockenga, Harold John
ISBN 13: 978-1-5326-7409-9

Publication date 2/22/2019
Previously published by Fleming H. Revell, Co., 1944

To
"A CERTAIN STARR"

SERIES FOREWORD

Harold John Ockenga: Voice of American Evangelicalism

HAROLD JOHN OCKENGA (1905–85) was one of the most remarkable individuals I have ever known. As a pastor and preacher, as a college president, as founder and president of two influential seminaries, as a popular writer of articles and books, as president of numerous organizations, and as one of the key leaders of the resurgent evangelical movement that swept across America and around the world during the mid-twentieth century, Ockenga's fame and influence were virtually unparalleled. "He was a giant among giants," reflected Billy Graham at Ockenga's funeral in 1985. "Nobody outside of my family influenced me more than he did. I never made a major decision without first calling and asking his advice and counsel. I thank God for his friendship and for his life."[1]

My own acquaintance with Ockenga came in 1978 when he invited me to join him as academic dean of the seminary where he was then serving as president. His passion for the spread of the Gospel around the world, his love for Christ and His church, his deep commitment to spiritual renewal, his compelling vision for what theological education needed to become, and his unquestioned life of integrity persuaded me to accept his invitation. While

---

1. Billy Graham, "Harold John Ockenga: A Man Who Walked with God," *Christianity Today*, March 15, 1985, 35.

working together at Gordon-Conwell Theological Seminary, Ockenga became my treasured mentor and friend. As we talked and prayed together, my appreciation for him deepened and my spiritual life was enriched.[2]

More than thirty years have passed since Harold John Ockenga walked among us.

Whole new generations have been born and have reached maturity with virtually no memory of this amazing leader and with only limited access to his most influential writings. The republication by Wipf and Stock Publishers of his major writings, including more than a dozen books and scores of articles, will now allow a new generation of readers to have access to the writings that helped shape an entire movement. Indeed, the book that you hold in your hands, like many of Ockenga's other publications, was eagerly read and put into action by the thousands of evangelical Christians who helped provide biblical guidance and fresh energy for mid-twentieth-century evangelicalism. With the appearance of this volume, by God's grace, it can once again provide guidance and fresh energy to a global movement in our own century—a movement that is increasingly in need of such godly guidance and wisdom.

Garth M. Rosell, Series Editor
Senior Research Professor of Church History
Gordon-Conwell Theological Seminary
South Hamilton, Massachusetts
January 1, 2017

---

2. Garth M. Rosell, *The Surprising Work of God: Harold John Ockenga, Billy Graham, and the Rebirth of Evangelicalism* (Grand Rapids: Baker Academic, 2008) 11–38.

FOREWORD

ORIGINALLY this series of sermons was to be called "Preaching in II Corinthians." However, as I worked over the material for publication the opening and closing words of the Epistle rang in my heart. "Blessed be God, even the Father of our Lord Jesus Christ, the Father of mercies, and the God of all comfort; who comforteth us in all our tribulation, that we may be able to comfort them which are in any trouble, by the comfort wherewith we ourselves are comforted of God. . . . Finally, brethren, farewell. Be perfect, be of good comfort, be of one mind, live in peace; and the God of love and peace shall be with you." The epistle was written with a fresh experience of God's comfort in Paul's troubled life. It depicts the comfort of God.

Paul suffered from some external attack or peril, so that he despaired of life. Paul was troubled within over the rebellion and sin in the Corinthian Church. Paul had a thorn in the flesh physically. Paul was accused of misuse of funds which he collected for the poor. Paul's apostleship had been questioned. Paul needed comfort from God if ever man did.

He received that comfort so that God always caused him to triumph in Christ. He was delivered from external danger, his message and prayers brought reform at Corinth, he was given grace for his infirmity, his request for money for the poor brought a great offering, and his apostolic authority was vindicated. God truly comforted him. His testimony was, "Thanks be to God, who always causeth us to triumph in Christ."

Multitudes are standing in need of such comfort today. Bereavement, separation, worry, fear, distress, loss, danger—all call for the comfort of God. As you read these struggles of Paul and the principles on which he won victory, God's comfort will be with you.

You will be surprised to find this one of the most evangelistic books in the Bible. Preaching through it will result in the salvation of many souls.

I wish to express appreciation to various publishers for permission to quote from their works, as noted. Also to Houghton Mifflin Company for permission to quote from "The Chambered Nautilus" by O. W. Holmes, and from *The Present Crisis* by J. R. Lowell. The quotation on page 12 is from R. C. H. Lenski's *Commentary on II. Corinthians.*

H. J. O.

Boston, Mass.

CONTENTS

		PAGE
I.	The Comfort Wherewith We Are Comforted of God (II Cor. 1:1-11)	11
II.	The Witness of a Good Conscience (II Cor. 1:12-14)	22
III.	"Yes and No" Men (II Cor. 1:15-20)	31
IV.	Anointed, Sealed and Endowed for Life On Earth and In Heaven (II Cor. 1:21-22)	40
V.	The Love Which I Have More Abundantly Unto You (II Cor. 1:23-2:4)	50
VI.	Unforgivingness, a Device of the Devil for the Destructon of Your Soul (II Cor. 2:5-11)	60
VII.	Christ and the Note of Triumph (II Cor. 2:12-14)	71
VIII.	That Which Sends Forth a Fragrance of Life and an Odor of Death, Who Is Competent to Explain? (II Cor. 2:15-17)	78
IX.	The Bible Every Man Will Read (II Cor. 3:1-5)	85
X.	The Old and New Testaments (II Cor. 3:6-11)	96
XI.	Removing the Veil (II Cor. 3:12-4:6)	107
XII.	The Prince of Darkness or the God of Light (II Cor. 4:1-6)	116
XIII.	His Suffering and Ours (II Cor. 4:7-18)	127
XIV.	At Home with God (II Cor. 5:1-9)	135
XV.	The Terror of the Lord (II Cor. 5:10-12)	147

		PAGE
XVI.	THE CHANCE OF BEGINNING AGAIN (II Cor. 5:13-19)	155
XVII.	AMBASSADORS FOR CHRIST (II Cor. 5:20)	166
XVIII.	WHO IS YOUR SUBSTITUTE IN THIS CONFLICT? (II Cor. 5:21-6:13)	175
XIX.	PERFECTING HOLINESS IN THE FEAR OF GOD (II Cor. 6:14-7:1)	185
XX.	REPENTANCE UNTO SALVATION (II Cor. 7:2-12)	195
XXI.	A MAN WHOSE PRESENCE WAS A COMFORT (II Cor. 7:13-16; 8:16-24)	206
XXII.	MOTIVATING YOUR MERCIES (II Cor. 8:1-15; 9:1-5)	215
XXIII.	THE CHEERFUL GIVER WHOM GOD LOVES (II Cor. 9:6-15)	221
XXIV.	THE WEAPONS OF OUR WARFARE (II Cor. 10:1-6)	229
XXV.	THE COMMENDATION OF GOD (II Cor. 10:7-18)	237
XXVI.	THE USE MEN MAKE OF THE DEVIL'S MASK (II Cor. 11:1-15)	244
XXVII.	JUST A PLAIN FOOL FOR CHRIST'S SAKE (II Cor. 11:16-33)	256
XXVIII.	THORNS IN THE FLESH (II Cor. 12:1-10)	263
XXIX.	NOT YOURS, BUT YOU (II Cor. 12:11-19)	270
XXX.	EXAMINE YOURSELVES, WHETHER YE BE IN THE FAITH (II Cor. 12:20-13:1-10)	277
XXXI.	PEACE, THE GIFT OF GOD'S LOVE (II Cor. 13:11-14)	282

I

THE COMFORT WHEREWITH WE ARE COMFORTED OF GOD

TEXT: *"Blessed be God, even the Father of our Lord Jesus Christ, the Father of mercies, and the God of all comfort; who comforteth us in all our tribulation, that we may be able to comfort them which are in any trouble, by the comfort wherewith we ourselves are comforted of God."*—II COR. 1:1-11.

THE SECOND EPISTLE to the Corinthians is the playground of Higher Criticism. Here this deadly method which originated in reference to solving the problem of the Old Testament comes into full play and manifests its inevitable results, its destructive nature. Higher Criticism originated with Julius Wellhausen, although it had its roots in movements which were one hundred years older than Welhausen. He, however, supplied the hypothesis which was able to correlate the theories and suppositions of other workers upon the Old Testament and to popularize them so that the last fifty years has been dominated by this theory. Thus Wellhausen may be called the father of Higher Criticism. The method of Higher Criticism is to dissect a book into different parts, supposedly written by different authors and later compiled into one book.

For illustration, the Pentateuch is supposed to have been written by many different authors, one in particular using Jehovah for God and another Elohim for God. According to the critics it is not supposed to have been compiled in its present form until the time of the exile or a thousand years after Moses is said to have written it. The criticism is based upon evolutionary naturalism and rearranges the books and teachings of the Bible in accordance with the evolutionary view of man's developing idea of God and God's righteousness.

Applied to the second epistle to the Corinthians, we have a very clear illustration of Higher Criticism's folly. The epistle has three parts. Part one is chapters 1-7, part two, chapters 8 and 9, part three, chapters 10-13. Tradition has always made the epistle a unit, but the three divisions are quite distinct one from another in topic matter and therefore have given rise to many theories concerning their origin. First it was said that chapters ten to thirteen were not a part of II Corinthians, were not even Pauline, although some radical critics declared them to be a separate epistle of Paul which was a philippic or a denunciation of his opponents. Then it was advanced that chapters eight and nine cannot belong together and were not part of the epistle. Next, chapter 6:14 to 7:1 was declared to be interpolated and not to be a writing of Paul. Finally the whole epistle was turned into a mosaic and made a very late compilation. It simply means that we have no epistle left to interpret to you at all. This shows that once a man launches on this practice of higher criticism, of placing himself as an authority above the Word of God, he soon comes to the place where he has no Bible left at all. It reduces the method to an absurdity and yet it is pursued by many in spite of the fact that we have not the slightest textual evidence to support criticism. Every manuscript of the Bible that was ever found gives us the second epistle to the Corinthians exactly as we have it today.

There is a real unity to this grand book and any one who will sit down and read it in the light of the Pauline relationship to the Corinthian Church will grasp that unity. It has been an experience of joy for me to find a recent Lutheran expositor unequivocably declaring this unity of this epistle of Paul. He expresses what has been my opinion for a long time:

"In part one Paul writes about his happiness, because, as Titus reports, matters are clearing up in Corinth, and Paul adds to this clearing up. In part two we see Paul's concern regarding the matter of the great collection. This is beginning to move forward again, and Paul writes to speed it forward successfully now, sending Titus and new additional brethren for this purpose. This leaves Paul's arrival which is to follow two or three months later. Paul writes about it in part three, tells of his fears, of what he does not want to meet unless he absolutely must, and in order that the last opposition to him may be removed writes at length about himself in a way that seems foolish to him, yet is necessary under the circumstances. Thus, as Zahn writes, 'The three sections of the letter treat respectively, the immediate past with its misunderstandings and explanations, the present with its practical problems, and the near future with its anxiety.'"

The epistle to II Corinthians is exceedingly valuable to us because it reveals to us the inward feelings and motives of the Apostle Paul. Here he lays bare his heart and reveals a compelling love, a fervent emotion which saturates even the sterner sections of the epistle. Of this great love our first exposition will be an adequate example. In the introduction an interesting contrast is made in the title which

Paul claims for himself, namely, "Apostle of Jesus Christ," and the title he gives to Timothy, namely, "the brother." The contrast implies that Paul himself is assuming all responsibility for that which is written and that he is speaking as an Apostle commissioned by God through the Lord Jesus Christ. It is a picture of Christ's ambassador, revealing his master as a representative man. On the other hand, the inclusion of Timothy is beautiful because Timothy had labored with Paul in the founding of the Corinthian Church, and though he was not an Apostle, but had the same status as the Corinthian believers themselves, there was a particular appeal from a brother in Christ. The letter itself was written to the saints, not those made perfect in holiness, but those with a new standing in Christ Jesus, sanctified by the indwelling Spirit and launched upon the Christian way.

To these, after his usual greeting, Paul declared the great comfort and consolation which had come into his life in contrast with the great tribulation and affliction which he had endured. Perhaps you thought that the word "comfort" was used redundantly in our text, but in five verses Paul mentions this great word, the root of which means the Comforter or Paraclete, ten distinct times. How wonderful it will be if we can understand the available source of comfort in the life of the believer. This particular word "comfort" is sometimes translated "console" and "consolation." It might even be translated "cheered," for there is that active meaning placed in it. Perhaps a word halfway between consolation and cheer would be encouragement. What a need there is of this comfort, encouragement and cheer in our world today!

Recently I called on one of our members who was sharing a hospital room with another woman. Just as I was about to pray, as is my custom in the sick room, I was introduced to this other woman and to her husband, who was present with her. Immediately her eyes filled with tears, her lip began to tremble and she blurted out the story of the loss of her little baby just a few days before. Then being able to contain herself no longer, she was convulsed with heart-breaking sobs. Her husband did his best to comfort her until I was able to bring the consolation of the Word of God. It makes no difference where we are in life or what our position, sooner or later we will need the consolation of God. All that others can say or do will mean nothing if we have not this. I repeat that these are days when men need comfort, encouragement from God. I have been reading the books of Rauschning, the German fugitive, who has attempted to analyze the Nazi movement for the enlightenment of thinking men. In his latest book, he speaks of the loneliness and the suffering and the despair of those fugitives who formerly had prominent positions and were leaders in a great nation, but now are gradually sinking down into the proletariat. Not only the fugitives from Germany, but millions of other men and women today need the encouragement and comfort of God. Therefore, it is with a sense of mission that I declare unto you these wonderful words of Scripture concerning the source, the purpose and the means of our comfort, our encouragement and our cheer in life's affliction.

I. THE SOURCE OF COMFORT

Paul designates God as "the Father of our Lord Jesus Christ, the Father of mercies and the God of all comfort." His thought begins with God, the triune God, who is the source of all good. In the very greeting of Paul, "Grace to you and peace from God our Father, and the Lord Jesus Christ," he declares that the two are made one source of grace and peace and are placed on an equality. Both names express the revelation which these Persons have made of themselves in connection with the work of saving us. And though the greeting is very brief it constitutes the basis of the entire Biblical and Christian theology. Thus also, when Paul says, "Blessed be God, even the Father of our Lord Jesus Christ" it is to give the declaraton of our Savior God, for we realize that in Jesus' human nature God was His God and for Him in His Deity God is His Father from all eternity. This God is the source of all compassion and comfort for the believer.

He is called the Father of our Lord Jesus Christ. The revelation of God as a Father was distinctly made by Jesus. It is true that in the previous conception of God He was once called Father, but in general He was considered as the Creator, the Judge and the altogether distant One, so much so that the Jews were reluctant even to pronounce the name of God and thus ultimately forgot what that Name was. Today we cannot even intelligently pronounce what the original name for Jehovah really was. God was holy, unapproachable, transcendent, and to be propitiated, before the day of Jesus, but in Jesus there came a distinct change in the conception of God. Jesus claimed that He declared God or exegeted Him. He showed Him to be a God of fervent love, of long-suffering and of kindness, a redeeming God, one whom He called Father. He even taught His disciples to pray, "Our Father who art in heaven." Necessarily, one would not think of God as Father without the factual revelation of the Trinity, especially through the Lord Jesus Christ. Since the time of Christ, the Christian experience of God has always primarily been one of Father. We are His children through faith in Christ. We are adopted into His family by regeneration. It is not true that we were all the children of God and that God is the Divine Father of all before we become Christians. Only the believer has the privilege of calling God Father. How natural, however, is this term in Paul's referring to God. God was his Father.

The first words of Paul were praise to the Father God. Said he, "Blessed be God the Father." This is the necessary and right attitude to God, that is, one of thanksgiving and praise. To bless God in the midst of many good things is easy, but to bless God in the midst of affliction and suffering, as Paul did, is not quite so easy, especially if we recognize God the Father to be the source of all things. With this thought of God, however, the flow of emotion in the fervent heart of Paul was revealed and we first sense that which runs through the whole epistle. Word had just come from Corinth, by means of Titus, that Paul's first epistle had been accepted and that many of the difficulties in that church were being corrected. Hence, Timothy and Paul shared their emotion of praise over what God had done and they testified to the mighty comfort of God which had come to them in their general tribulation.

The next title given is, "The Father of compassion" or "pity." This reminds us of the verse in Psalm 103, "Like as a father pitieth his children, so the Lord pitieth them that fear him." This picture of God as Father stands in the midst of praise for the great common blessings or mercies which are received from God, that is, healing from disease, life itself and all the blessings attendant upon life. It is a recognition that God sends the rain upon the just and the unjust, the sunshine upon the good and the evil. God bestows His common benefactions upon us all. The title unquestionably describes the tender feeling of God towards men and His willingness to do good unto them, a conception which was needed by the Corinthians as much as by Paul and Timothy. But this is not the only side of God's nature. Many people like to hear about the God of compassion and the God of pity, but they are not willing to accept the conception of the God of holiness and of judgment which is expressed in wrath. No such unbalanced thinking may be attributed to Paul. God for him was the source of every blessing, but also was the source of judgment and chastisement.

The mercies spoken of here by Paul seem to me to be not so much the common mercies of life as the special mercies referred to in the book of Romans, when he said, "I beseech you therefore brethren by the mercies of God that ye present your bodies a living sacrifice." Those mercies referred to were God's sending of His only-begotten Son to become a substitute for us, to bear the curse of the law and to make an exhibition of God's justice upon Calvary that God might remain just and yet be the justifier of sinful men. The first mercy there declared is the mercy of God's justification of the sinner. Then he declares the mercy of the new life is in Christ Jesus, that of grace, of hope, of love. Again he declares God's mighty mercy in the provision for our sanctification by the gift of the Holy Ghost. And finally the mercy which is in God's plan for universal salvation of both the individual and the world. By these mercies Paul was able to plead with men. God's greatest compassions and comfort are always manifested through the Lord Jesus Christ, for the entire Gospel is soteriological, that is, deals with our salvation.

Here, as in the epistle to the Romans, these mercies must be acknowledged by the saints, presenting themselves as a living sacrifice to the God of compassion and mercy and comfort. Paul so dedicated himself that he passed the sentence of death on himself that he might no longer trust himself but only on God who raised him from the dead. He was ready to meet tribulation, because he knew that the Father was with him.

Finally, Paul speaks of God as "the God of all comfort." Literally, this is the God of comforting. Fatherhood and comfort are brought together. No one has the ability to comfort as a parent can comfort its child. Usually we think of a mother comforting her child, but the father is truly as great a source of comfort and encouragement as a mother. Hence, God for Paul was the source of understanding. He could go to God in his affliction and his distress and know that he would be relieved. God was the God of help. As a doctor removes the cause of distress or the weight of oppression from a patient, so the Father is able to help His children. He was the God of security and while God was present there was no need of fear. The very Divine attributes contributed to this, for God knew all the conditions. God was able to perform His will in connection with these conditions, and we have the source of our comfort, encouragement and cheer in the God and Father of our Lord Jesus Christ, the Father of mercies and the God of all comfort.

II. THE PURPOSE OF OUR COMFORT

This comfort available is expressed in the following words, "Who comforteth us in all our tribulation, that we may be able to comfort them which are in any trouble, by the comfort wherewith we ourselves are comforted of God." We suggest first that this purpose is expressed in our knowledge that tribulation and comfort go together in Christ. Hear the word, "For as the sufferings of Christ abound in us, so our consolation also aboundeth by Christ." Tribulations will come to the believer. If we are heirs of God we shall be heirs of His suffering as well as of His glory. God evidently permits tribulation to come to us for several purposes. We must know tribulation in order to be able to give comfort, for unless we ourselves have been comforted of God how can we ever comfort others? One need only read Paul's and Timothy's experience in Asia, which is described as being pressed out of measure, above strength, insomuch that they despaired even of life and passed the sentence of death in themselves, that they might not trust in themselves but in God who raised the dead, to realize what a terrible affliction they must have passed through. We think that we cannot identify this with the persecution raised by Demetrius the silversmith in Ephesus, for Paul in another place said that he fought with the beasts at Ephesus. Thus he may have had a much more severe trial than that which is mentioned in the Acts, but whether it was persecution or danger of death or mere opposition by other believers, Paul learned that God could comfort him in the midst of his tribulations. This kind of tribulation which repeats itself in the lives of ministers and people today brings them together in true fellowship and harmony.

The second purpose of tribulation is the sanctification of the believer. That God should make men perfect as He did the Captain of our salvation through suffering is rejected by such men as H. G. Wells, who puts into the mouth of Noah in his conversations with Almighty God a complaint that God permits the righteous to be afflicted and to suffer in this world. But as Christ suffered for us, so the sufferings of Christ will abound in us. The very sufferings of Christ on the Cross will be continued in His Church. It does not mean that Christ suffers in us today, but that we are completing the sufferings of Christ and for the sake of Christ in the world. Jesus said, "If the world hate you, ye know that it has hated me before you." What happened to Christ will in a measure also happen to us. His sufferings and His consolation will be repeated in us. Paul said,

"I rejoice in my sufferings for you, and fill up that which is behind of the afflictions of Christ in my flesh, for his body's sake, which is the church." As He is, so are we in this world, and as He suffered so we shall have tribulation.

But our joy is that comfort is available for us as it was available for Christ, and the very nature of our relationship to Christ is that the comforting will correspond to our suffering. Was Christ strengthened, encouraged and cheered in all of His trials, such as Gethsemane and Calvary? Then as God comforted Him we also may be comforted by God. Hence we read, "It behooved him to be made like unto his brethren, that he might be a merciful and faithful high priest in things pertaining to God, to make reconciliation for the sins of his people. For in that he himself hath suffered being tempted, he is able to succor them that are tempted." The connection, however, between our comfort and our tribulation is Christ and thus the God of comfort or the God of Christ is our God because of the mediator.

When one Christian suffers, others suffer, and we become partakers of their sufferings. If one Christian is consoled, so shall all be consoled and partake of the consolation. If, therefore, we partake of the sufferings of the body of Christ you may be sure that in compensation we will have the consolations of God.

The second purpose in our tribulation is that we may comfort those who are in any trouble by this same comfort wherewith we are comforted of God. God uses those whom He comforts to transmit His consolations to others who are in trouble. There are disease, material loss, crippling of the body and death itself. Many are the kinds of trouble. Thus Jesus said, "Blessed are they that mourn: for they shall be comforted." If you would comfort those in trouble it must be with the comfort of God. This encouragement or comfort is really being done by God, although human beings are His agents, such as Paul and Timothy were. There is a mighty gulf existing between the hollow comforting by one who has not the comfort of God but who has passed through the same experience of bereavement and trial and who can only tell what he feels as he went through it and the comfort which is from God through a believer. The first is idle, inefficient, hollow and void. The second, in bringing God and God's divine comfort through Christ into the life of a sufferer, is able to comfort effectively. All other comfort or comforters are a sham. Beloved, if you would find your comfort, your cheer or your rest, draw your strength and your comfort from God. What a blessedness there is for those who are able thus to comfort the sorrowing and the troubled in this world! This thought enables us to endure affliction gladly in preparation for a wider ministry as the representatives of God.

The third purpose in our affliction and tribulation which God permits to come is that it is for the salvation and the comfort of others, that is, the church. The first and the most important part in our affliction is the salvation of others. Paul says, "Whether we be afflicted, it is for your consolation and salvation." All that he endured, the peril of the elements, the peril of the sea, the peril of robbers, the suffering of scourging, fasting, cold, hunger, nakedness, many travels and finally death, was to bring the message of salvation unto others. What a contrast between what God expects us to bear for others and what we are willing to bear. Many of us profess to be the servants of God, but are grossly surprised when affliction comes to us, yet we are told that by much tribulation we must enter into the kingdom of God, that is, of course, the ultimate form of the kingdom. Our affliction, then, in many cases, excluding the affliction which God sends to us because of the need of chastenment for our own sins, is for the salvation of others. We also note here that the first part of comfort for those receiving comfort is salvation. He says, if we are afflicted it is for our comfort and salvation. Without salvation there can be no comfort. Unless a man is saved from his sins and the burden and guilt of them he cannot begin to know the comfort of God, for only grace and peace of God can come to men in their salvation, but once saved, this comfort, with its embodiment of encouragement and cheer, is in the midst of our affliction enabling us to endure unto the end. To have this mighty example of Paul and Timothy being comforted in enduring what God asked of them, which is probably far more than will ever be asked of any of us, will impart confidence, courage and cheer to us in the bearing of our burdens, for God is able to comfort us in like manner.

III. THE MEANS OF OUR COMFORT

This Divine consolation and comfort is extended to us in three ways; first, by the Person of Christ. "Our consolation also aboundeth by Christ." We have made plain before that Christ is the mediator between God and the believer in this Divine comfort. God comforts us, but only through the truth and the work of Christ, as the mediator between God and man. Unless one has truly seen the sufferings of Christ and partaken of them he will not know the consolation which is in Christ Jesus. Truly, if we are to be heirs of God and joint heirs with Christ we shall be heirs not only of His glory but also of His sufferings. Both the sufferings of Christ and the consolation which is in Christ will be repeated in us. Therefore, Christ is truly the source of succor, strength and deliverance to all believers in need of comfort. We may truly say that Christ is the archtype of the Christian and as He was so are we in this world. The living Christ abiding in us is able to make personal the means of our comfort.

The second means of comfort is our trust in God. Paul said, "We had the sentence of death in ourselves, that we should not trust in ourselves, but in God which raiseth the dead, who delivered us from so great a death." There is an open confession that Paul had needed an experience which would bring him low, so that he would cease to trust in himself and would trust in Almighty God and in Him alone. Unquestionably, this experience came to him providentially at the very moment when he was having trouble with the Corinthian Church. He had been disciplining that church. He had been asserting his apostleship and he may have fallen into the error of trusting in himself and in his mighty position, but here he tells us that the experience which befell him led him to trust only in God. What the nature of that experience was we are not told. It seems to us that it goes beyond anything that is related in the Acts. It may have befallen him at Troas. At any rate, Paul and Timothy came to the point in their lives where they were so oppressed and weighed down that they absolutely despaired of life and believed that death was certain. They went so far as to pass the sentence of death in themselves, believing that their only hope was now in being raised from the dead. And yet in the midst of that experience when they were pressed beyond measure, above all strength and power which they had in themselves, God mightily delivered them. Perhaps it is well that we do not have the experience related for us, for we might be laying too much emphasis upon it. All we know is that God delivered them, does deliver and will deliver. Paul had such a confidence and it became to him the source of mighty consolation. For those who will rest wholly in God, placing their trust absolutely in Him, there will always be this confidence of one who is able and willing to deliver.

The third means of our comfort is the Holy Spirit. Commentators are agreed that the comfort spoken of here is not of a nature to be appropriated at one's discretion, but only as the operation of the Spirit who is the true source of mercy and of consolation. The Holy Spirit is called by Jesus, the Comforter, or the Paraclete. The word used here for comfort by Paul is, *parakaleo*. Ten times, then, the name of the comforter is used in this passage. That is not without meaning. Paul here unquestionably intended to call to our attention the fact that if we would have the Divine comfort it must be through the Comforter. Remember that when Jesus said to His disciples, "Let not your heart be troubled. Ye believe in God. Believe also in me," He went on to say that He was going to leave them and in leaving them He would send them another Comforter, one who would do His work, who would give them peace, who would guide them, who would teach them all things and who would ever be with them. Therefore, they should not let their hearts be troubled. Now, this Comforter was actually sent by Jesus at Pentecost. So Peter said, "Having received of the Father the promise of the Holy Ghost, he hath shed forth this, which ye now see and hear." That Comforter now works in the believer, to do God's good pleasure. The Spirit working as Comforter enables the distraught soul to find peace, giving assurance of forgiveness in the midst of great conviction. The Spirit enables the impotent believer to receive Divine help in his infirmity. The Spirit enables believers in all difficulties to trust God, and gives guidance in bewilderment. He gives teaching in ignorance. He gives Divine Presence in loneliness. Thus, by the Person of Christ, by a trust in God and by the possession of the Spirit, we may receive this great comfort.

The reception and experience of the comfort was partly dependent upon the prayers of these Corinthians for Paul. He said, "Ye also helping together by prayer for us, that for the gift upon us by the means of many persons thanks may be given by many on our behalf." Further deliverance, further comfort, further confidence were all to be expected by Paul because of the prayers of Christian people. Here is an example of the blessed opportunity of a Christian ministry of any believer, for God's servants, whether preachers, missionaries, or laymen, and of the bond which unites us together in our dependence upon God and one another. "Blessed be God, even the Father of our Lord Jesus Christ, the Father of all mercies, and the God of all comfort; who comforted us in all our tribulations, that we may be able to comfort them which are in any trouble, by the comfort wherewith we ourselves are comforted of God." Let not your heart be troubled.

II

THE WITNESS OF A GOOD CONSCIENCE

TEXT: *"For our rejoicing is this, the testimony of our conscience, that in simplicity and goodly sincerity, not with fleshly wisdom, but by the grace of God, we have had our conversation in the world."*—
II COR. 1:12-14.

CONSCIENCE IS THE WORM that never dies. It is the flame that will never be quenched. Conscience is as positive and distinct a fact in man's moral history as is the morning star in the sky.

What is conscience? Conscience is the faculty of the soul for self-judgment as to the moral quality of its actions, whether good or bad, taken together with a sense of obligation to do what is right. Judgment is a work of the intellect in discerning the relations between objects, the judgment of conscience being the relation of acts or qualities to a certain standard of right and wrong. This judgment may be passed on others, as well as on self, but its moral significance rests only in the self-approval or self-condemnation of our own action. Such a thing as social conscience exists when we sit in judgment upon the actions of our fellows. This social conscience is the developing moral standard among men, and it also conditions the individual conscience. When we speak of conscience it is in reference to the self-approval or self-condemnation which is an inalienable part of life and without which existence would be utterly different from that which we know it to be today.

What is the ground of conscience? The ground of conscience is a sense of obligation, and it is this which makes conscience important. In all matters of right and wrong man affirms that he must do the right. He has a sense of oughtness which is inborn in him. He knows that he has certain duties. Duty is not a dream. The sense of ought is not fiction. The moral authoritative imperative may be perverted but it may not be destroyed. Thus right and duty are correlative and to know the right is to possess the duty to perform the right. The fact of the sense of duty is universal to men and this rests back upon conscience. In these judgments of self, man ascertains the degree of respect which he can hold for himself. If his conscience approves him, he may have self-respect. If it disapproves him, he will have self-aversion.

Conscience, then, is grounded in the personality of man. This sense of obligation inheres in personality. A person is so constituted that he ought. Personality includes the power of rational judgment. Rational judgment implies the duty of judging as truly as it is possible and then the necessity of action. The power of acting on rational and worthy grounds cannot exist without the duty to act. If a person possesses the power to distinguish between right and wrong he also possesses the duty to act in accordance with the right.

Therefore, we press the sense of ought to a deeper ground than that mentioned in personality alone, namely, on the nature of God Himself. In this great universe there is a rationality expressed in universal mind which may be called God. From this ultimate personality the personality of man is derived. If God is a personality then the sense of ought exists in God and it is in conformity with His absolute and perfect goodness which rests in His own nature and which is the ultimate standard for all character and all goodness. Therefore, in the Person of God whose image in personality and in moral agency man bears, we have the ultimate source of ought. Thus, after the rationalist Kant has bowed God out from all of his philosophical thinking, he realized that, in some way, he had to account for the sense of ought in man's life. Therefore, he said that there must be a lawgiver on whom the sense of ought is grounded and that lawgiver can be no other than God.

The standard of conscience must be some test or norm of right and wrong. What is it that makes right right and wrong wrong? The ultimate standard of this can rest only in the perfect goodness as it exists in God Himself. One cannot think of an infinite God without perfect goodness. This goodness, then, becomes the standard of the judgment of right and wrong as it is found in man. Everything unlike God Himself shall be judged in man. The revelation of this standard of perfect goodness was given to us in the law, in the person of Christ and in the gospel. Universally, man's moral judgment assents to the righteousness of the law and of the person of Christ. However, we are told in the Scriptures that this work of God was also written on the constitution of man. It may have been dimmed by sin or perverted and warped, but it can never be wholly lost. It will vary greatly as a standard between different individuals because of this dimming of the knowledge of God's righteousness, but the standard of self-judgment for any individual will be the highest and best that he knows. The Bible is universal in declaring that this will be the standard of his ultimate judgment. Those "which have not the law, do by nature the things contained in the law, these, having not the law, are a law unto themselves: which show the work of the law written in their hearts, their conscience also bearing witness, and their thoughts the meanwhile accusing or else excusing one another." Jesus said, "And that servant, which knew his lord's will, and prepared not himself, neither did according to his will, shall be beaten with many stripes. But he that knew not, and did commit things worthy of stripes, shall be beaten with few stripes." It is axiomatic that obedience to conscience or to the best which one knows is the easiest way of receiving further enlightenment and clarification of the standard of right and wrong.

The correlate of conscience and of obligation is free agency. Both conscience and obligation would lose their meaning without free agency of man. The theologian A. A. Hodge said:

"A man acts from the springs of his own active power. . . . He can never be made to will what he does not himself desire to will. . . . His desires are not necessarily either rational or righteous, but are formed under the light of reason and conscience, either conformable or contrary to them, according to the permanent, habitual dispositions of the man, that is, according to his own character."

A man acts according to his desire, which may be reasonable and righteous or may not be, but he has the freedom to act. Man must have the power to choose to act if he is to have a responsible life. Without this we could not speak of conscience or of obligation. Man is the one in the midst of all appetites, desires, convictions and judgments who determines what he will do and who puts his determination into effect. This determination is the power of the will. Man is free to decide whether and how he will act, although there are certain external compulsions to this will. Much enters into every man's life which lies beyond the sphere of his volition, such as, his birth, his parenthood, his country, his physical health and numerable other things. These all affect his will and are somewhat of compulsion. Moreover, the very disharmony of man's internal power often hinders his will, so that it cannot act. He may be torn between two desires but we affirm that he is free to decide whether and how he shall act. Conscience depends upon personality, upon God, upon a standard of goodness and upon free agency, all of which are taught in the Bible and are confirmed in universal human experience.

I. The Essence of a Good Conscience

Paul speaks of "the testimony of our conscience, that in simplicity and godly sincerity . . . we have had our conversation." This word "conversation" comes from a Greek word which is equivalent to the German word *wandeln,* meaning to walk or to behave oneself. It really designates a mode of life or of conduct. Thus conscience, whether good or evil, is connected with a life or a mode of living, a conduct of oneself. It is bigger than merely talking. It embraces the whole of one's life. Evidently Paul was certain that conscience bore a good testimony or an approving testimony to the kind of life and behavior in which he indulged. Paul was able to face himself, others and God with a clear conscience for his actions. Whenever there is conflict between one's manner of life and his conscience his is a case of a house divided against itself. It is a source of weakness, of neurosis and of defeat in his experience.

Could you testify to a good conscience concerning your conduct in this world? Does that harmony exist in your life between your moral judgment and the standard of the best which you know for yourself and others? Recently a lady brought her son to me on a certain problem. In the midst of my conversation with him she said, "You had better lecture the mother also, because she simply is not living up to the knowledge which she has." Here was a woman who openly confessed that in her own life she had this conflict between a standard of righteousness and the kind of life which she was living. There can be no peace in such an individual's life, whether it refers to his social contact, his business life or his personal actions.

There is a difference, however, between the actions of conscience in a regenerate and an unregenerate man. In an unsaved man the standard of goodness is more or less perverted, dimmed and deteriorated, but it is still sufficient to condemn him. For those whose personal standard is greatly perverted it is necessary to preach the law of God and the righteousness of God revealing His requirements for man. Once this is seen, the man knows that he is not right with God, has an inner clash between God's goodness and His sinfulness which makes him very miserable. In the saved, the indwelling, living Christ restores the Divine standard and likeness. The conscience becomes purged from dead works, in which the individual formerly trusted, to service for the living God. It is turned from a perversion to the true knowledge. The interesting thing is that a conscience in a Christian becomes more and more tender or quickened to rebuke the individual. That is because the image of Christ and the goodness of God through Christ are more real in the individual's life. Many baffling questions may still remain, even in the life of a Christian, which can be judged only according to what is called the Church conscience or the communion of the saints. These things may be called matters of conscience, things which in themselves are not right or are not wrong, but which must be judged according to the day in which we live and their influence upon other people.

It is a wonderful experience for one to be able to say as Paul did, "I have lived in all good conscience before God until this day." His life had unquestionably conformed unto his conscience. Paul determined that he would not defile it.

The kind of life which is so adjusted by conscience is here described by Paul. He said, "In simplicity and godly sincerity." Here is the suggestion of the specific character of a Christian conscience. Simplicity comes from the word which means holiness or sanctity. This holiness is a first requirement of the law and Paul had lived in holiness according to his conscience. Sincerity joined with the phrase "of God" or "godly" means, according to the lexicographer Thayer, the purity which God effects by the Holy Spirit in one's life. It is that which a master produces with the stroke of his brush, namely, a causal relationship. Hence, the suggestion is that Paul had conformed to the Divine righteousness in his own life.

The only way this can be brought about is through the influence of the formative principles of Christianity upon the Christian conscience. The first of these principles is faith. By faith the moral consciousness is no longer bound by the law, but is brought under the personal example of Christ and is mastered by Him. When the living Christ enters the life and masters the conscience it intensifies the sense of personal responsibility and it imparts to the individual a new sense of freedom. The believer has this freedom because he comes to delight to do the will of God. God places within him a thirst after holiness and righteousness and he finds his satisfaction in doing holy things. Thus he automatically walks according to faith and according to his conscience.

The second principal influencing conscience is love. In a truly regenerate man the love of Christ is now made the constraining force for Christian conduct and conscience. The law has been supplanted by a new principal. This love is the principal of moral discernment and it abounds in good judgment. Thus, whenever one takes a course which is devoted to selfishness he may be suspicious of whether it is in conformity to the right. Love forgets self and love quickens the Christian conscience and guides it in the actions of life.

The third principle influencing conscience is hope, that is, the Christian conscience is Messianic. It lives and it works in hope, in expectation of fruitfulness in the future. Christian conscience motivates the life of the believer in the knowledge that the good which it follows will ultimately overcome the evil. Hence, a Christian conscience is a healthy, happy and optimistic rule of life, even when it is in contact with sin and evil. It brings the assurance that he who follows it is on the winning side.

Conscience operating under these Christian principles produces a specific kind of life. It is a life which is at its beginning more or less conformable to the Divine image and becomes by the working of the Holy Spirit more conformed to that image which is the ultimate standard. "We all, with open face beholding as in a glass the glory of the Lord, are changed into the same image from glory to glory, even as by the Spirit of the Lord."

Paul defines the source of this life which shall be witnessed by a good conscience as "not with fleshly wisdom, but by the grace of God." Fleshly wisdom dictates a course of life which is quite contrary to the Christian conscience. It speaks of compromise, of adaptability and of pleasing all men. When one's conscience conflicts with the mores of the locality or day, fleshly wisdom says compromise, adapt yourself, do not offend men, all of which type of wisdom Paul fully repudiated. He declared that he sought to please not men but God. Fleshly wisdom dictates a despicable opportunism, a characterlessness of conduct and a vacillation of conscience which God's standard could never approve, and to break with this kind of life, often designated, "when in Rome do as the Romans do," in which earthly preferments are resident, is almost impossible for the natural man. He simply has not the conviction to do so. Even the Christian living in the flesh is not able to wrest himself free from conformity to worldly standards. Only in the grace of God under the new rule of life, which is the power of the Spirit, may one so yield his members instruments of righteousness unto God as he once yielded his members instruments or unrighteousness unto sin. Correctly, Paul here designates that he had the testimony of a good conscience because he walked in the grace of God.

II. A Good Conscience the Source of Gratification

The text begins with the words, "Our rejoicing is this, the testimony of our conscience." The word translated "rejoicing" is really "boasting," and yet there is a close similarity between the two, revealing something of gratification in a good conscience.

Conscience and its gratification is a personal, subjective element. This sense of gratification cannot be measured scientifically, for we have no quantitative norm by which to compare our pleasure or pain in conformity to conscience with that of another man, although each of us does have a subjective experience by which we can compare our past pains and pleasures with present or future ones. There certainly appear to be people who have so warped and seared their consciences by perversion that they temporarily are inoperative, so that these persons enjoy the pleasures of sin without any sense of self-condemnation. How free they actually are from such condemnation of conscience we cannot judge. Hence, our appeal concerning conscience must be somewhat intangible, except as God witnesses to His truth in the life of the individual.

We can speak with certainty, however, of the pain of a troubled conscience. As the conscience judges our actions it is accompanied by vivid emotions, pleasurable in view of that which is right, and painful in view of that which is wrong, especially when our conscience is engaged in reviewing the state or actions of our will. Sometimes it is almost as if a second person inside us sat in judgment upon us and we were able to carry on conversation either by way of trying to excuse ourselves or rationalize our actions. These self-judgments of condemnation have a peculiar character among judgments of our mind. They are moral and they bring pleasure and pain, satisfaction and shame, rejoicing and remorse. When our experience is that of pain it is remorse. This is an inner sorrow due to the consequences of our sins if we are unbelievers, and to the very nature of sins if we are believers. It results in shame, in burning self-aversion, in perplexity, in disappointment and even in a sense of lostness. Perhaps you have never had that experience, never felt such self-condemnation of conscience, but it has been known many times that those who seemingly were dead to self-condemnation suddenly were aroused by the Spirit of God to terrific anguish after many years of hardness of heart. The history of the Christian movement records seasons when hardened sinners have been so smitten by their consciences that they have fallen upon their faces in agony in public meetings and thought that they were slipping immediately into hell. Such occurred during the ministry of Wesley, of Jonathan Edwards and also of Charles G. Finney.

On the other hand, there is the intense pleasure of a satisfied conscience. Whereas a troubled conscience brings pain and agony and a sense of the judgment of God, a satisfied conscience brings confidence of salvation and peace of heart and rest. External pleasures, such as stimulation, excitement and beauty, cannot begin to compare with the internal pleasures of a conscience at peace with God. Contrast this quiet equilibrium or integration in a real Christian conscience and life with this inner controversy that continues in the life of either an unbeliever or a backslidden Christian. Real happiness does not result from anything in man's relation to man, but in his relation to God. Thus the catechism said, "Glorify God and enjoy him forever." When God is glorified and obeyed in the individual life, there is a harmony with the righteousness of God which is the source of peace and joy. It is a wonderful state of inner rest, integration, self-approval and contentment. This testimony of a good conscience may rightfully be the source of a good man's boast or rejoicing.

III. THE TESTIMONY OF A GOOD CONSCIENCE

Paul added, "And more abundantly to you-ward. For we write none other things unto you, than what ye read or acknowledged; and I trust ye shall acknowledge even to the end." Here is a reference to the social aspects of conscience.

There is a social test of one's actions, namely, the approval of the brethren. Paul and Timothy had been brought into question by this Corinthian Church for their actions. They had had something of a controversy with them, but in all of their actions they had clear consciences. It was Lincoln who said, "Do the right as God gives us to see the right." Thus Paul had acted. God had guided him. God had shown him what he wanted him to do and Paul acted in accordance with that right. Had Paul been divided in his mind and conscience at the time he was having the conflict with the Corinthian Church his state would have been very precarious, but his good conscience, the knowledge that he was true to God's law and God's nature, sustained him and re-established his authority in the Corinthian rebellion.

Happy is the man whose conscience approves him in all of his social relationships. What testimony does your conscience give to you concerning your marital relations over the years? Are things there which your conscience constantly points out to you that must be made right? What about your conscience concerning your business conduct through the years or about the relationship with your neighbor? If conscience condemns, it is wisdom to make an adjustment immediately that you may have peace of soul. Conscience may be called the voice. It is the inner, still small voice, and it will continue to have a controversy with you until you have acted in righteousness. The voice of God is His means of calling you in your relationship to your fellow man to His righteous standard.

Paul also spoke of the social conscience in the sense that the Corinthians approve of them. They knew and they acknowledged that Paul and Timothy had acted in conformity to the Christian social conscience of the day. There is a naturalistic social conscience of each age, which if we disobey brings a social disapproval and judgment. In the matter of morality today multitudes of people are doing deeds which in the days of early New England would have caused them to wear a scarlet letter as Hester Prynne of Hawthorne's tale was compelled to do, yet in our day they go scot-free. On the other hand, our social conscience is such that those who freely possessed and used slaves in colonial days would now be under condemnation. Some writers go so far as to say that the individual conscience is the reflection of the social conscience and that "no individual can make a conscience for himself. He always needs society to make it for him." We must admit that there is such a thing as the social conscience. Hence, also there is such a thing as the Christian social conscience, which is a check upon the individual conscience, and often when our own individual conscience is not sufficient leadership, we are compelled to conform to certain standards because of the Christian conscience.

No one can act thoroughly independently of the social conscience and no Christian can repudiate the Christian conscience. The testimony of the approval of our fellow men means too much to us as social beings.

The final test of conscience, however, is to be at the day of the Lord Jesus. Paul says, "As also ye have acknowledged us in part, that we are your rejoicing, even as ye also are ours in the day of the Lord Jesus." There will be a mutual witness of Christians in the day of the Lord Jesus Christ, the day of reckoning for the believer. Paul said, "We must all stand before the judgment seat of Christ to receive for the deeds done in the body." The very presence of individual conscience in us now is prophetic of a higher judgment at a future time. God has given that conscience to every man that he might answer before the judgment bar of God. Christians shall not escape a similar judgment for they too must answer at the judgment bar of Christ. Our consciences at that time must stand the objective test. If we have wilfully lowered or perverted them, we shall find them conforming and acknowledging the goodness of God and our judgment in accordance therewith. No man is answerable only to his own subjectivity. This is one of the errors of national socialism which has caused it to run riot over the world. H. W. Goering said, "I am subjective. I belong to my nation. I do not recognize anybody else in this world. Thanks to my Creator for creating me without the responsibility of objectiveness." But there is an objectiveness in the Divine judgment, the standards of Divine law and the ultimate nature of God Himself according to which every one of us will be judged.

Back then to our introduction. Jesus said that in hell there is a worm which dieth not. There is a flame which is not quenched. We believe that worm and that flame to be conscience and memory. If your conscience has a controversy with you now it is but a foretaste of the pain of hell that shall come. Better for you that you should fight beasts or that you should struggle for a living or that you should be unrecognized among your fellow men than that you should have the pain of controversy with your conscience. We therefore beseech you by the mercies of God to let Christ by His own precious blood cleanse your conscience from dead works to serve the living and true God.

III

"YES AND NO" MEN

TEXT: *"For the Son of God . . . was not yea and nay, but in him was yea."*—II COR. 1:15-20.

RECENTLY AT A LUNCHEON table of business men, I overheard a conversation between two prominent individuals. The words that caught my attention were, "He is a 'yes' man." The words were spoken disparagingly and most people hold a "yes" man in rather ill repute.

There is another type of man, however, who is even more distressing to us mentally than a "yes" man. I speak of a "yes and no" man. A "yes and no" man is one on whom it is impossible to put your finger. He is ever shifting ground. You may find him first in one position and then in another position. There seems to be no principle or foundation under his life.

Such individuals are exasperating enough when they are in the common intercourse of life, but a terrible disappointment is involved when they are the leaders of the church and the subject about which they are saying "yes and no" is an essential element of our faith. Then there is need to be positive. While we instinctively despise every form of evasion in ordinary social and business interchanges, yet as a church facing the world and called upon to deal in a forthright fashion with the facts of the Gospel, many are no longer scrupulous. Whereas Christ taught us that our communication is to be yea, yea, or nay, nay, from other quarters we have learned the dark art of saying yea and nay both together and all at once. It was this terrible accusation which was made against Paul when he changed his mind in reference to a journey.

He acknowledged that he had desired for sometime to come unto the Corinthians in order that they might enoy a second benefit of his presence and of the Gospel which he preached. That second benefit, by the way, was not the second blessing inaugurating a holiness experience, as some people teach. It was merely a second benefit of his apostolic labors in the Gospel. You may be sure that Paul preached the whole Gospel when he was with the Corinthians for eighteen months, and now upon his projected return to Corinth he was to give them a second benefit of such labors in the Gospel. The benefit which they had first received and which was brought to them in Christ was that they were saved from heathenism. This second benefit would be that they would be more established in Christ.

Paul had stated this purpose along with his intention of going from Corinth to Macedonia and then back again to Corinth and from there to Judea. However, when he came to Corinth, it was via Macedonia because of some compulsion which forced him to change his mind. The reason for that change was that he did not at that time desire to come to Corinth, for he would have had to come with disciplinary measures and he preferred to wait until the Corinthians themselves straightened the affairs of their house. This is small basis for the accusation that Paul was guilty of confusion and changeable. It could only have been made by some one with ill will toward Paul, for it amounted to the common statement that Paul was not a man of his word and this is a serious charge on a minister of the Lord. The accusation really was that Paul was changeable, undependable, vacillating and a "yes and no" man. This means that he was not a man of his word, but was one who lied when it suited his purpose and that he used fleshly wisdom so that his yea statements and his nay statements could not be separated and it was impossible to rely upon him.

Paul utterly repudiated this charge. He scorned to give any actual explanation for the action of a change of mind concerning his mode of journey, for well did he know that if he should give it, his enemies would seize upon it and call it another means of evasion. "Don't explain. Your friends do not need any and your enemies will not believe it, anyway."

That was the ground of Paul's response.

Paul's refutation of the charge was based upon the God whom he served, the Christ whom he preached and the Spirit whom God had given unto him. Thus he rested his plea for consistency of action and judgment in his service of the triune God. Paul had an aversion to such fickleness, either of word or conduct. Similar hatred of undependability is essential in all men, but especially so in a Christian. We should shun the "yes and no" attitude as we would shun the plague, as weakness, as deterioration of character, as deadly to the soul, as insincerity and as a moral defect. Any such attitude militates against one's witness for Christ.

I. THE CONDITION OF "YES AND NO" ATTITUDE TAKEN BY MANY ON THE BIBLE AND TRUTH

In spite of what I have said above, many men habitually assume the "yes and no" attitude concerning the most essential things of our Christian faith. By doing so they negate the very truths which they ought to preach. Others take the "yes and no" attitude in the matter of their own faith and therefore have absolutely no assurance and no witness toward the Lord Jesus Christ.

First, we find this toward the Bible itself and the question of its inspiration. These "yes and no" men take the position that while the writers of the Bible were inspired of God, it is impossible to say "the Holy Spirit did so inspire, guide and move the writers of Scripture as to keep them from error." This attitude is found in many who have been impressed by the modern sceptical attitude, called the scientific mind, which has made its attack upon Scriptures. These "yes and no" persons have never thought their way through. They are not willing to give up the Bible as God's Word and as the source of their religious knowledge and yet they will not acknowledge it to be a dependable book. The result of this attitude on inspiration means that the dependability of the Bible is open for debate. We can trust it. Yet we cannot trust it. What other kind of inspiration is there which can give us a trustworthy Bible in the place of the doctrine of the full plenary inspiration of the Word of God? The church has always taught that "the Bible is the Word of God" and the world has always taken the stand that "the Bible is man's word." There is a great gulf between these two and the "yes and no" attitude tries to compromise between the world and the church.

The second matter upon which the "yes and no" attitude manifests itself is the birth of the Lord Jesus Christ. The Bible unqualifiedly teaches that Jesus was born of the Virgin Mary, without sin, without a human father and is the Son of God. Yet the "yes and no" attitude takes the position that though Christ was not born of a virgin, God was manifest in the flesh. Thus it denies the Virgin Birth but it affirms that God was in Christ. What kind of manifestation of God this is nobody knows. Certainly by it the essential Deity of the Savior is lost and He becomes a mere man, such as any other man in whom God might be residing in an immanent sense, yet these individuals affirm that Christ is divine, divine but not virgin born.

The third vacillating position is in reference to miracles. Instead of accepting the Biblical plain teaching that Christ actually performed miracles over men and over the elements, these "yes and no" men tell us that He wrought mighty works, but that he never performed a true miracle. Either Jesus did or He did not do miracles. The miracles simply are not folklore interpreting a great personality. It is impossible to say both "yes and no" to the miracles. Moreover, God either can or He cannot do miracles today. Why delude ourselves with the idea that there is a position halfway between on these great subjects.

On yet another subject the "yes and no" attitude becomes very important, for we are told, "Although Christ did not die to satisfy Divine justice His death was vicarious." This word becomes meaningless when a satisfaction to Divine justice is removed. How was it vicarious? What can such a word mean? It is emptied of all of its meaning. Either Christ died for you or He did not die for you. Either He took your sins upon the Cross or He did not take them upon the Cross. Now which did He do? Christianity which is Biblical is positive in presenting to you a Savior who died upon the Cross to save you from sin.

The next great matter of fact upon which people have taken the no-concern attitude is the resurrection. They tell us that Christ's body did not rise from the dead, but that His spirit did. What kind of resurrection is this? No Christian ever taught that the spirit of man dies. History has something to say upon these facts which can not be gainsaid. The Bible, Christianity and history are unequivocable in their affirmation of the resurrection of the Lord Jesus Christ. There can be no "yes and no" attitude taken here. Yet one meets it constantly. Thus also there must be a positive teaching in Christianity on immortality, heaven, hell, the new birth and other great doctrines. A few years ago a prominent minister said, "A man dogmatic in his religion is fairly well outlawed from intelligent society." That may have been true twelve years ago, but just the exact opposite of it is true now. Recently I sat at a table with three very intelligent men from the business world. Each of them is head of a particular business. The question why a particular authoritative branch of religion seems to be growing in the New England area arose. One of them replied, "There has been so much confusion in the world through science, politics, philosophy, that the average man now takes the attitude to the church, 'Dish it out and I'll accept it.' " In other words, even intelligent persons today want the church to have a message which is dogmatic and definite and historical and Biblical. If our analysis of that is true, we may affirm that in this church you have heard for nearly a century and a half the great truths of the creation, man's fall, original sin, God's covenant, the new birth, the judgment, heaven, hell, the justice of God and the justification of the sinner by faith, preached without exception by every minister. On this positive message we have expected constant conversions and we have had constant conversions.

No more than a church testimony should be yea and nay or a ministerial testimony be yea and nay should an individual word be yea and nay. Let common honesty of your yea being yea and your nay being nay follow you in your business and your home and your social dealings with your fellow men. Anything else is utterly unacceptable to us.

II. Contrast with the Everlasting Yes in Christ

Paul declared, "As God is true, our word toward you was not yea and nay." The Person of God is faithful. This statement men intuitively accept when they receive the concept of God at all. If there is a God who is perfect and infinite, He must be faithful and true.

Nevertheless, this true God used Paul, Timothy and Silvanus as instruments in bringing the everlasting Yea to the Corinthians. That Yea is described by Paul in these words, "The Son of God, Jesus Christ, who was preached among you by us, even by me and Silvanus and Timotheus, was not yea and nay, but in him was yea." Christ was the everlasting Yes preached by Paul and his companions to the Corinthians. It is utterly incompatible to think of a true and faithful God and a false and unworthy servant. If God used these men as instruments of the everlasting Yea they certainly were not devoid of the truth. The Corinthians had trusted their preaching and found God to be true. They had come to a living experience of Him by means of the Christ whom Paul preached. During the eighteen months of Paul's ministry in Corinth multitudes had come to trust the great "Amen—Christ." We reiterate that this transmission of the everlasting Amen could never have been made by "yes and no" men. God is still ready to witness to His eternal Word preached by true servants, by saving those who will receive that Word. Wherever God finds a true servant He has a channel of revealing His personality to others.

Not only the Person of God is a great Yes or the truth, but the Person of Christ is also the great Yea and Amen. "Amen" was Christ's own word because it described Himself. It was one of His names. "These things saith the Amen, the faithful and true witness." Many times did Jesus use the word "Amen" in His ordinary teaching. Thirty-one times in Matthew's gospel alone He said in introducing his words, "Amen, amen, I say unto you." Twenty-five times in John's gospel this peculiar expression, translated in our unique King James' version, "Verily, verily," occurred. What it actually means is "So be it—yes." Thus Christ may be called the great yes man, or the everlasting Yes. In Him we have only "yea," namely, that which is definite, decisive, positive and unchangeable. No wonder, then, that Christ urged His disciples to let their communication be "yea, yea, or nay, nay."

Our business as the servants of God and of Christ is to be as Christ is in this world, that is, to be definite and positive and decisive in our attitude. I am not here to wrangle with you or to bandy opinions back and forth in a speculative way, but I am here to seize you and to save you, even as Christ came to seek and to save the lost. I am not here to please you and to conform to your desires but to convict you, to convince you and to convert you to Christ. In a lesser sense every true Christian must be an unequivocable, dependable, steady "Yes" like Christ is.

Paul carries the thought a step farther, saying, "For all the promises of God in him are yea, and in him amen, unto the glory of God by us." Have you seen Jesus? Then you have seen the fulfilment of the promises of God, for they are all yes in Christ. Think of the ways in which Christ was the "verily" of God and thus of the promises. In the very beginning of the Bible there is a promise of a Savior, that the seed of the woman should bruise the head of the serpent. That was reiterated time and again. To Abraham it was said that his seed should prove a blessing to all the nations. To David it was promised that his seed should sit upon the throne forever. Now we read in the New Testament that Mary should call her child's name Jesus, for He should save his people from their sins. Do you find in Jesus a Savior? Does Jesus save you? I know that your hearts respond with "Amen." Christ is the Amen to the promise of a Savior.

In the Old Testament we have a promise of a great shepherd. David said, "The Lord is my shepherd. I shall not want. He maketh me to lie down in green pastures. He leadeth me beside the still waters. He restoreth my soul. He leadeth me in the paths of righteousness." Was Jesus a good shepherd, leading His sheep in the paths of righteousness? Do we know Him and His voice? Does He comfort us and anoint our heads with oil? What did He say?

"I am the good shepherd: the good shepherd giveth his life for the sheep. . . . I am the good shepherd, and know my sheep, and am known of mine. As the father knoweth me, even so know I the father: and I lay down my life for the sheep. . . . My sheep hear my voice, and I know them, and they follow me: and I give unto them eternal life; and they shall never perish, neither shall any man pluck them out of my hands."

Have you found Him to be your shepherd? Again your hearts respond with "Amen." Christ is the great Yea of the promise of a shepherd.

In the Old Testament there was the promise of life. Job in his suffering said, "I know that my redeemer liveth and that he shall stand at the latter day upon the earth: and though after my skin worms destroy this body, yet in my flesh shall I see God." Abraham was willing to place his only begotten son, Isaac, upon the altar as a sacrifice in fulfillment of what appeared to him to be a contradictory command because, as the Scripture writer says, he believed that God could raise him from the dead. Abraham and Job believed in a resurrection as did David. Who then removed the great negation—death? Who answered the question, "If we die, shall we live again?" Who confirmed the fact of life after death? Surely you have read and you know the great truth in the New Testament of the resurrection of Jesus from the dead. Surely you know that in Christ death has lost its sting and the grave has lost its victory. Thus your hearts answer, "Amen, the Christ is everlasting life."

Therefore, I bring to you Christ's "verilies." If I choose them from John's gospel alone, I have a great message. Hearken:

"Verily, verily, I say unto you, Whosoever committeth sin is the servant of sin. . . . Yes, yes, I say unto thee, Except a man be born again, he can not see the kingdom of God. . . . Amen, amen, I say unto you, He that heareth my word, and believeth on him that sent me, hath everlasting life. . . . Amen, amen, I say unto you, He that believeth on me, the works that I do shall he do also; and greater works than these shall he do; because I go unto my father. . . . Verily, verily, I say unto you, He that receiveth whomsoever I send receiveth me; and he that receiveth me receiveth him that sent me. . . . Whatsoever ye shall ask in my name, that will I do. . . . Truly, truly, I say unto you, The hour is coming, and now is, when the dead shall hear the voice of the son of God: and they that hear shall live. . . . Verily, verily, I say unto you, Before Abraham was, I AM. . . . Yes, yes, I say unto you, Hereafter ye shall see heaven open, and the angels of God ascending and descending upon the Son of man."

We declare unto you that as God is faithful, as Christ is the great Amen, as all the promises are yea and amen in Christ, that this gospel presented by faithful ministers of the Word is the great affirmation of God. Does your heart say "Amen" to it, or does it criticize and repudiate it? This is the hour for you to make your great affirmation, to say yes to God.

III. THE CONFIRMATION IN THE TRUTH

Paul then declared how that a minister or persons become part of the everlasting Yea rather than "yes and no" men. Said he, "Now he which stablisheth us with you in Christ, and hath anointed us, is God; who hath also sealed us, and given the earnest of the spirit in our hearts." God had established Paul with the Corinthians in Christ. In writing to the Romans Paul introduced his tremendous epistle with the statement of his purpose in desiring to come to Rome, namely, "that I may impart unto you some spiritual gift, to the end ye may be established." He concluded with this benediction, "Now to him that is of power to stablish you according to my gospel, and the preaching of Jesus Christ, according to the revelation of the mystery, which was kept secret since the world began . . . to the only wise God, be glory through Jesus Christ forever." Between those two references to the establishment in Christ of a believer, Paul declared the great means by which it is done, namely, in Christ. By the propitiation of Christ the believer is enabled to overcome his sins, for they were carried in Christ's body on the tree. By identification with Christ the believer is able to die unto sin and rise unto righteousness. By the inhabitation of Christ the believer is able to overcome the temptations of worldliness. Thus it is that in Christ one is established, which means in grace or being saved or being redeemed. Paul had accepted Christ and these Corinthians had accepted Christ, who is the verily of God and thus they in turn also became true or a "verily." All "yes and no" attitude was removed from them. They were established in the great Yes. God is willing to establish you in this truth by Christ through His gospel now. The everlasting Affirmation, the great Yes may be yours, and you, in turn, may become an affirmation of God.

Such individuals God has anointed, sealed and given the earnest of the Spirit in their hearts. These are very suggestive phrases and we shall examine them further later. Suffice it to say now, let no one attack the anointed of God, for he cannot do so with impunity. We have not forgotten that when Saul twice fell into the hands of David and David's men advised him to put Saul to death, David said, "The Lord forbid that I should stretch forth my hand against the anointed of the Lord." Each time he spared Saul. When the Amalekite came to David in Ziklag, announcing that Saul and Jonathan were dead, and presented Saul's crown and bracelets as tokens of the truth of his message, saying, "So I stood upon him, and slew him, because I was sure that he could not live after that he was fallen," David commanded that the Amalekite should be put to death, saying, "How wast thou not afraid to stretch forth thine hand to destroy the Lord's anointed?" Let no one also tamper with a seal, whether it is the seal of the state or of God. That seal is final. He who is sealed is God's messenger and his word is true. Moreover, let no one deal lightly with the earnest of the Spirit which is the foretaste of glory. This is God's internal witness that one is approved of Him.

Hence, Paul calls God to record concerning the reason for his change of mind. God knows and God does record. God is the final judge and He will witness whether you are a "yes and no" man or whether you are a great affirmation to His truth. The day will come when all such Laodiceans who are neither hot nor cold but are "yes and no" men will be spewed out of Christ's mouth. Therefore, let this be the hour of your "yes" to God, that forever you may be conformed to His image and able to say "no" to the world.

"Yes and no" religion is transient, accomodating, compromising, distasteful. No suspended judgment concerning God and God's truth can be permanently held by man. You must say "yes" or "no" not "yes and no." If you are not for Christ, you are against Him and you are giving comfort to His enemies. Now is the time for you to cry, "I am Thine, oh, Lord. I give myself to Thee."

IV

ANOINTED, SEALED AND ENDOWED FOR LIFE ON EARTH AND IN HEAVEN

TEXT: *"Now he which stablisheth us with you in Christ, and hath anointed us, is God; who has also sealed us, and given us the earnest of the Spirit in our hearts."*—II COR. 1:21-22.

THE TEXT SPEAKS of our being established of God in Christ by the Holy Spirit. Here we behold three wonders.

First, there is the wonder of being established, of becoming steadfast in Christ and of being a pillar in the temple of God. The text declares that God takes vacillating, unstable, untrustworthy men and makes them as immovable, dependable and certain as a rock. God takes "yes and no" men and transforms them into great affirmations. For an illustration one would have to go no farther than Simon Peter, who was as unstable as water, but who became the rock who strengthened his brethren. Once a man has been so established by God, like Paul, he may feel secure on this eternal foundation. Paul laid no claim to a unique steadfastness which in the nature of the case was denied to others. Rather, he said, "God stablisheth us with you in Christ." He, they and all Christians may be permanently established in this grace. They may be rooted and grounded in the great Yea and Amen. It is interesting to note that the present participle is used in the verb "stablish" whereas the aorist tense is used for the other verbs in the text. This shows that the establishing is a continuous action and that it is accomplished by means of the three works referred to in the other three verbs of the text and connected with the Holy Spirit, but whatever the reason and whatever the means, that God can take weak, defeated, sinful, succumbing men and can save them and establish them in righteousness is a great marvel of human experience. It might be called the chief wonder of the world.

The second wonder presented in our text is that of the Trinity in redemptive activity. One can never cease to marvel at the beauty, the harmony and the completeness of the plan of redemption through a triune Godhead. Any system of theology which presents God as other than triune mutilates the wisdom of God in the plan of redemption. God the Father is the source. His position is emphasized by an inverted order of the sentence. Paul says, "Now he which stablisheth us is God." God is really in the predicate of this sentence and yet He is the source of the establishing, the anointing, the sealing and the giving of the earnest of the Spirit. It is no less a one than God Himself who makes this establishing effective. When a life is God-centered and God-established, it has a strength that no other source can provide. But the text also proclaims that Christ is the way of salvation and establishment. "He stablisheth us with you in Christ." These simple words, "in Christ," designate the mediator between God and man, the means or the way. It was Christ who reconciled sinners unto the Father, who brought the prodigal back to God. The phrase "in Christ" is the most familiar designation of those converted from the world and Satan to God, of those who have passed from darkness into light. To be "in Christ" describes a truly saved man who has been forgiven of his sins at the Cross of Calvary, justified by faith and identified with a resurrected and living Christ. But the text goes one step farther and declares that the Holy Spirit is the means of this establishment. Here, as we shall see, the Spirit is the instrument of the threefold work effecting the establishment of the believer. Thus we again bow in holy awe and wonder before the Biblical revelation of a triune God active in our redemption. Mystery though this Trinity may be, it is absolutely essential for the salvation of man.

The third wonder suggested in this text is the threefold part of the Spirit's work in salvation. The story is told of a Salvation Army lassie who was conducting personal work on the edge of a street meeting in England. She approached a man standing on the edge of the crowd and said, "Are you saved?" With a kindly look and a twinkling eye, the gentleman looked down at her and said, "Do you mean *sesomai* or *sodzomai* or *sosomai?*" The lassie looked up in astonishment and perceived a smile in the eyes. The gentleman went on to say, "Do you mean, have I been saved, or am I being saved, or shall I be saved?" The girl was talking to the great churchman, scholar and Christian, Bishop Westcott, who, in turn, merely emphasized the three phases of salvation represented in our text. To this real distinction in the matter of salvation belong the three phases of the past, present and future work of the Spirit of God. The text speaks of our being established in the present by possessing the seal of the Spirit and our being established in the future by the earnest of the Spirit. This establishing is the communicating to the believer whatever is in the possession of Christ. This occurs by an ingrafting of the individual to the Lord but by an outward reception into the public community of the church. The result is that the life of Christ is the life of the believer through the Holy Spirit. Our intention is to look at these three phases of the work of the Spirit.

I. The Past—"Anointed"

Anointing with oil is a symbol often used throughout the whole of the Bible. The use of oil was symbolic of the Holy Spirit. Thus Samuel persuaded Saul to tarry behind in the land of Zuph while his servant passed on. Then Samuel took a vial of oil and poured it upon Saul's head and said, "Is it not because the Lord hath anointed thee to be captain over his inheritance? . . . And it was so, that, when he had turned his back to go from Samuel, God gave him another heart." Thus also when Saul had failed to obey God as king, Samuel was sent by the Lord to the house of Jesse. There he reviewed the various sons of this Ephratite of Bethlehem and finally anointed David in the midst of his brethren, and the Spirit of the Lord came upon David from that day forward. Thus also when the priests were first consecrated to the service of the tabernacle, Moses was commanded to make for them exquisite garments for glory and for beauty. God commanded him then to anoint Aaron and his sons and consecrate them and sanctify them that they might minister to God in the priest's office. The anointing was the symbol of the Divine consecration and sanctification by the Spirit. In fulfilling this, Moses first made a sacrifice of a bullock for a sin offering and applied the blood of it to the tip of Aaron's right ear, to the thumb of his right hand and to the great toe of his right foot and did the same to

Aaron's sons. Then Moses took the anointing oil and sprinkled it upon Aaron and upon his garments, upon his sons and upon his sons' garments with him and sanctified Aaron and his sons. Thus were the priests consecrated to serve the Lord. Similarly, when a leper was declared cleansed from his leprosy, the priest offered a lamb as a sin and burnt offering, the blood of which was also placed upon the right ear, the right thumb and the right toe of the body of the individual and then the oil was poured into the palm of the priest's hand, so that from it he could dip out that which would be sprinkled before the Lord and upon the individual to be cleansed. This was the means of cleansing of one possessed of the plague of leprosy.

The symbolism represented the consecrating, sanctifying and setting apart of an individual unto God. First always came the cleansing by the blood and then the anointing by the Holy Spirit. Whereas the blood of an animal represented the blood of the Savior, the oil represented the Holy Spirit. When one is cleansed by the blood of Christ and anointed with the Spirit sanctification is begun in his life. This consecration and sanctification are necessary for a pure life as well as for service in the Lord's work.

The anointing of the Spirit is the common symbol of the possessing of the gift of the Holy Spirit which is common to all Christians. "If any man have not the Spirit of Christ he is none of his." The Scripture says, "The Lord is the Spirit," and to be anointed and sealed by the Spirit is to bear the image of the Lord, even of Christ, though that image may be very inconspicuous in the beginning. The anointing, of course, does not end with merely possessing the Spirit. There may be fresh anointings which lead on to great holiness and sanctification of life.

The anointing is simply symbolic of the spiritual rebirth or the new birth. Jesus said to Nicodemus:

"Except a man be born of water and of the Spirit, he can not enter into the kingdom of God. That which is born of the flesh is flesh; and that which is born of the Spirit is spirit. Marvel not that I said unto thee, Ye must be born again. The wind bloweth where it listeth, and thou hearest the sound thereof, but canst not tell whence it cometh, and whither it goeth: so is every one that is born of the Spirit."

The new birth, then, is by water and by the Spirit. Water represents the human side, namely, our true repentance and utter abandonment of all sin, our faith in what God says Christ did for us and our obedience to God's commandments. Water represents what we are to do in this matter of being born again. Being born of the Spirit, however, is God's part. This is the Divine anointing or the Divine baptism upon the individual when he repents, believes and obeys, just as Peter said, "Repent and be baptized in the name of Jesus Christ for the remission of sins, and ye shall receive the gift of the Holy Ghost." The time of the anointing with the Holy Spirit is not necessarily the time when we are baptized with water, but it is identical with a baptism by the Holy Spirit. One cannot be born again without what is called the baptism of the Spirit.

The Lord Jesus Christ was called "The Anointed One." He said, "The Spirit of the Lord is upon me, for he hath anointed me to preach the gospel." These were the words with which Jesus began His ministry. Later, when Peter preached the gospel to the household of Cornelius, he said, "God anointed Jesus of Nazareth with the Holy Ghost and with power." Christ, then, was the anointed One, but we believers also are anointed. Said John, "Ye have an unction from the Holy One, and ye know all things." That unction, of course, is an anointing of Christ. This makes us anointed like unto the anointed Christ. In the Greek there is a play on words in this text. The word for Christ is *Christon* and the word for anointed is *Chrisas*. Paul said, *"Christon kai Chrisas."* In other words, Christ is the anointed One and hath anointed us. The similarity of our position with Christ is thus brought out. God sanctifies us as He sanctified Christ by the anointing with the Spirit. Christ was inducted into His high office and position of prophet, priest and king by this anointing. Thus also we become kings and priests unto God in Christ and are called to our spiritual offices by the anointing of the Spirit. It is by the Spirit dividing Himself into us severally as He will that we are enabled to undertake the offices of Christian service.

Once this anointing is performed, the Spirit remains on us. It is true that new and fresh anointings for particular tasks may be sought and received, but the original anointing is never lost. In the New Testament this act is never ascribed to any one but God. God anoints us with the Spirit. This gives an unction from on High for service in God's kingdom. Unction is a strange word. It is hard to define. But the unction upon an individual may be recognized when it is present, and it carries its own authority. It was this that constituted Paul's authority. He was particularly anointed of God for the office of an apostle. There was an intensification of the gift of the Spirit on Paul for his special work, and that unction rested in Paul.

Synonymous with this term of anointing are other descriptions of the same experience in the Word of God. The first description is "being born again, not of corruptible seed, but of incorruptible, the Word of God which abideth forever." We have already mentioned somewhat in detail this matter of being born again which is so often repeated in the Scriptures. The Spirit is the agent in the new birth. The second description synonymous with anointing is "the baptism of the Spirit." We do not mean by this a second baptism, for every believer is baptized by one Spirit into the body of Christ. I am aware that such godly men and such effective evangelists as R. A. Torrey and Charles G. Finney prayed for and claimed that they received the baptism of the Spirit separate from their conversion or their saved experience, but I am persuaded that this is not Biblical language. There may be fresh anointings, but there is truly but one baptism of the Spirit into the body of Christ. But I would rather be wrong in the use of my terminology and truly be anointed with the Holy Spirit of God, as were these two men, than right in my terminology and lack the baptism of the Spirit. The third phrase is "the witness of the Spirit." This is God's wonderful seal, comparable to the Old Testament circumcision, whereby we know that we are God's possession. We are told that if we are children of God "the Spirit beareth witness with our spirit." Likewise also the Scripture says, "God hath sent forth the spirit of his son into your hearts, crying Abba, Father." And again, "He that believeth on the Son hath the witness in himself."

In each case where the Scripture speaks of the witness, it speaks of our being sons of God and heirs of God, all of which is constituted by our being born again or anointed by the Spirit into this body of Christ. Yet a fourth phrase which describes this is "indwelt by the Spirit." Paul said, "Know ye not that ye are the temple of God, and that the Spirit of God dwelleth in you?" Again he said, "Know ye not that your body is the temple of the Holy Ghost which is in you, which ye have of God, and ye are not your own? For ye are bought with a price: therefore glorify God in your body, and in your spirit, which are God's." We conclude, then, that anointing with the Spirit, being born again by the Spirit, baptism by the Spirit, possessing the witness of the Spirit and being indwelt by the Spirit all refer to that initial work of grace whereby we become children of God or are saved. That is past for those who are Christians.

II. THE PRESENT—"SEALED"

Our text next says, "Who hath also sealed us." What is this seal?

Paul describes it in Ephesians, saying, "After that ye heard the word of truth, the gospel of your salvation: in whom also, after that ye believed, ye were sealed with that Holy Spirit of promise, which is the earnest of our inheritance until the redemption of the purchased possession." Here the seal is defined as the Holy Spirit. There is no other seal in Christianity but the Holy Spirit. Water baptism cannot take the place of this. Thus there is no question but that the Holy Spirit is the subject referred to here by Paul. The seal is given by God in the person of the Holy Spirit at the same time as our anointing, but it designates a different purpose. Let us look at that purpose from God's side, from the human side and from the church's side.

The purpose in giving a seal unto the believer from God's side might be described as enacting. The verb "hath sealed" is in the middle voice in the Greek and thus is reflexive and implies hath sealed us for Himself. God seals His purchased possession for Himself. When it is evident that Christ hath purchased us with His precious blood and we become children of God, God places upon us a seal of His possession. It designates ownership by God. It is the public attestation that the transaction is completed. We sing:

" 'Tis done, 'tis done, the great transaction's done.
I am my Lord's and He is mine."

But it is necessary that there be some seal to this. That seal gives its authentication. There can be no question about the authenticity of the transaction. The believer and God both may always point to the seal if any doubt or question arises as to one's salvation. That seal speaks of the Divine administration in the life. From now on God is the Lord, the master, the owner and the keeper of that life. This gives us the recognition that the sealed ones belong to God. It is the covenant sign by which they are identified as His. It gives assurance that God has extended His grace to the ones sealed and that the believer is ultimately to be conformed to the image of His Son.

From the human side this might be described as enabling. This reference of Paul in our text is very brief, but, thank God, we are not dependent upon this one reference for our understanding of the entire matter. The work of the Spirit in the soul is greatly enlarged in the Bible. To be sealed by the Holy Spirit is to enable us to walk in the Spirit and to bear the fruit of the Spirit. The only way to understand this fruit of the Spirit is really to contrast it with the fruit of the unspiritual nature. Once we walked in the lusts of the flesh. Now

Christ has set upon our souls, bodies and minds the seal of His purity. Once we were filled with passion, given to angry words and hasty deeds. Now we are sealed with the meekness and gentleness of Jesus. Once we were grasping and even dishonest. Now we have been sealed with the liberality of Him who though He was rich yet for our sakes became poor that we through His poverty might be rich. Once we sought vengeance for any wrongs. Now we stand aside and give place to Divine wrath, and even pray for our enemies. Once we sought our own will. Now we seek the will of God. This is all the evidence of being sealed by the Spirit. This constitutes guidance in our everyday life. That is not a past nor a future fact. It is a present fact, and unless we can daily depend upon the Spirit of the living God to guide us in our decisions we are not being enabled of God to live as He wants us to live.

Finally, the seal of the Spirit enables us to be filled with the Spirit. Now, to be filled means that we shall empty ourselves of all other things that Christ may fill us with His Spirit. Only in this way do we ever attain to the close and beautiful fellowship with God which is possible and essential for victorious, Christian living, for powerful work and for the performance of the Divine will.

The purpose of the seal of the Spirit for the kingdom or the church might be described as empowering. Here the entire Scriptural teaching concerning the gifts of the Spirit for the church in the form of prophesying, teaching, governing, healing, helping, etc. have their meaning. God has provided a power. He has said, "Ye shall receive power after that the Holy Ghost is come upon you." He has commanded us to tarry until we be endued with power from on high. He has given us a tremendous task, namely, to make disciples of all men everywhere. This task is impossible without the empowerment of the Holy Spirit. When God sets His seal upon a man He is empowering that man for His service.

III. The Future—"The Earnest"

Paul said, "Who hath given the earnest of the Spirit in our hearts." The earnest of the Spirit might be called the first down payment. It is an assurance of payment in full which is to come. It actually was used and is a technical word to describe the payment of a small sum of money to clinch a bargain or to ratify an agreement. It was used from the earliest times of the Old Testament. Most of us ought to be able to understand that terminology today. We need only use the word instalment. The first instalment is a token of a good many other instalments yet to come. Now, in this case it is God who is giving the first instalment on a future fulness and it implies the Divine obligation to give us more. The fulness is our inheritance. The seal of the Spirit is the earnest of our future inheritance in Christ. We might illustrate this by saying that illumination is the earnest of everlasting light. A spiritual quickening in one's life is the earnest of everlasting life. The comfort given by the Paraclete or the Holy Spirit is the earnest of everlasting joy. The present happiness in the Spirit is the earnest of everlasting happiness to come. Thus the fulness is yet future, but we already have a taste thereof. A certain excitement is implied in this text in the words, "in our hearts." Here an emotion, a stirring, a quickening is suggested in reference to this experience which precedes the subsequent repose. Many are those who having received the anointing and the seal and the earnest were thoroughly affected in their emotions. Such was Dwight L. Moody's experience of baptism with the Divine love. Such was Charles G. Finney's experience, in which waves of glory swept over his soul in the little law office at Adams, New York, and such has been the experience of many individuals. I myself may testify to an experience only a few months ago in which when returning from the morning service I could do nothing but laugh and weep from the very waves of glory that swept over my soul by a baptism of Divine love.

Now, the essence of this pledge or of this earnest is the Person of the Spirit Himself. The Scripture says, the earnest "of the Spirit" and this is an appositional genitive. That is, it describes the Spirit as the pledge. It reveals that God gives Himself in the Third Person of the Trinity in order to connect us to Himself or to the great Yea and Amen. If this is only the pledge, then the fulness must also be of the Spirit. It must be a greater development of the Spirit. It must be an order for which the Spirit alone can qualify us, namely, ultimate immortality. Here we have a suggestion of our final identification with God. True that we shall be like Him. True that we shall be conformed to the image of His Son. True that we shall sit with Him on His throne. We have here the suggestion of how all things are "of him and through him and to him," and how, finally, we shall all be taken back into the bosom of the eternal God, that is, all the redeemed.

Here, again, we must mention purpose in reference to the earnest of the Spirit. This Spirit we are told is the foretaste of future glory.

What that future glory is no man can tell, for "eye hath not seen, nor ear heard, neither have entered into the heart of man, the things which God hath prepared for them that love him." We know that the inheritance is "incorruptible, and undefiled, and that fadeth not away." It is called glory. Therefore, we understand the meaning of the promise, and in the meantime we, "with open face beholding as in a glass the glory of the Lord, are changed into the same image from glory to glory, even as by the Spirit of the Lord." Day by day and hour by hour through the sanctification and the indwelling of the Holy Spirit we shall be conformed more and more unto that glory until we shall bear the full image of our Lord. Thus our triumph at present and our triumph in the future will be through the Spirit and whatever there is of victorious life or of sanctification must inevitably be connected with the Holy Spirit or the Third Person of the Trinity. Have you neglected the Spirit in your life? Have you honored Him? Have you surrendered to Him? Have you obeyed Him? If you would enjoy being anointed, sealed and in possession of the earnest of the Spirit, you must be born again.

This new birth is conditioned, we are told, on our repenting and our believing. Repent and ye shall receive the gift of the Holy Ghost. It is conditioned upon our asking, for if we being evil know how to give good gifts, how much more shall the heavenly Father give the Holy Spirit to them that ask Him? It is conditioned on our obedience, for the Holy Spirit is given to those who obey Him. If, then, you are willing to repent, to believe, to ask and to obey, Almighty God will anoint you with His Spirit, will seal you with His own image and will give you the earnest in the third Person of the Trinity of your great inheritance and glory to come, namely, immortality with God. May it be so for His Name's sake.

V

THE LOVE WHICH I HAVE MORE ABUNDANTLY UNTO YOU

TEXT: *"For out of much affliction and anguish of heart I wrote unto you with many tears; not that ye should be grieved, but that ye might know the love which I have more abundantly unto you."*
—II COR. 1:23-2:4.

I HEREBY RAISE a voice for love in a world wilderness of hate, jealousy and vengeance. The text warrants this word in behalf of love.

We have here a glimpse into a pastor's heart. St. Paul bares his soul to us and we behold all the tenderness and affection of love. The language which he uses to describe his emotions as he wrote the first epistle to the Corinthians is hardly extravagant. Part of that epistle defended his own authority as an Apostle. Cardinal Newman, while writing his *Apologia Pro Vita Sua*, wrote to Sir F. Rogers, "During the writing and reading of my part three I could not get from beginning to end for crying." He wrote to Mr. Holmes-Scott, "I have been writing without interruption of Sundays five weeks. I have been constantly in tears, and constantly crying out with distress." Whenever a man draws the veil away from his soul it is with reluctance and sometimes with grief. Here Paul draws aside the veil concerning the spirit in which he wrote the first epistle to the Corinthians. His apostleship had been questioned by some of them, and widespread evil existed within the church, so that it was out of affliction, with many tears and with anguish of heart, that Paul wrote his letter. The glimpse we get into his heart reveals the effect of sin in the lives of his converts upon his own soul. Paul was no stoic. He felt deeply and he expressed the emotion which he felt.

Here we have ample evidence of why the Apostle Paul was so effective in his ministry. He put his whole soul into it. He was indignant, grieved. He wept and he loved alternately, and he was unashamed to manifest it unto men, even though it would be written for future generations. When we contrast this with our modern restraint, with the niggardly way in which we express our emotions, whether of commendation or affection, we get a clue as to why we are not more effective.

Here in this text it is our purpose to single out what is of spiritual value to us and relegate the critical disputes about Paul's visits, letters and hypothetical controversies with the Corinthians to the studies of scholars and to academic papers, for we believe that in these epistles we have adequate information to account for all about which Paul was writing. There are some who take the attitude that because Paul did not mention his tears in his first epistle to the Corinthians this present description could not apply to it, but we suggest that if divisions, carnality, immorality, lawsuits, confusion in worship and excesses at the Lord's table, to say nothing of incest, were not enough to grieve the founder and father of that church to tears, what would it then take? Therefore, we assume that Paul was writing in reference to the first epistle to the Corinthians and to the condition which it was designed to correct.

Dare I take this emotional aspect from the apostle's life and heart for a sermon on love among Christians? It is with hesitancy that I do so. Will this be called by supercilious hearts and by lifted eyebrows "emotional" or "sentimental" or "womanish"? Perhaps I should confess that so much of the university, of the sophisticated world and of the customary has bound me that I am often afraid of emotion and of being personal. If you can accuse Paul of emotionalism in this passage, then you will be able to accuse me too, for I am going to express my feelings to you for once. I dipped my pen in the milk of human kindness to write this sermon. If for seven years I have been your pastor and have felt love, grief and joy over you people I have never told you. I have merely preached the truth to you and allowed the Holy Spirit to apply it as He would. But how unlike Paul this is; he poured out his heart in such love that all future generations could read of it. To fail to express love is like the suitor who in attempting to win his greatly desired one said, "I am not the world's greatest lover, but perhaps other things can make up for that." No, they cannot. If we love, we must say so. Perhaps it is because I have put so little soul in my preaching and work that I have wooed and won so few to my lovely Lord. What a poor representative of the living Christ! But now my courage mounts with this study of the Apostle Paul, who in plain words wrote of his fervent affection for the people, saying, "That ye might know the love which I have more abundantly unto you." This text and passage are essentially a love story of a pastor and his people.

Have I then loved the people whom I serve? The answer is "Yes," with a love bringing grief and tears over certain aberrations at times, and joy over righteousness which is almost constant; a love which has resulted in pain and in delight; an abiding love, which on several occasions has prevented me from accepting invitations to labor elsewhere. As Paul did, I also call God to a record upon my soul that love has motivated my services.

We have a real duty in dealing with men in loving affection. How little we have manifested this love in our lives, in our church, in the relationships of life, and yet it is the first requirement of God. He said, "Thou shalt love the Lord thy God and thy neighbor as thyself." It is also the first fruit of the Spirit, leading the long list of Christian graces. Are we really Christians at all when we examine ourselves and find the lack of love which has existed in our lives or at least the expression of it? Think of the divisions among Christians, the practices of jealousy, of littleness, of selfishness, of criticism and of pride. All of us are guilty of some of them in a measure. We, too, as James said, "fight and war and have not because we ask not." We have not sought the good pleasure of our God from whom is every good and perfect gift.

How easy and how cheap it is to denounce evil. It is easy to seek out wrong, to work up a passion and wrathfully to denounce either individuals, communities or nations. This is the temptation of a preacher. We have a news report of an awful condition in one of the nations and it would be an easy thing to single that out and to denounce it before the world. But nothing would ever be gained by doing that. It is altogether too easy to pick faults in the community, the church, and the nation, to point them out, to criticize, to denounce, but when we have finished all this, we are still far from removing the evil or from winning the evildoer to our Lord. On the other hand, how difficult it is to get in and to carry the load, to change things, to bear the burdens of men. Yet the Lord Jesus carried sin in His body to the Cross. He loved the sinner and He overcame the evil. I think as I read this text that Paul was like our Lord. Thus I suggest to you that love was the secret of Paul's authority in his Christian service and that this love in contact either with sin or righteousness brought to him grief or joy.

I. Love the Basis of Authority in Christian Service

In the Christian religion there must be no lordship of human beings over our souls. Paul said, "To spare you I came not as yet unto Corinth. Not for that we have dominion over your faith, but are helpers of your joy: for by faith ye stand." Paul was an apostle, authenticated with miraculous gifts, given the care of the Gentile churches and endowed by God for this task, yet Paul refused to exercise dominion over individuals' faith. Paul acknowledged that his authority was purely spiritual. Paul was the great preacher of spiritual liberty. He taught that the days of bondage were over for a Christian and that he was no longer a slave of men or of tradition or of law. Only a spiritual authority which commended itself to the individual was of any value in the church. Each believer, according to Paul, stands or falls before the Lord alone. "By faith ye stand." Ultimately, there can be no final judgment of any believer in this world. He receives his commendation or condemnation before the judgment-seat of Christ. This is a tremendous liberty, the principle of which is faith, and that faith must produce the kind of works which are not a perversion of liberty. Thus where evil deeds arose within this church, Paul did not resort to compulsion or to commanding, as some clerical hierarchies might do. He did not legislate for their faith. Paul merely emphasized the tremendous responsibility to God and to one another which Christians have and a counterbalancing force to this liberty. Thus, as he says in another instance, "Ye have been called unto liberty; only use not liberty for an occasion to the flesh, but by love serve one another."

We may be sure that no ecclesiastical or professional hierarchy has any dominion over our faith or over our souls. The mere fact that some of us have received orders does not permit us to command others in spiritual things. Even education or knowledge of the Bible or position in a church does not grant us authority to do this. There is no priest or mediator who stands between the soul and God. The only mediator between man and God is Christ Jesus. The believer himself has been constituted a high priest unto God and is able to offer up spiritual sacrifices. Though none is able to exercise dominion over us, yet many are able to help or hinder us in our Christian life.

This liberty, then, not only gives us independence, but it also gives us responsibility. It must not be anarchic. There is a spiritual authority to the Word of God and also to him who proclaims the Word of God and of him to whom God has given gifts in His service. It is well for us as individuals, then, to accept the teachings, the criticism, the guidance which are given in love from the Word of God and which are essential to brotherhood. The Corinthians had had this to learn, and the loving dealings of Paul completely restored the purity, harmony and obedience of the church in the Word of God. It is true that there is an alternative method of dealing with the people of God, namely, to come with a rod, but love accomplishes more.

The Lord gave us the example of the love way. The Lord laid down the law of redemptive love in His own vanquishing of sin by taking the burden and the guilt of sin on Himself at the Cross. Calvary, in which there was so much suffering and grief which is familiar to us, is always described in the Bible in the terms of the love of God. "God so loved the world that he gave his only begotten Son, that whosoever believeth in him should not perish but have everlasting life." "When we were yet without strength, in due time Christ died for the ungodly." "Herein is love, not that we loved God, but that he loved us, and sent his Son to be the propitiation for our sins." Yes, the Cross is the manifestation of the limitless love of God. Too many think of Jesus as a third party stepping in between God and man to propitiate a vengeful deity. That is not the Biblical conception at all. God Himself took upon Him human flesh in order to reconcile sinful man unto Himself. It was God who suffered and who took death and pain up into His Divine nature.

> "See, from His head, His hands,
> His feet, sorrow and love flow mingled down!
> Did e'er such love and sorrow meet,
> Or thorns compose so rich a crown?"

That Cross of Calvary is the evidence of the loving, suffering heart of God in meeting the sin of man.

The way of love was also demonstrated in the life of Jesus. Far from revealing a weakness of character or body, the life of love can come only from the strongest of men. Thus the Bible speaks of Jesus as one who was able to love the rich young ruler who came seeking the way of salvation, one who loved Mary, Martha and Lazarus, the little family of Bethany, one who having loved His disciples loved them unto the end. The service of the Lord Jesus to the publicans, the outcasts, the needy, the sick and the impotent was a service of love incarnate. Because Jesus loved, He suffered in the presence of the evil which was so widespread in the world.

The one characteristic which imparts moral authority to our words and deeds, whether in the pulpit, Sunday school or the home is love. A loving heart will do more than learning, discipline and pleading. It is the parent who loves who is able to exercise an authority over children. This way of love commends itself unto us so that its authority is recognized.

If Paul adopted the way of love in following the example of the Lord Jesus Christ, then surely it is also our privilege to work in love. As Christ was, so we are to be in this world. We do not imply that our love is able to redeem men. It is merely the way of life. The Bible says, "None of them can by any means redeem his brother, nor give to God a ransom for him." But we do believe that when the believer accepts the way of love there will be a sacrifice in his life. It means giving without expecting. This sacrificial, loving element in the Christian life reveals that the mind of Christ is in us. "We can not be the Son of God, dying for the world, but we must necessarily present the Son of God who died for the world." This means that in love we shall take the path He took and may really say, "I am crucified with Christ. Nevertheless, I live. Yet not I, but Christ liveth in me."

On this principle Paul was able to say, "The love of Christ constraineth us; because we thus judge, that if one died for all, then were all dead: and that he died for all, that they which live should not henceforth live unto themselves, but unto him which died for them, and rose again." This constraining love of Christ may be considered in two senses, the objective and the subjective. In the objective sense Paul says he did the things which marked his life because he loved Christ and he did them for the love of this Christ. On the other hand, considered subjectively, the love of Christ becomes the motivating power. That is, it is Christ in him, giving him this love and enabling him so to serve his fellow men.

This love is the only adequate motive for Christian service, but we hold that it must be divinely given. It was of this love that Jesus asked of Peter, "Lovest thou me?" Peter could not trust himself with the profession of this divine love, given and inspired of God. All he could profess was a human love or fondness. Yet Paul here declares that he had a divine love for these Corinthians. Such a love will always commend itself as the basis of authority in spiritual leadership. Just as Paul won in Corinth over Satan's devices to undermine his authority and to disrupt the church, so we too may win by love over the devices of Satan which would be applied in our lives.

II. GRIEF—THE REACTION OF CHRISTIAN LOVE TO SIN

In this passage we catch a glimpse of what sin in the Corinthian Church did to the Apostle Paul. We behold his fears, his successes and his affections in reference to the Corinthian Church. When he first went to Corinth it was with fear and trembling, in physical weakness and in reticence, yet it was also in the power and demonstration of the Spirit, not trusting in human wisdom. As a result of this, within eighteen months God gave Paul a tremendous success in Corinth, and multitudes were converted out of heathenism.

It is altogether natural that he should have conceived during that eighteen months a great affection for this city and church and such a dominating position over the whole of Achaia. Now that sin should arise within the church brought him great grief and sorrow. Think of the sins which arose in that body of Christ. They were divided over the subject of baptism and the methodology used in preaching by Paul and by Apollos and by other representatives of the church. This manifested their carnality. Some of them repudiated Paul's authority and teaching and despised the weakness in which he came to Corinth. Others were influenced by the doctrine of Christian liberty, and slipped into immorality or into idolatry. Still others entered into quarrels one with another and went so far as having suits before the law, Christian with Christian, bringing the name of Christ into disrepute. When the Lord's Supper was practiced some became drunk and unworthily partook of it. Still others misused the gifts which were bestowed of God for His church in public worship. Confusion resulted. As great an error as any was the doubting of the resurrection of the body, due no doubt to the Gnostic teaching as to the essential evil of matter. Crowning the aberrations of this congregation was one great case of incest which the people had failed to discipline. Is it any wonder that when Paul learned of this condition of the church that he was filled with sorrow, that he profoundly wept, that he had great grief over it? A burden descended upon his spirit until the Church at Corinth should be rectified in all of its errors, in its sinful practices and its misdeeds.

When we think of what sin in the Corinthian Church did to Paul, how much greater must the grief be in the heart of a loving God when He sees sin in the Christian. If sin at one time raised a Cross on Calvary, is it not true that wherever the love of God meets sin a cross is set up and God suffers afresh? Of course, not a redemptive suffering this time, but now still a suffering because of sin in the presence of love. We are told that those who sin willfully after they have received the knowledge of the truth crucify Christ afresh and put Him to an open shame. This is equivalent to an open repudiation of the Lord Jesus Christ and must bring sorrow to the loving heart of God. Yet there are Christians or at least those who name the name of Christ who cause the unbelievers to blaspheme the name of God because of their profession. Then also we are warned against grieving the Holy Spirit, whereby we are sealed against the day of redemption. Sin even in a believing heart and life cannot go uncondemned, and the Holy Spirit who is given unto us is said to endure grief when we choose evil rather than good. Likewise also sin does despite unto the grace of God. It is an equivalent to our definitely inviting God to punish us, to chastise us, to put us under the rod. All of the grief and suffering of sin are not caused in the lives of others. It sometimes comes back and reverts to us.

Thus sin also brings grief to a pastor's heart. Instead of joy, the presence of sin in a congregation brings a burden, discouragement, heaviness and grief. The congregation is a source of a pastor's gladness or of his sadness and to know that some of the Christian flock are turning back to evil, to drink, to lust, to carelessness, to defrauding one another, to pride is to increase the grief of a pastor's heart. He who truly loves his flock and witnesses the inroads of sin in such a manner will find himself sleepless at night, greatly burdened in prayer and grieving over those who have sinned against God. This is not confined to a pastor's heart alone, for there are many who are not pastors but merely friends or teachers or parents who are burdened in excessive sorrow over the sins of their children or their pupils or their friends. I could testify now to friends who have within their hearts a permanent sorrow because of the unbelief, the rejection, the indifference of their own children to the Gospel of Christ. If you are living in sin this day just remember that you are causing sorrow, that you are bringing pain, shame and sadness either to the heart of your parents or your pastor or to God Himself. Those who should make you glad are unable to do so because in turn they are sorrowed by your unbelief or your sins.

III. Joy—The Reaction of Christian Love to Righteousness

Paul describes a minister as "the helper of your joy." Christianity is a religion of joy. Joy actually is the chief end and element of the Christian life. Thus the catechism rightly says that we are to glorify God and enjoy him forever. Do you enjoy God or do you desire joy now in your own heart and find it lacking? How much joy is really present in your life if you are a believer? Is it joy unspeakable and full of glory as the Apostle describes it? Or, as Paul says, do you rejoice because the love of God is shed abroad in your heart through the Holy Ghost? Unquestionably many of us are false witnesses to the Gospel of Christ on this point before the world. We do not have the joy of the Lord.

It is sin which mars the joy in the life of Christians. If we wish to know why Christians are joyless, we must say that sin is the answer. There may be the sin of insensibility to the great act of Divine love upon Calvary. Some of us have begun to grow blind to the great things which lie at the basis of our faith. That is, the love of God in Jesus Christ; that love in which He died for us upon the tree. It has begun to lose its newness and its wonder and we often speak of it without real apprehension and without feeling. Our hearts do not burn within us any more. We have no real joy in this truth. But also we can have no joy without it, and usually it is because we have been pampering self or have been indulging in some practice of worldly pleasure or we have been catering to evil and we have lost our first love. David said, "In thy presence is fulness of joy; at thy right hand there are pleasures forevermore." This should describe the life of a Christian. Never pity a Christian, even though he may be sacrificing on many points. He, you may be sure, is having the time of his life. He is having joy unspeakable and full of glory.

Now, he who effectively removes sin from a believer's life is a helper of his joy. Therefore, sermons which you hear which search out sin, hypocrisy, evil-speaking, lying and weaknesses help your joy. Thus it is necessary for us to preach about depravity, about carnality, about self-judgment, about Divine chastenment, about fruitlessness, if we are to produce joy in your lives. We want you to have the joy of healing which comes after surgery. I have told you of a professor friend of mine who was so concerned over an operation under which his child had to go. He had spent sleepless nights in prayer and it was not easy for him to allow that little child to undergo the knife, but he called me several times afterwards. Each time he was exuberant, praising God, because his little girl was up and walking around the room in the hospital and he knew that she would get well. It is not easy to apply the knife, but when it is done, it is for the purpose of producing joy in the healing of your soul.

There is a union of grief and of happiness in pastor and people. Paul said, "If I make you sorry, who is he then that maketh me glad, but the same which is made sorry by me? . . . I should have sorrow from them of whom I ought to rejoice." Paul was reluctant to bring these Corinthians into sorrow because of their sin, because it would make him sorrowful too unless they repented. To preach a people under conviction so that they are miserable and would rather stay away from church gives a pastor no joy. To see people sad makes him sad also. A true pastor with a heart of love can not help but feel the keen pangs of conviction that come upon people who live in sin. He weeps with those who weep. Therefore, the only avenue for the restoration of joy either to a pastor or people is the repentance of backsliders and the conversion of sinners. I tell you there is no joy like that of seeing men accept Jesus Christ as Savior or like that of hearing testimony of restored blessing in the lives of individuals.

Therefore, in love let us be helpers of one another's joy. As from time to time your pastor points out to you the way of holiness and of life, may it be to help you to great joy and may your repentance and your contrition be such as to give him joy and glory. Together let us seek such an outpouring of Divine love in its infinitude and overwhelming omnipotence that our joy may be fully renewed, that we may bask in the Divine favor. This is the greatest evangelistic force in the world. When people see our joy they will seek our Savior, for they wish to have joy too. It is the right of joy to reign in the Christian community and that joy is the reaction of love to righteousness in the lives of individuals.

No wonder then that Paul dismisses this particular situation with the words, "To whom ye forgive anything I forgive also: for if I forgave anything, to whom I forgave it, for your sakes forgave I it in the person of Christ." Forgiveness! That is the most beautiful word in human language and forgiveness comes from love. If love meeting sin erects a cross, where there is a cross comes forgiveness. Titus had brought Paul the report that the Corinthians had accepted his authority and disciplined the sinner, which had produced repentance in that sinner and which also had resulted in the rectification of the evils within the church and the acknowledging of Paul's authority. No wonder Paul experienced joy and was able to write, "My joy is the joy of you all." Now, in turn, Paul urged them to forgive the repentant sinner and to restore him to fellowship even as he, the Apostle, in the Person of Christ forgave him. Here then we see something of love in action, love which turns to grief in the presence of sin, love which turns to joy in the presence of righteousness and love which results in forgiveness when there is repentance. This is God's way and we have spoken of it in order that you may know the love which we have more abundantly toward you.

VI

UNFORGIVINGNESS, A DEVICE OF THE DEVIL FOR THE DESTRUCTION OF YOUR SOUL

TEXT: *"To whom ye forgive anything, I forgive also: for if I forgave anything, to whom I forgave it, for your sakes forgave I it in the person of Christ; lest Satan should get an advantage of us: for we are not ignorant of his devices."*—II COR. 2:5-11.

THE FORGIVENESS of a great sinner is the subject before us in this Scripture. It is absolutely impossible to reconstruct all the details of this sin, to identify the sinner and to describe the means of discipline and of forgiveness. Numerous great Bible scholars identify the individual referred to in this text as the man guilty of incest in the Corinthian Church. An equal number of great scholars feel that this identification is impossible and that Paul is referring to some one who had wronged him during his visit at Corinth. Whichever view may be true is rather inconsequential to the truths contained in the text. It is neither necessary nor advisable that we should know the individual to whom Paul was referring. In fact, Paul refers to the matter in a most delicate and careful way. He speaks of the one who committed the sin as "any one" and "such a one." The fact that Paul neither named the individual nor the sin which he committed in this text shows that it is better to immortalize the truth which underlies this relationship than the sinner himself.

There is no value in reviving past sins when they once have been confessed to God and to the brethren and have been cleansed and forgiven by God's grace. For the church or for third parties to bandy about lightly such sins is to smack of scandal mongering, something which should be greatly avoided. For individuals to revive sins in open confession on numerous occasions is to defile the pure consciences of their auditors or even of themselves, after they have been cleansed, and to place a stumbling-block in the way of innocent men. I shall never forget the effect of such a confession meeting upon my mind in the year 1935. I visited a meeting at Victoria Hall, Geneva, during the session of the League of Nations in that important year when the League was considering whether it should be strong in applying sanctions against Italy for invading Ethiopia. At this particular meeting individuals from South Africa, from London and from other parts of the world stood on the platform and confessed numerous sins which should have excluded them from accepted society. Now, it is quite possible that they had committed those sins, but they should have confessed them privately and to individuals sinned against, not on a public platform. The whole thing was revolting in the extreme, as are other practices of this same group. With nothing ought we deal more delicately than with confessed sin. A man who has passed through a religious experience may have his head in the clouds but he should also keep his feet on the ground by remembering the practical implications of the things which he is doing and saying. We ought to take a lesson from the Apostle Paul in the manner in which he dealt with sin.

This particular instance of the necessity of forgiving sin was the possible means by which Satan might get an advantage over the church, the Christians and the Apostle himself. Christianity is a serious business. It is a struggle against principalities and authorities under the leadership of the prince of darkness himself, who is not only personified evil but is a person called Satan. Many and great attacks can be made by this hierarchy of evil powers upon believers from many different angles. We are specifically told, "Your adversary the devil, as a roaring lion, walketh about, seeking whom he may devour." In this mighty struggle it is easy to lose the advantage, to be defeated, to be taken in snares or traps unawares. The church or the individual who is overreached by Satan, outwitted or outmaneuvered is unfitted for service or for testimony. For this reason Paul said, "I keep under my body, and bring it into subjection: lest that by any means, when I have preached to others, I myself should be a castaway." In this case Paul recognized a device by which Satan could easily have gotten the advantage over him and the church.

Satan has many devices of which we should not be ignorant. A device usually suggests craftiness, subtlety, wicked purposes and wrong intentions. With Satan every device is malign. This is implied in the exhortation, "Fret not thyself because of him who prospereth in his way, because of the man who bringeth wicked devices to pass." Daniel describes the man of sin at the end of the age as one who "shall forecast his devices against the strongholds, even for a time." In passing we ought to glance at several of these devices of Satan.

One device of Satan is sickness. In the case of Job Satan used this device to attack Job and to force him to sin against God in rebellion and bitterness. He believed that by this means he could make Job curse God and die. In the case of Paul he also used sickness (apparently) to buffet him so as to make him weak for the service of the Lord. The ease with which Satan gains the advantage over believers by sickness is apparent. Sometimes he permanently afflicts one who could be delivered by prayer and hence is able to keep such a person incapacitated for spiritual work. Such was the woman whom Satan had bound with a spirit of infirmity for eighteen years and whom Jesus loosed from her infirmity. On the other hand, Satan uses the sicknesses which God permits to come to us for His own glory to incite us to bitterness or to complaint or to rebellion and thus to turn what should be to the glory of God to the glory of Satan himself. Not all sicknesses come from Satan or from God. Many of them come from our own foolishness and sin. Such was the sickness which existed among the Corinthian Christians in their lack of true temperance at the love feasts. Satan often uses sickness as a device to attack our souls.

One hardly needs to mention temptation as a device of Satan. Satan tried by means of temptation to destroy the Lord Jesus Christ. We read concerning Jesus' forty days in the wilderness that "he was tempted of the devil" and that when the temptation had ended "the devil left him." Some temptations come directly from Satan as a means of destroying the soul, but Satan's great ally exists in the lust of our own flesh. James says, "Every man is tempted, when he is drawn away of his own lust, and enticed." By this temptation Satan causes some who have received the Word of God to fall away. God has given us innumerable promises in the Scriptures that He will succor us in the hour of temptation if we will but turn to Him. For this reason Christ was tempted in all points like as we are, that He might succor us in the hour of our need. God will never permit us to be tempted above what we are able, but will always provide a way of escape. Jesus said, "I will keep thee from the hour of temptation."

A third device of the devil may be called deception. "Satan himself is transformed into an angel of light." Thus it is his device to deceive the whole world by inspiring all the deceptions of false religions and by ensnaring souls in error. The last great attack made by Satan will be through his emissary, the false prophet, who will do lying wonders at the end of the age. Satan is called by Jesus "the father of lies." It is no wonder, then, that he should deceive us in every possible way. The only possible explanation for the numbers who embrace errors and anti-Biblical systems of thought which are so prevalent is the deception of Satan. This is permitted by God, for Paul said, "Because they received not the love of the truth, that they might be saved. And for this cause God shall send them strong delusion, that they should believe a lie: that they all might be damned who believed not the truth." It is only necessary for Satan to get men to believe a lie in order to get an advantage over them and to hinder the work of God's servants. It is much more difficult to convert men from half truths than from heathenism. I think of a movement which originated in Boston and has spread over the world, which has much truth in it concerning the healing of the body, a truth which the orthodox church has largely neglected, much to its own loss. But joined with this truth on healing is the great error concerning the atonement, namely, the denying of the efficacious work of the Lord Jesus upon the Cross in behalf of sin. In fact, the movement denies the existence of sin. This is a deception of Satan whereby he is willing to heal a man's body in order to destroy his soul. How much better to have both body and soul healed by the Lord Jesus Christ in connection with His true Gospel!

Then Satan uses the device of opposition to Christian work. One need only refer to the parable of the tares in which the enemy or the devil sowed evil seed amidst the good seed in order to divide, to impede, to hinder and to destroy the effect of the good seed. That is Satan's method at all times. He even is able to impede the prayers of God's people. Daniel was hindered in his prayers for three weeks, before the answer came, by the prince of the kingdom of Persia, namely, the prince of the power of the air or Satan. It is Satan's purpose to inspire unbelief or prayerlessness or indifference in the Christian or even discouragement and despair in order to hinder God's work. We must constantly remember that we struggle not with flesh and blood but with principalities and powers, with spiritual wickedness in high places and that therefore we need the whole armor of God.

These devices of the devil demand constant watching, prayer, spiritual preparedness and union with Christ in order for us to triumph always in Christ Jesus and to make manifest the savor of his knowledge in every place. Such triumph is possible, for Satan our great foe has been defeated by the Captain of our salvation. Christ, "having spoiled principalities and powers, made a show of them openly, triumphing over them in it," namely, the blood of His Cross. Therefore, God is able to give us the Divine armor described by Paul in Ephesians 6:11-18, and the victory may be ours. "For whosoever is born of God overcometh the world: and this is the victory that overcometh the world, even our faith."

The particular device of Satan used in this case described in our Scripture lesson is unforgivingness. The Corinthians had evidently written to Paul asking whether they should forgive the sinner who had been disciplined by the church. They had been tempted to the unforgiving attitude by a minority within the congregation, and had the minority succeeded in the unforgiving attitude Satan would have gained a distinct advantage over the whole Christian movement. The disciplined individual had been guilty either of incest or of withstanding Paul's authority or both, and thus had stirred up division between the church members. It seemed sufficient to some to cast him out permanently, but such natural reasoning would have been a device of Satan to hurt all concerned. Unforgivingness is a most common device for Satan to use to get advantage of us. Therefore, this subject demands an exposition from the Scripture. It was my intention to pass on to that magnificent text in the 16th verse but the Spirit of God forced me back to this subject of unforgivingness. Hence I am led to believe that it is needed by some.

I. THE PLACE OF FORGIVENESS IN CHRISTIAN TEACHING

The fountain head of all forgiveness is God. The ground work of all forgiveness is found in the unmerited love and mercy of God. By our attitude toward others we reveal how much we have made that love our own. Christianity is a religion of grace, of the unmerited favor of Divine love resulting in forgiveness. God is a god of grace. That is, He is predisposed in our favor. God is not some Shylock exacting his pound of flesh in the fulfilment of a debt. He freely forgives all who call upon Him in repentance. God, however, remains completely just in so forgiving all sinners who seek Him. His love has been expressed in His justice no less than in His mercy. "God was in Christ, reconciling the world unto himself."

The Cross is the manifestation of this grace. God Himself satisfied the demands of His moral universe, so that He might be free to forgive sin. Thus we read, "Whom [Jesus Christ] God hath set forth to be a propitiation [mercy seat], through faith in His blood, to declare his righteousness for the remission of sins that are past, through the forebearance of God; . . . that he might be just and the justifier of him which believeth in Jesus." God showed that forgiveness came at the price of awful suffering. It was not arbitrary leniency. God revealed that love meeting sin brings a cross and where a cross is, there is forgiveness. Calvary provided the forgiveness of God for all sin, showing His love, His suffering and His favor toward all men. "He is the propitiation for our sins: and not for ours only, but also for the sins of the whole world." Such a doctrine involves the Trinity in its full work of redemption. Its practical result is that there is no sin which can be committed in life which is too great for the forgiveness of God. The heart of the Gospel is that through this man [Jesus Christ] is preached unto you the forgiveness of sin.

God not only gave to us the revelation of how He is able to forgive our sins, but He gave us an example of forgiveness in the Person of Christ. If we carefully watch the Lord Jesus Christ in the Gospel narratives of His life, we see that He went about forgiving sin. In the case of the man of palsy who was brought to Jesus lying upon a bed, He said, "Son, be of good cheer. Thy sins be forgiven thee." This was the preliminary to the process of healing His body. Likewise also, when Jesus spoke to the woman of the streets who followed Him into the house of Simon and washed his feet with the tears of her repentance, He said, "Thy sins are forgiven." Jesus not only forgave sins but He also taught His disciples that they must forgive the sins which had been committed against Him. Thus he taught them that when they stand praying they must forgive and that the condition of the acceptability of their own prayers was that they should forgive their fellow men their trespasses. This teaching made such an impression on Peter that he was willing to go far beyond the teaching of the rabbis of his own day and suggest that he should forgive his brother who sinned against him seven times. But Jesus laid down the principle of endless forgiveness when He said, "Not seven but seventy times seven." The Lord reinforced His own teaching about forgiveness by praying for the forgiveness of those who nailed Him to the rugged Cross saying, "Father, forgive them, for they know not what they do."

This practice of forgiveness is enjoined on the believer. Jesus commanded us to forgive if we would be His followers. Think of His words, "If ye forgive men their trespasses, your heavenly Father will also forgive you: but if ye forgive not men their trespasses, neither will your Father forgive your trespasses." Paul adds, "Be ye kind one to another, tender-hearted, forgiving one another, even as God for Christ's sake hath forgiven you." This is as much a commandment of God as any one of the Ten Commandments. Jesus, in expounding the Ten Commandments, said, "Love your enemies, bless them that curse you, do good to them that hate you, and pray for them which despitefully use you and persecute you; that ye may be the children of your Father which is in heaven." Likewise, this practice of forgiveness is made the condition of the answer to our own prayers. If we forgive we shall be forgiven, but if not we shall not be forgiven by the heavenly Father. If we have something in our hearts which we are holding in unforgiveness our hearts will condemn us and God is greater than our hearts, and thus we know that we shall not receive the answer to our prayers. Jesus said, "If ye keep my commandments ye are my friends." Surely this is one of His commandments. Let us re-emphasize the fact that forgiveness in attitude conditions our own forgiveness, namely, that our attitude toward others reveals how much we have made the love and attitude of God our own. If a man reacts with unforgiveness after he professes to be saved by Christ, he reveals the true nature of his heart as hard and unregenerate rather than tender and transformed. Though we are not saved by what we do, our actions will reveal the condition of our hearts. An unforgiving person is an unsaved person, or, at least, he is under Divine condemnation and he is in a backslidden condition.

Forgiveness is the most beautiful manifestation of Divine love which we have, for it means suffering, sacrifice, redemption and service. It is the one act of love which is most near to the Divine characteristics. The *Sunday School Times* printed an illustration on this very subject. A wealthy business man in Boston, a devout Christian, married a beautiful woman and gave her a beautiful home. She fell, through the besetting sin of drink. One day she left home, never to return, leaving a note behind saying that her life was not in keeping with her husband's sterling Christian character. He immediately employed men throughout the land to search for her. Copies of her photograph were left in various cities with undertakers, with these instructions, "If her body should ever come to you, buy the finest clothes that money can buy, give her the finest casket possible, bank it with flowers and send for me." And when at last an undertaker called him, and he through his tears, gazed upon the face in the casket, he said, "Oh, Nellie, if you only knew how I loved you, you would have come back to me." When the funeral was over, he went to the marble works and contracted for a costly monument. When asked what should be inscribed on it, he said, "I want you to inscribe on it just one word—'Forgiven.'"

II. THE PERIL OF UNFORGIVINGNESS

The coupling of tender-heartedness with forgiveness and hard-heartedness with unforgivingness is quite consistent in the Scriptures. Each of us is tempted to relentlessness. It is the tendency of the natural man to seek vengeance. Shakespeare makes Shylock say, "I will better their instruction," when speaking of his enemies and the vengeance he will work upon them. There is a natural desire in men to inflict pain for pain, to exact an eye for an eye and a tooth for a tooth. It is difficult to escape this tendency when a deliberate wrong is done to an individual, but there is no place for this self-righteousness and Pharisaical hardness in the Christian life.

The right for vengeance or to repay wrong belongs unto God and God alone. He says, "Vengeance belongeth unto me. I will repay." This relegating of vengeance on those who do us wrong to God demands a great step of faith. We must actually believe in God. Paul said, "Give place unto wrath," by which he meant that we are to step aside, not taking our vengeance in our own hands but committing it unto God Himself. If there is any retaliation to be taken by a believer it must be doing good for evil and thus heaping coals of fire upon a person's head, that is, bringing him to shame and contrition. Yes, the Sermon on the Mount has meaning for us today.

Assuming the right to repay or to commit vengeance lays us open to Divine judgment for all of our sins. This practice is the repudiation of the principle of grace. The Cross of the Lord Jesus Christ not only means our forgiveness from sin through the grace of God, but demands our forgiveness of others through our own favor and grace. To repudiate that is to negate our own privilege of being forgiven by God.

Thus we call unforgivingness a sin. It is, first of all, a violation of a Divine commandment, a worse violation, we believe, than murder. Unrepented murder will shut one out from the kingdom, but so will unforgivingness, and unforgivingness has a greater deception and is a greater trap than murder, for more people fall into it. Thus by it Satan is able to destroy more souls. We have said that it is a repudiation of the Christian principle of grace. We are told to be forgiving one of another as God for Christ's sake hath forgiven us. If God for the sake of Christ has forgiven us then we for the sake of Christ must forgive others. It is in this sense that Paul here speaks of himself as forgiving "in the person of Christ." It has been said that this was Paul acting in the eyes of or under the sight of God.

Not at all. Paul is in Christ Jesus, and being in Christ, for the sake of Christ and His love and redemption and the principles of grace, Paul knew that he must forgive. To refuse to forgive would be to deny the God who bought us and to repudiate our salvation.

This attitude is amply described by Jesus in the parable of the two debtors. His lord forgave a servant an immense debt, which was beyond the power of any one individual to repay. This represented the debt of the individual sinner to God. This same servant who was forgiven refused to forgive a debt which was so paltry and meager that a few days labor would be able to repay it. He cast his debtor, a fellow servant, into prison until he should pay the debt. The parable says that when the lord of that servant heard it, he summoned the wicked servant before him and said, "Oh thou wicked servant, I forgave thee all that debt, because thou desirest me: shouldest not thou also have had compassion on thy fellow servant, even as I had pity on thee?" And his lord was wroth and delivered him to the tormentors until he should pay all that was due to him. Jesus added, "So likewise shall my heavenly Father do also unto you, if ye from your hearts forgive not every one his brother their trespasses."

The result of unforgivingness is to be lost, to be destroyed, to be utterly and finally ruined for eternity. We unqualifiedly state that he who forgives not, whether an unbeliever or a professing Christian, is lost and will bear the penalty of all of his sins and not of this one sin of unforgivingness alone. This leads him to face the penalty of his sins and the demands of justice alone, without the mediation and the substitution of the atonement of our Lord Jesus Christ. It is an awful fate to contemplate. In plain words, Jesus said that the unforgiving man would be condemned to hell far quicker than he who was guilty of adultery, of murder or of thievery, for the one who is unforgiving compels God to apply the principle of judgment and justice to his own destiny. What, then, is that which we forgive in our brethren in comparison with what God forgives us for all eternity? Do you not see now that all Satan's devices tend to utter and final destruction of the soul and that this one is one of the most subtle of all?

III. THE POWER OF FORGIVENESS

We understand the power of forgiveness in two ways. First, the power to forgive, and second, the power of forgiveness over others. Perhaps someone whose heart is embittered and incensed toward another, will want to know how he can have the power to forgive when his heart is in such condition. The first means is that of prayer. Have you ever tried to pray for him who wronged you? Yes, you tried it and your lips are sealed. The heavens are as brass and you are unable to express your thoughts, for your heart is bitter and hard and is not right with God. Then it is time for you to pray unto God to teach you the spirit of Christ and to give you his Holy Spirit, making you feel something of the love of God, in order that you may pray for the brother who wronged you and that by that prayer and by that forgiveness you may be able to win him unto the Lord and righteousness. You will find sooner or later that God will melt your heart and will bring you in unison with your Lord and give you a taste of that which Jesus experienced upon Calvary.

> "My enemy had done me bitter wrong,
> And at forgiveness all my soul rebelled.
> The thought of vengeance surging hot and strong
> Like bitter water deep within me welled.
> I sought to drive it from my heart with prayer;
> 'Oh, Father, help me to forgive!' I cried.
> But my hurt soul still brooded silent there
> The hurt of unjust dealings, wounded pride.
>
> "Then a new prayer I taught my heart to say
> Forgetting hurt to self and vengeance sweet,
> 'Oh, Spirit, enter thou his heart this day
> Make it with justice and with truth to beat.
> Give him a mind that cannot others wrong,
> A will and purpose like unto Thine own.
> Be Thou his guidance, all the way along,
> Let Thy sweet spirit in his life be shown.'
>
> "Then the old truth I saw, as dawn of day;
> We cannot hate the one for whom we pray!"

The second answer we give to you as to how to forgive is by the enabling Spirit of Christ. Paul forgave "in the person of Christ." What we cannot do in ourselves Christ can do in us. Are you born again? Are you in Christ and is Christ abiding in you? Then you can do all things through Christ who strengtheneth you and this, the Scripture says, is according to the will of God. Thus we infallibly tell you that the Spirit of Christ will enable you to forgive. If Christ was forgiving in this world and we are truly His representatives in the world, then we also must be forgiving. "Let this mind be in you, which was also in Christ Jesus."

The third suggestion is that you may forgive or have the power to forgive by love. John said, "We have known and believed the love that God hath to us. God is love; and he that dwelleth in love dwelleth in God, and God in him." Micah said of God, "He retaineth not his anger forever, because he delighteth in mercy." God delights in mercy manifested in the Christian as well as in Himself. A true Christian will grieve more over the wrong done to the sinner's own soul than he will do because of the wrong done to himself. He will love like Christ.

> "Oh, give us hearts to love like Thee,
> Like Thee, oh Lord to grieve
> Far more for others' sins than all
> The wrongs that we receive."

Thus it will be by loving that we shall conquer.

> "Should friends misjudge, or foes defame,
> Or brethren faithless prove,
> Then, like Thine own, be all our aim
> To conquer them by love."

The power of forgiveness means not only to forgive but the influence exercised by forgiveness over others. The forgiving attitude humbles, softens and breaks the hardest, sinning and evil heart, but selfish pride and relentlessness exacting from others restitution only hardens them and drives them on. Thus Paul here said that there was a danger in unforgivingness of sending this disciplined sinner to hell through his despair. Satan would use this device for the claiming of a soul.

We have commonly believed that Stephen's prayer for the forgiveness of his persecutors who put him to death resulted in the conversion of Saul of Tarsus. Well it may be, for Saul later became the great expounder of Stephen's gospel presented before the Sanhedrin.

In Countess Alexandra Tolstoy's biography of her father, called *The Tragedy of Tolstoy*, she tells the story of an experience in his childhood. It is as follows:

"Masha seldom scolded me. One day I was reading Mayne Reid's *Headless Horseman*. It was bedtime, but the book was so fascinating that I continued to read in bed, though it was strictly forbidden. Not until Masha was actually at my bedside did I realize that somebody had come in. Instinctively I blew out the candle. Masha became angry. 'Aren't you ashamed? Not only do you do something forbidden but you want to hide it, you want to lie!' Masha's voice sounded unkind and harsh, and she almost slammed the door as she went out. 'How wicked and unjust Masha is,' I thought to myself, and burst into tears. Finally, I stopped crying, and my thoughts went wandering off to the American prairies. I dozed. 'Sasha, are you asleep?' Masha was sitting on the edge of my bed. 'Forgive me,' she said. 'You know, I thought that I must have been wrong. If you are afraid of me, it means I gave you a reason for it; perhaps I had not been kind to you.' And all of a sudden my feelings of offense and irritation vanished and were replaced by contentment and repentance. I felt ashamed of having wished to deceive Masha and overjoyed because she was so good and she forgave me for it. 'I won't, I won't do it again,' I whispered through my tears. She stroked my head, and even though the room was dark, I knew that tears were in her eyes, too, and that her face shone with kindness."

We conclude with the words of Jesus, If you would be forgiven, forgive. "If thou bringest thy gift to the altar and there rememberest that thy brother hath ought against thee, leave there thy gift and go thy way. First be reconciled to thy brother and then come and offer thy gift." Let not Satan destroy your soul by the device of unforgivingness.

VII

CHRIST AND THE NOTE OF TRIUMPH

TEXT: *"Now thanks be unto God, which always causeth us to triumph in Christ, and maketh manifest the savour of his knowledge by us in every place."*—II COR. 2:12-14.

A NOTE OF TRIUMPH and of victory in Christian warfare is necessary. In the text a metaphor is used of the Roman triumph as similar to the experience of the Christian.

Paul uses this metaphor of the triumph to describe certain aspects of the Christian life. He had seen enough of these Roman triumphal arches and probably some of the processions so that it was an apt figure for his use. To this he referred when he said, "He ascended up on high, he led captivity captive, and gave gifts unto men." Likewise also when he spoke of Christ spoiling principalities and making a show of them openly, "triumphing over them in it." This is the meaning of our particular text.

The comparison of Christianity to warfare is most appropriate. In fact, this is probably the most repeated metaphor in the Bible and in hymnology. We are enjoined to fight against Satan, against the world, against temptation, against self and against mere inertia. We are told "to be a good soldier," to "fight the fight of faith," "our warfare is not with fleshly weapons," and to "contend earnestly for the faith." Any one who seriously tries Christianity, knows that war is the best description of it. There are many other figures of this Christian life used in the Bible, but none so good as war. War depicts the sacrifice, the toil, the suffering, the expenditure of money and effort, the self-denial, the heroism which is connected with Christianity. One need only think of the sacrifices which have been made by missionaries and are being made today to realize that this is a war of no mean proportions. The holy war of Christianity demands from its soldiers all that a worldly war demands from those young men who are laying down their positions, giving up homes and loved ones and going into encampment for the possible reason of shedding their blood for the country. Yet this very fact of the warfare of the Christian against sin, evil and Satan is often forgotten by Christians who desire to take their ease in Zion. But heaven was never attained on flowery beds of ease and it never will be, for Christianity is warfare. The conflict comes before the victory, the suffering before the triumph, both in the individual Christian's experience and in the church. Without great dangers, sufferings and struggles no triumph would ever be celebrated in a military way, and without danger, conflict and struggle there would be no triumph in an individual life.

We are constrained that this note of triumph is needed by many who embrace Christ's cause today. If there is an absence of the note of triumph it is because we have entered no war, made no sacrifices, have met no obstacles, have undergone no jeopardy for Christ. Who would ever think of the Premier of Hungary or the King of Rumania enjoying a triumph after their ignobly capitulating to the Axis powers? One need only contrast this with the heroic struggle put up by Greece and the Netherlands to know who deserves a triumph. It can come only to those who wage warfare. The note of peace at any price, appeasement of evil, compromise, retrenchment, and of defense has been the note of the church as it has been the note of a nation. For such there can never be a triumph. There can never be intoxicating joy of victory and of glory and there can never be any trophies in their train. For the church we say, away with such inglorious, anæmic, vacillating leadership and spirit in individual lives.

"Cross of Christ lead onward, through the holy war;
By this sign we conquer, now and ever more.
Not of man the power, not to man the fame;
We are victors only in our Leader's name."

I. Paul's Victory in the Christian Warfare

Think of the mighty afflictions and deprivations under which Paul passed in his Christian warfare. As he wrote this second epistle to the Corinthians from Macedonia he remembered vividly his recent terrible trial at Ephesus, when his ministry was concluded by a riot in the amphitheater led by Demetrius the silversmith. At that time his life was in danger, but as he now writes some new danger had come to him in Asia, the nature of which we do not know. He describes it, "We would not, brethren, have you ignorant of our trouble which came to us in Asia, that we were pressed out of measure, above strength, insomuch that we despaired even of life: but we had the sentence of death in ourselves." Some terrible experience had seized the apostle Paul which led him to even despair of life. Distress came to him from still another condition, however, namely, the spiritual confusion and turmoil which existed in the Corinthian Church.

A great contrast is here brought out between the life which Paul lived and what people imagine the Christian life to be. These afflictions which Paul mentioned are but a small part of the general afflictions which he underwent as a good soldier of the Lord Jesus Christ. Paul had taught himself to endure hardness as a good soldier, for he was compelled to undergo much. He said:

"Even unto this present hour we both hunger, and thirst, and are naked, and are buffeted, and have no certain dwelling place; and labor, working with our own hands: being reviled, we bless; being persecuted, we suffer it: being defamed, we entreat: we are made as the filth of the world, and are the offscouring of all things unto this day."

On another occasion Paul declared:

"We are troubled on every side, yet not distressed; we are perplexed, but not in despair; Persecuted, but not forsaken; cast down, but not destroyed; always bearing about in the body the dying of the Lord Jesus, that the life also of Jesus might be made manifest in our body."

Yet again he describes his experience by saying:

"Are they ministers of Christ? I am more; in labors more abundant, in stripes above measure, in prisons more frequent, in deaths oft. Of the Jews five times received I forty stripes save one. Thrice was I beaten with rods, once was I stoned, thrice I suffered shipwreck, a night and a day I have been in the deep; in journeyings often, in perils of waters, in perils of robbers, in perils by mine own countrymen, in perils by the heathen, in perils in the city; in perils in the wilderness, in perils in the sea, in perils among false brethren; in weariness and painfulness, in watchings often, in hunger and thirst, in fastings often, in cold and nakedness. Beside those things that are without, that which cometh upon me daily, the care of all the churches."

The preaching which describes the Christian life as all smiles, airy, breezy and full of nothing but pleasures was not the kind of preaching Paul gave and not the experience which he had. Paul had no plaster smile upon his face for every one whom he met. There were times when he was deeply concerned over matters in these churches. He did not try to cover up his agitation and his concern over the Corinthian Church and its difficulty. There was no absurd, self-deception about all men being good, about there being no sin and no sorrow in the world. Paul knew that the world was full of sin and sorrow, and he had had plenty of both as his own share.

Yes, if Paul's life is anything of a standard for us we may conclude that this life is a war, a fight to the death against sickness, sorrow, temptation, loss, failure, need and evil. It is a false idea to affirm that one is a Christian because God has blessed him with a family, home and happiness, as some contend. Paul had none of these things and yet Paul was the first Christian, and many have followed in his train.

Yet Paul declared that the Christian way was the way of victory. He himself contended that he was more than conqueror in all these things through Christ who loved him. When one can come off victor in this conflict and even more than a victor, he has resources which enable him to say something to us. One who out of the midst of these disturbing experiences can say, "Thanks be to God who always causeth us to triumph in Christ," has a message and a note to sound for our day. This was merely another vindication of God's present help which was evident in all of Paul's life unto the very end.

This victory is held out by this great Christian as the average believer's privilege. He said, "We are more than conquerors." This victory or triumph is not something reserved for a choice few, such as Bishop Taylor or John Wesley, but is available for all, for every believer. Any man who will enter his Christian heritage may be more than a conqueror through Christ who loves him. He may have a daily triumph as a foretaste of the great ultimate triumph that is to come. Many crowns are promised in the Word of God to the overcoming soul. He shall have an incorruptible crown that fadeth not away, a crown of life, a crown of glory, a crown of righteousness laid up for those who love His appearing, but the daily crown of victorious living is one of the best.

Jonathan Edwards was a good illustration of such victory in the midst of disturbing circumstances.

H. Bramford Parks, writing Edwards' biography concerning the time his ministry was terminated at Northampton and his congregation was turned against him, said:

"Never in his life did Edwards shine more nobly than in these eighteen months of martyrdom. He treated the townspeople as reasonable beings, who would listen to intellectual argument; but that was a mistake, not an error of character. Never for a moment did he falter in his belief that his cause was right; he was convinced that his enemies were the enemies of God, and when necessary he did not hesitate to say so in unqualified words, but in the whole controversy he showed no trace of bitterness or personal rancor; the account which he wrote of it is not only sober, just and good-tempered, it is actually amusing; he looked down upon his enemies from the pinnacle of his own untroubled conscience as if he were a God. An onlooker remarked in his diary that he never saw in Edwards the slightest trace of anger or grief; he seemed like a man of God whose happiness was beyond the reach of his enemies; by nothing, he added, were the townspeople more infuriated than by their obvious failure to ruffle his serenity." *

Jonathan Edwards was more than conqueror in the greatest crisis of his life.

II. THE MEANS OF VICTORY IN THIS WARFARE

In this epistle Paul gives three great means of victory; first, God; second, Christ; and third, spiritual weapons of warfare.

The Apostle commences his pæan of praise by saying, "Thanks be to God." God was placed as the source and center of all of Paul's victory. The belief in God and God's purpose is able to hold one steady when the billows break over the barque of his life. To be able to believe in God, whose hand is at the helm, who is the disposer of destiny, who has an all-embracing will, is to give one stability in trouble. A woman who has suffered exceedingly from an accident recently wrote, "I did not make nearly so good headway so long as I rebelled against my affliction. Now I am leaving it all in His hands and really I begin to see light on the whole process, and I am coming through with a better understanding than I have ever had." God is necessary not only to keep us on the course, in this warfare, but also to provide the strength to continue it and the promise as to its

---

* *Jonathan Edwards, The Fiery Puritan*, Minton, Balch and Company, New York. Quoted by permission.

end. For this reason the Apostle wrote, "All things work together for good to them that love God, to them who are *the* called according to his purpose." This belief in God gives inner resources which can be obtained in no other way.

The confidence that nothing can befall you without God permitting it is the greatest element in your victory or triumph over circumstances. If you are willing to stop fighting mentally, spiritually and inwardly against your lot, if you will use this mighty but dissipated energy to get well, to conquer obstacles, to do something for others, you may have victory. Remember that God controls the events of your life and God is able to give you the victory.

But Paul also ascribed this victory as coming "through Christ." The Bible holds out no promise of your victory or your triumph outside of Christ. Without Him you are a pawn of wicked forces doomed to defeat, battered by caprice, and though you may think of your head as being bloody but unbowed, as Henley did, you are menaced at every step and moment of life by death itself. Who is able to deliver you from death? Only Christ.

Christ has won the great triumph. He is the victor. Paul declares that on the Cross He triumphed over all principalities and powers openly, that He spoiled them as a conqueror spoils the vanquished, that he made a show of them openly, as Julius Cæsar or Titus made an open shew of those vanquished in their great battles. Hence, you may be sure that there was something more to Calvary than merely a demonstration of God's love to men, something more than the death of a martyr for the truth which He preached, something more than a political offender dying because He opposed the powers that be. On Calvary a spiritual battle was won, and following it the Lord Jesus Christ led captivity captive and before the universe demonstrated His supremacy over all spiritual enemies. God Himself once and for all defeated our enemy, the accuser, the angel of death, by submitting to death on Calvary and emptying it of its sting.

Thus Christ is the secret of the believer's victory. When we are united with Christ all that He overcame is vanquished for us. We know that He overcame temptation, sorrow, sin and death, and thus we believe He can overcome them for us. It is the living Christ in us who affords Divine activity on our behalf, which gives us the victory. Thus Paul could say and we can say with him, "I can do all things through Christ who strengtheneth me." If God withheld not His own Son but freely delivered Him up for us all, how shall He not also with Christ freely give us all things? In Christ, or regenerated, we are on the road to victory.

A third factor enters, however, into the means of our victory, and that is our willingness to wage warfare with spiritual rather than carnal weapons. These spiritual weapons include prayer. One may be sure that day and night Paul was interceding for this Corinthian Church and that through his intercession the Spirit of the living God was mightily persuading the Corinthian Christians to obey the Apostle's exhortations and commandments. Yet another spiritual weapon is the Word of God, which is sharp and powerful and is able to cut between the thoughts and the intents of the heart. Expert use of the Word of God is a weapon of spiritual victory. Likewise, the blood of the Cross may be used as a weapon of victory. It was the shedding of this blood, namely, the giving of life of the Son of God in sacrifice which won the great victory and which repeats victories in individual lives today. Finally, we would but mention the Spirit of the Lord as a weapon of warfare, for he who possesses the Spirit of Christ knows the mind of the Lord, is able to do his work in the power of the Spirit, is most equipped for Christian warfare.

III. THE VICTORY IS WON BY FAITH

The Apostle John declared, "Whatsoever is born of God overcometh the world: and this is the victory that overcometh the world, even our faith. Who is he that overcometh the world, but he that believeth that Jesus is the Son of God?" One has defined the world as all that antagonizes God, God's kingdom, His cause, His people and His law. Whatever dims the sense of the Divine or devitalizes faith is properly speaking the world. "Whosoever is overcome by the world is one who lets the present outweigh the future, who allows self to crowd out God and the perishable to overshadow the eternal." If we, in turn, overcome this world, we must have victory over pain, over anxiety and over death itself, with all that is included in these three great words. We do not say that a man will never be concerned, but we do believe that in God he will have the victory over his concern. We do not say that a man shall never have pain, but we believe that in God he shall have victory over his pain. We do not say that man will never die, but that in Christ he has victory over death. Thus also we are to overcome poverty, ignorance and weakness, so prevalent in the world. We are to triumph over temptation, sin and even the gates of hell itself.

The principle declared by John which gives us victory over the world is our faith. The beginning of this faith is the actual conviction that Jesus Christ is the Son of God. I do not mean by that that Jesus is divine, or that Jesus was a superman, but that Jesus actually was the Son of God, as the Bible declares Him to be, that He was born of a virgin, lived a sinless life, performed miracles, died on the Cross as a substitute for men and man's sin, rose again and is now exercising the powers of Deity. To all those who thus believe on Christ and commit themselves to Christ, God gives the promise that they are born again and that whosoever is born of God overcometh the world. That is the promise made to those who are regenerated, that is, to those who have received the Divine life by faith in Christ and who have become kindred with God. Is it not wonderful how the Bible begins so much of its teaching with this essential step of being born again? It is so here and it is so with all the matters of the kingdom.

Thus this promised victory is a faith victory. It is by faith that we are united to the great Victor, Christ, and it is this Christ who always causes us to triumph.

VIII

THAT WHICH SENDS FORTH A FRAGRANCE OF LIFE AND AN ODOR OF DEATH, WHO IS COMPETENT TO EXPLAIN?

TEXT: *"We are unto God a sweet savour of Christ, in them that are saved, and in them that perish: to the one we are the savour of death unto death; and to the other the savour of life unto life. And who is sufficient for these things?"*—II COR. 2:15-17.

THE GOSPEL, is an odor, both a deadly fume and a delicate perfume, metaphorically speaking. The Gospel is compared to such a heavenly fragrance given by God for the sake of affecting the sensibilities of men. Paul said, "Now thanks be unto God, which maketh manifest the savor of his knowledge by us in every place." Here occurs a spontaneous change of figure from that of the Roman triumph to the sacrifice suggested by the waves of incense from innumerable altars which filled the air at a triumphal procession. At a triumph incense arose from a thousand altars. Flowers were strewn in the way before the conqueror. Laurels were carried by the conqueror and by his soldiers. Incense might be compared to the odor of the dumb offerings, which was thought by the offerer to be pleasant to God and to men. The tabernacle ritual of the Old Testament included certain offerings of incense unto the Lord which were described as a delight unto Him.

Men also have various reactions to odors. The distillation and preparation of perfumes is an industry of great antiquity. It is the difficulty in the manufacture of pure perfume that accounts for its value, but nothing is so irrepressible and pervasive as fragrance.

The Gospel is described as a fragrance manifested in men who are God's representatives, ambassadors on earth. The savor of God, whether good or bad, depends upon those who profess His Name and on their faithfulness in declaring the Gospel. When we think of the uncounted flowers which are crushed in order to provide a drop of perfume, we realize that the fragrance of the Gospel came from the Cross of Christ, from His suffering and the suffering of His servants like Paul. Wherever a single soul is identified with Christ a fragrance of the Gospel goes forth. By this the knowledge of God is manifested everywhere, in every place. What that fragrance is depends upon the men who manifest it.

The Gospel of the sweetness of God's redeeming love is seen by all who look upon Christians or who hear the message of salvation. This fragrance is first connected with preaching, with the making known of the truth of God, and also by the life of those declaring it. It is important for us to note what an overwhelming effect this fragrance has upon the life of men. Therefore, we shall attend to this Gospel in its particular faculty of being the savor of life or of death unto men.

I. THE DIFFERENT EFFECTS OF THE GOSPEL ON MEN

Paul said, "We are unto God a sweet savor of Christ, in them that are saved, and in them that perish: to the one we are the savor of death unto death; and to the other the savor of life unto life." What is the fragrance or perfume of the Gospel? It is declared to be the savor of His knowledge or of the knowledge of God in Christ. In other words, it is the plain Gospel. It is what Christ revealed of God and what God said that Christ did upon the Cross and is able to do in us. This plain gospel of redemption and of regeneration is the savor of God in us. Thus the savor or the odor cannot be presented without either preaching or testimony concerning this Gospel, and how easy it is for us to be willing to present the Gospel without the sweetness, the winsomeness and the attraction of it. We are willing, and sometimes anxious, to present judgment and wrath rather than the loveliness and the beauty of it.

The text declares that this savor appears differently unto men. It is interesting to note that when one shuts off his olfactory nerve artificially that he is unable to discern many tastes that otherwise are quite common. This has proved that many of our tastes are connected directly with smell. Hence, it is quite a correct translation of this word, meaning pleasing fragrance, to call it a savor. To some men the Gospel is a savor of death and to others it is the savor of life. The Gospel becomes a noxious odor to those who are perishing. Strange to say, some are repelled by the gospel. They dislike it. They turn away from it in disgust. This aversion to the Gospel is not due to anything in the odor of the Gospel, that is, in the Gospel itself, but, as in the case of any perfume, the difference is in the man, who either likes or dislikes it. God does not use the perfume to work death, but rather to bring life. If it works death, the responsibility is not in God, but in the man who perishes. Thus it is that the Gospel blinds some, hardens others and stirs up the corruption and the exasperation in the human heart. Whenever this happens we may be sure that the person is perishing. If the Gospel, as plainly declared in the Scripture, stirs your ire, your hatred, your revulsion, if you are not willing to hear about the blood of Christ, about the atonement, about the Spirit of God, about the supernatural graces of God and about the great doctrines of the Christian faith, it is a sign that you are perishing.

But this same Gospel is a delightful fragrance to those who are saved. What a delicious aroma is to the nostrils, what blending colors are to the eyes, what sweetness is to the taste, what graceful contour is to the touch, the Gospel is to the believing heart. It is a source of great satisfaction. In fact, the saved love to contemplate the Gospel. They are willing to sing,

> "Tell me the old, old story,
> For those who know it best,
> Seem hungering and thirsting,
> To hear it like the rest.

"And when, in scenes of glory,
I sing the new, new song,
'Twill be the old, old story,
That I have loved so long."

To move in an atmosphere perfumed by the love of Christ is like passing through a room touched with the world's most delicate perfume. It is this fragrance of the knowledge of God in Christ which should be diffused everywhere among men by Christians. Paul declared that God made manifest the savor of his knowledge by him and his fellow workers in every place. Does God leave a trace of the Divine fragrance where you have been?

This savor accomplishes certain things in men. Paul said, "To the one we are the savor of death unto death; and to the other, the savor of life unto life." Death is wrought in some by the Gospel. What ought to be to life, namely the Gospel, or the person of Christ, is found to be to death in those rejecting and refusing to believe. This occurs in those who perish. The word "perish" is a present active participle designating that the act is not completed and that those who are now perishing may turn to Christ and to life, for they are not yet in their final state. The death described as ensuing from this fragrance of death is eternal and is the opposite of eternal life, but does not designate annihilation.

On the other hand, life is wrought in some by the Gospel. It is a savor "of life unto life." The Gospel and Christ are life to some. They impart life to those who believe. Any believer knows that the Gospel quickens, gives hope and results in eternal life. Likewise, this is described as an uncompleted action. It is a savor of life unto those who are being saved, and the implication is that these likewise might turn from their uncompleted process and perish.

Here is a mystery. The same element works both life and death in different people. As the heat hardens the clay and softens the iron, so the Gospel saves some and appoints others to death. This we believe is due to the good or bad wills which are worked upon. We can never say that God arbitrarily appoints some unto life and some unto death. Beyond this we cannot go, for it is a mystery. But it is the same with the effect of pain, which mellows some and embitters others, depending upon their personalities. That some draw death from Christ and the Gospel is due, we believe, to man's action and not to God's, for God tells us to convert and to believe and be saved. Why man acts so in rejecting the Gospel and having a distaste for it we cannot say. His action appears to us as unreasonable and as insane as that of suicide. What God ordained to life our wickedness turns into the most awful instrument of judgment, namely, death. This is not a description of two unalterable classes, except in their reaction to the Gospel. They are being saved and are perishing, but their condition may be changed according to their reaction to the Gospel.

II. THE DEPENDENCE OF THE GOSPEL ON GOD FOR EFFICACY

Paul asked, "Who is sufficient for these things?" This implies the inefficiency of human instruments. Men are neither competent to explain this difference in the effect of the gospel nor are they able to change it. Having ministered the gospel, we must leave the final answer of it unto God. But the Bible declares that in God's judgment every man will be revealed as being without excuse if he perishes.

Man's labor in preaching, pleading and convincing sinners is insufficient for their salvation. The conversion of sinners does not depend upon our own worthiness. Only the practice of speaking from God in the presence of God in Christ qualifies the ministering individual, not the power inherent in himself. If the saved, the being saved or the perishing of others depended upon us entirely, the responsibility would be terrible. We believe that the power of the Gospel is independent of the worthiness of the preacher. No preacher is in himself sufficient for these things.

On the other hand, men must be true to the gospel of Christ. Paul said, "We are not as many, which corrupt the Word of God: but as of sincerity, but as of God, in the sight of God speak we in Christ." The figure used in the expression "corrupting the Word of God" is that of a huckster, or a wine dealer, or a merchant who adulterates his product in order to make greater personal profit. That Paul accuses many preachers of doing this is a serious matter. We are confident that there are many adulterated, corrupted, diluted gospels preached today which are no gospel at all. There is a gospel which is reduced in its value and its price, a gospel without a Virgin-born Christ, a miracle-working Christ, a Christ who rose from the dead, a gospel which is based upon no authoritative Bible, a gospel which has no supernatural power, a gospel which proclaims prayer as merely a psychological exercise. These, my friends, are all adulterated gospels, which are being traded for some personal profit of him who declares them. Only sincerity, integrity, purity of motive in reference to *the* Gospel constitutes a sufficiency or a capacity to do this work.

The sufficient One, therefore, for this work of determining whether the Gospel shall be unto life or death is the Holy Spirit, who empowers the Gospel. It is God who works the change in the heart as the Gospel is preached and as the individual believes. Man is saved by the power of the Spirit attending the Gospel message. That this Gospel message may be given by a Spirit-filled and empowered individual is a wonderful help, although we believe that God could use the Gospel presented by an unregenerate preacher to convert a man. Nevertheless, how much more God will use it in its sufficiency when it is attended by the labors of a Spirit-filled servant. Ultimately, however, it is God alone who divides between the saved and the lost and who knows the reason why.

This leaves an impression of awe and reverence upon us when we deal with the Gospel. The Gospel is as deadly as radium, which may bring wonderful healing if correctly used, but if misused may bring death. It is as deadly as some of the new drugs which are used to combat pneumonia, lukemia and other enemies of mankind. We simply must not toy with the Gospel. There is a finality to the issue from this Gospel, either of life or of death, and this is eternal. When we think of these as the goal of the ministering of the Word we know that we are performing a delicate service, something like that of the surgeon who opens the very heart of a man in order to bring about his healing. But one slip may mean death. Hence, the responsibility for us to be as competent and sufficient, as pure and as sincere as it is possible to be.

III. THE DIVINE ACCEPTANCE OF THOSE WHO BELIEVE THE GOSPEL

One aspect of this brief passage has been omitted by us, namely, that expressed in Paul's words, "For we are unto God a sweet savor in Christ." Those who have the knowledge of God manifested in them become a benediction unto God, a sweet savor or a fragrance unto God Himself. The life of a believer is a perfume redolent of Christ in which God takes pleasure, for He sees the manifestations of His Son in the believer. This very text reveals that not only the preaching of the Gospel but the acceptance and the living of the Gospel is important to the fragrance in one's life. Have you not been in the presence of Christians whose lives seem to be to you a breath of heaven? Thus the lives of us all should be. Regardless, then, whether our efforts bring life or death unto others if we have the knowledge of God manifested as a pleasing savor in us, this is sufficient for our Lord.

But this knowledge of God must be translated into character in order to be a fragrance pleasing unto God. We have need of sincerity, that is, in Christian profession, in our preaching and in our service. Men, we believe, want the Word of God spoken and obeyed in pulpits and in the lives of Christians. When they find it not, they have a tendency to become insincere in their own lives. The sincerity and the meekness of Christ ought to be found in the believer if he is to have a fragrance of life. This life is lived, Paul said, in the presence of God, ever before His eyes. Only such a life can have a good savor unto men. It is empowered and enabled by God, for it is "of God or from God." And it is also in Christ. There can be no other means of becoming a Divine heavenly fragrance unto men, the means of life, unless it be through Christ and the regeneration provided by Him for the believer.

This knowledge of God manifested in us and translated into character is what bestows upon us the fixation of fragrance. Some perfumes are valueless because though their aroma is pleasant it is so transitory. For this purpose the very rare musk is used to extend its life and quality. Unless your savor be a fixed one, not vacillating and transitory, it is valueless.

No better illustration of this savor of life unto life and death unto death exists than the sacrament of the Lord's Supper. We have been told many times that it is the means of grace or the means of condemnation. He who eateth or drinketh unworthily, not discerning the body of the Lord Jesus Christ, drinketh to himself damnation. On the other hand, it is the means of the very greatest blessing. This is because the sacrament proclaims the Gospel to us, because it is the Gospel, which, if we believe and confess and partake in sincerity, communicates to us its fragrance. Thus, as we approach the table of the Lord let us examine ourselves. Let us judge ourselves. And let us prepare spiritual sacrifices to offer up as a holy priesthood, that the fragrance of this incense may be pleasing unto God.

IX

THE BIBLE EVERY MAN WILL READ

TEXT: *"Ye are our epistle . . . known and read of all men."*—II COR. 3:1-5.

THE PRACTICE of using letters of recommendation is not new. Paul asks, "Need we, as some others, epistles of commendation to you, or letters of commendation from you?" Evidently some one had raised the question of Paul needing some letter of recommendation from the Jerusalem Church and that in place of it he was writing self-commendatory letters. It was the custom in the Early Church to use these epistolary commendations of workers when they transferred from one section of the Church to the other.

A clear example of this is given in the case of Apollos, who, having labored at Ephesus, desired to go to Corinth, and the brethren wrote a recommendation of him to the brethren in Achaia, so that he would be freely received on his arrival. According to the Scripture, Apollos warranted this courtesy. Likewise, in the case of Phebe, who was going to Rome, Paul wrote a letter of recommendation, saying, "I commend unto you Phebe our sister, which is a servant of the church which is at Cenchrea: that ye receive her in the Lord, as becometh saints, and that ye assist her in whatsoever business she hath need of you: for she hath been a succorer of many, and of myself also." This brief commendation is included in the epistle to the Romans, and the journey of Phebe to Rome was the occasion of Paul's writing that marvelous epistle dispatched by the hand of a simple deaconess in the Achaian Church. This form of introduction was evidently widely used by the Corinthians, just as it is widely used by us with validity today.

The practice of writing letters of recommendation today is greatly abused. Did you ever write one with your tongue in your cheek, thereby putting a person in the wrong light or in the wrong position, because you were not firm enough to refuse a word of commendation? Certainly it is difficult to refuse the request for a word of commendation in some cases, and yet we have need of common honesty and firmness in these things. We ought not to speak about something we do not know, and we ought never to recommend a person whom we know to be either undependable or unfitted for the particular task for which he is applying. On the other hand, we must be generous in our consideration of our fellow men and always give them the greatest benefit of the doubt. A testimony to the misuse of such letters of commendation is the fact that many church letters of transferal are absolutely valueless. We have no idea when a man joins our church on recommendation from another church whether he is a Christian or not, for we do not know what the other church required and we do not know also whether this individual was a faithful member or not. This is a tragic situation, and the perversion of a very valuable practice compels us to examine every person who applies for membership in our church.

But worst of all are letters of self-commendation which Paul's enemies implied that he was sending to Corinth. "Do we begin again to commend ourselves?" Letters of self-commendation, instead of helping and pleading one's cause, usually have the opposite effect. In the course of my ministry numerous committees seeking new pastors have sought my advice, and usually they revealed that scores of men either have their friends write recommending them to such committees or they themselves write, advocating their own cause. If such men only knew the adverse impression which is given to the official committee of a church seeking a new pastor in such a case, they would never have resorted to that practice. It simply dooms their effort in advance to futility and rejection. Paul needed to write no such letters.

The repudiation of such a charge was made by Paul on the basis of the nature of the work which he had done among them. Paul considered them to be his "epistle," known and read of all men. To think that he needed a letter of commendation to the church of which he was the spiritual father was highly incongruous. When Paul first came to Corinth to labor, there was no Christian Church and there were no Christians. He found an immoral, degenerate people living in rank heathenism. In fact, in writing to them later he described them as fornicators, idolators, adulterers, effeminate, thieves, covetous, drunkards, revilers, extortioners. But, by the grace of God, they had been utterly transformed and made into a church of the Lord Jesus Christ. Their sins were forgiven and their characters were changed, so that, as Paul wrote to them at this moment, they themselves were adequate testimony to the kind of work which he was doing.

Yet we have already seen that there were elements who had worked their way into the Corinthian Church and were now trying to undermine his influence. They, in turn, used commendatory letters from some important personages at Jerusalem, where, as we may learn in the Acts of the Apostles and in Paul's epistles, many enemies to the Gospel were centered. Carefully does Paul later declare that these enemies were not Peter, James and John, who were the pillars of the Church and who agreed with him as to the nature of the Gospel, but were many thousands of Judaizers in Jerusalem who were determined to put an end to the kind of gospel which Paul was preaching. In the last verse of the second chapter Paul had described the men who came with commendatory letters as hucksters who adultered the Word of God for their own profit and who depended not on the fruits of their labors, but on commendatory letters to give them authority over the churches. There will always be some who will seek to ruin a good minister's work for perverse reasons, and the usual means employed by them is the same that was employed against Paul, namely, the undermining of his reputation in the eyes of his congregation. He who steals a minister's name ruins his character and takes all that he has. In any other profession a man may go on with a sullied reputation, but it is not true in the ministry. We have known of several cases of earnest servants of the Lord being forced from their pulpits by these very evil practices.

Nevertheless, this occasion caused the presentation of an important truth, namely, that the fruit of a man's labors is the greatest attestation which he can have. The very changed characters and actions of the converts of Paul in Corinth was a sufficient letter of commendation for his work. Thus Paul said, "Ye are our epistle written in our hearts, known and read of all men." Just as an epistle opened the hearts of those to whom it was written concerning the bearer, making them one in service, so Paul claimed that the Corinthians and he were joined together in heart by the work which God had done in their behalf. In other words, Paul carried an epistle in his heart, namely, the Corinthian believers. No other epistle of commendation was necessary. This truth may be enlarged to the Church Universal, in which the adherents of our cause become our greatest commendation or our greatest hindrance. Innumerable are the men and women who will never take the trouble to listen to me preach, or to read our creed at Park Street Church, but will judge the church by what they cannot help but see in you while you are in your home and in business and in amusement. You become the letter of commendation or of criticism of the church to which you belong and of the Lord whom you profess. Thus in a very real sense you are the Bible whom every man will read every day and every hour of your life.

I. THE CHRISTIAN IS A MESSAGE FROM GOD TO MAN

Paul said, "Ye are manifestly declared to be the epistle of Christ." Christians, then, are a message from Christ to our fellow men. God has written a Bible which men do not read. That Bible is composed of sixty-six books written over a period of at least fifteen hundred years. It contains the only source of light, of the knowledge of God and of righteousness in the world. It is God's revelation to men inspired by the Holy Spirit, who moved on holy men of God, causing them to speak and write according to the will of God. From this great book is derived the knowledge of the justice, mercy and love of God toward men. From this book we get the ultimate truth about whence we came, why we are here and wither we are going, or, as Bunyan put it,

> "This book it chalketh out before thine eyes,
> The man that seeks the everlasting prize;
> It shows you whence he comes, whither he goes,
> What he leaves undone; also what he does:
> It shows you how he runs, and runs
> Till he unto the gate of glory comes."

This great book tells us about the nature of the world, the nature of man, the fact of sin, the means of redemption and the ultimate goal of humanity. Thus, through the Bible we see ourselves, we see God and we find a means of reconciliation between God and man.

This Bible which God has written has left a glorious record of its progress in the fruitage of moral influence, character transformation, uplift of civilization and extension of righteousness. The translations, numbering more than a thousand languages, the great Testament campaigns to place parts of the Bible in vast, unreached areas of humanity, the Gideon efforts to put the Bible in all the hotel rooms and schools and army camps, the millions of copies which are sold every year and taken into home, classrooms, studies, libraries, innumerable other places, constitute a glorious story and history. We sometimes congratulate ourselves on this wonderful record of the Bible as the best seller of all books, but the tragedy is that the Bible is purchased, but is not read. Only too often the Bible is left to lie in a home upon a table gathering dust, or is inserted in a book rack and rarely removed, or is left on a shelf of reference in the schools.

The Bible, as a fetish or a charm or some holy book to be left lying around the house, is of utterly no value at all. In order to be effective it must be read.

Unbelievers do not care to read the Bible and refuse to do so. Usually, only some extreme need will drive them to the Bible, or else some intellectual curiosity. The Bible usually is read only by believers and then only too often is neglected. The good test of just how much the Bible is read and how unashamed to read it people are, is to ask yourself whether you would be willing to read it in a subway train on your way to work every morning. I have had individuals stop me when they saw me reading the Bible on a train or in some other public place and say, "I thought you must be a minister or you wouldn't have had courage enough to read your Bible in public." The Bible simply is not read. Yet the Bible is God's primary message to men and without it Christian work will ultimately flounder. It is God's plan. It is God's revelation and it is God's witness in the world, though perhaps it is one of the most neglected books.

But God has written a Bible which men do read. It may not be the Bible of sixty-six books, but it is a Bible just as effectively as is this other Bible. Every man reads the mind, character and actions of the lives of those round about him. This reading is automatic, spontaneous and uncontrollable. It comes about as mind clashes with mind, character rubs shoulders with character and actions come into conflict with actions in daily life. The resulting impression is irresistible. It is the effect of personality upon personality in the daily intercourse of life. As a result of it we have a very definite impression of the minds, character and actions of those with whom we come in contact. As thinking implies combining, comparing and abstracting concepts, the process of passing some judgment upon people we meet goes on automatically in our minds. It is like thinking, and we can not help it. Hence, every man is involuntarily influenced and affected by the lives of those round about him. We simply do not live or die unto ourselves. We leave an impression upon those whom we meet.

Every life, therefore, gives some kind of message to other men, either good or bad. One's life can be a letter of Satan, of worldliness, of sin, of evil, to thousands of people every day. Look upon the faces of some who serve Satan. See how they are seamed and seared. Listen to the voices of those who speak round about you. Watch carefully the actions of people whom you meet. Soon you will become aware that the things which you took for granted were actually leaving a very definite imprint upon your own mind, either elevating you or degrading you. On the other hand, one may be a letter from Christ, displaying all the virtues, the holiness and the character of our lovely Lord. Such a person likewise leaves an indelible imprint upon those with whom he associates every day. It was of this character of Christ that the Corinthians were now a message to all who passed by Corinth, telling that God was able to take a group of wicked pagans and transform them into men and women bearing the image of Christ. This was a sufficient commendation to any who knew of the Corinthian Church.

Every believer's life is read constantly as to its testimony to God, to the Christian faith and to the Christian way of life. Recently, strange as it may seem, three of the people to whom I talked concerning Christ advanced the argument against Christianity that the lives of certain Christians did not correspond with what they understood Christianity to be. One highly educated young man even went so far as to say that in the midst of the vices which he practiced he believed himself to be more of a Christian in his attitude toward his fellow men than were two other professing Christians to whom he referred. For years he had been reading the lives of those Christians and he himself did not want to be like them. A young couple confessed that they were on the verge of abandoning Christianity and at the moment were passing through a life-and-death struggle concerning Christianity for the simple reason that other Christians were by their actions literally driving them away from Christ. They were reading their fellow Christians. A third man about whom I have been praying and to whom I have been speaking off and on for some time refused pointblank to become a Christian because of all the hypocrites that he knew were in the churches. Yes, you are our epistle known and read of all men. That is, by the public in general. Hence, we see the absolute necessity of being not a hearer of the Word but a doer of the Word. If we are to profess the name of Jesus Christ, we then become a Bible read by men. What a terrible thing it is to give the wrong message, to leave an impression which you did not want to leave, but, because of some irrepressible emotion or thought, affected men adversely.

Just what message do you give to men about God? Do you give a lie to God's nature, promises and works? If God has revealed Himself in the Bible as a God of justice, mercy and love, do you in the Bible of your life reveal that to your fellow men? If God has promised to give you deliverance from sin and victory in your daily life, are you showing deliverance and victory to your fellow men? If Jesus came to work the works of the father and His life is the Biblical standard thereof, are your works conforming to those? We have all too many professors of Christianity who are censorious, cheating, careless, inconsiderate, wrathful and impure. God has committed His reputation to their keeping, and the masses of men by them are kept from our lovely Christ because of the unchanged lives of those who profess to be His followers. Is it not a tragedy, then, that church members, the followers of Christ, are to a large extent no different from the world in the way that they do business, occupy political office, govern their homes, conduct themselves in ordinary intercourse with their fellow men?

Do you confirm the written Word by being a good witness to the power of God to change a human life? What is the use of our preaching about the supernatural grace of God in regeneration if those who profess to be regenerated are unchanged? What is the use of our saying that the mind of Christ must be in you and the beauty of Christ must be on you and the works of Christ be done by you, if the Spirit of Christ whom you profess to have received does not work this transformation within you? Remember that we are His witnesses. This Jesus said to His apostles and this He said unto Paul, "I have appeared unto thee to make thee a witness." In this sense God's revelation is not completed and awaits your work. The sixty-six books of the Bible are completed and there will never be anything added unto them, but there is a constant revelation of God in human personality and character in the Bible that every man reads. That book will never be completed until the last Christian life on earth is finished.

II. THIS MESSAGE IS WRITTEN BY GOD

Paul said, "Ye are manifestly declared to be the epistle of Christ ministered by us." There is a real sense in which Paul was the human agent who made this letter what it was. God uses human hands, words and minds to do His work, even as He did in making the Biblical revelation. When the Bible was written, God did not dictate it. He spoke through holy men of God as they were moved by the Holy Ghost. Thus, also, in writing these present day Bibles God uses human instruments. Just as He used Paul to write the Corinthian epistle, He also used the Corinthians to write an epistle for others. So it is that God works. In every conversion, in every church, in every Divine movement of history men have been used. We cannot emphasize and re-emphasize too much that nothing is ever done except through human agents. Wherever God finds some one He can use, some one whom He can command, some one through whom He may speak, He begins writing, sending messages and speaking to men. Sometimes through one man He will speak to great masses of men. It was by His being able to write upon the heart of Paul that He could through Paul write upon the Corinthians and through them both do an even greater work that ensued.

It is no wonder, therefore, that false ministers or hucksters may worm their way into God-founded churches, for this is one of Satan's ruses. But the true ministers whom God has used will be evident to all. In, through and on the Corinthian Church, the name of Paul was inscribed, and the name of anyone else would never be inscribed, for he was its father and founder. Yet it is good to remember the qualification that Paul raises, namely, "not that we are sufficient of ourselves to think anything as of ourselves: but our sufficiency is of God." God may use these human instruments, but there is no efficacy in them alone. If we are to be sufficient as a savor of life unto life and of death unto death, then that sufficiency must have its source in God and Him alone. No man can change another man's character permanently in Christian conversion. That is the work of God and of God alone. The Divine seal was upon the ministry of Paul, constituting him a sufficient and able minister of the new covenant. Any man may walk in that apostolic succession.

Secondly, this epistle was written by the Spirit of the living God, "written not with ink, but with the Spirit of the living God: not in tables of stone, but in fleshly tables of the heart." Here we have a reference to the ancient method of writing. Let nobody display his ignorance by ever saying that there was not writing in any age in which the books of the Bible were claimed to have been written. There was an effective writing for at least a thousand years before the time Moses lived. Men had written on papyrus with pen and ink long before the days of St. Paul and they had written with a stylus upon stone or clay as early as 3000 B.C. the books rescued by archeology which we still have in libraries. The reference "not in tablets of stone" is to the method of engraving stones and then pouring in metal which preserved them through the centuries. Anyone can write either with pen and ink or with stylus on stone, but how different it is to write on fleshly hearts of men so as to change them. Only the Spirit of God is sufficient for this, for it is an omnipotent work, a work of which any human would despair. For this reason, any story telling of the transformation of a human personality appeals to the minds of men. Witness Shaw's story, *Pygmalion*, in which a London guttersnipe is taken and transformed by him in six months time into a cultured lady. This may be done in stories, but in real life it is not done expect by the Spirit of the living God.

It is the Spirit of God who attends the ministry of men, convicting sinners by the Word, converting them unto Christ and changing their characters and lives. Only the Spirit of God is able to renew the human mind, to quicken the soul and to enable the saved one to put off the old man and to put on the new. That means dropping the old habits and assuming an utterly new kind of life. It is this Spirit of the living God who sanctifies and who makes a man holy. Thus it is the Spirit who wrote the letter of commendation of Paul by changing the lives of the Corinthians.

Passing on from the writing by physical means and by changing human hearts to the two great covenants represented thereby, Paul proclaimed a great truth, namely, that the letter, or the thing written, kills and the Spirit maketh alive, or quickens. The letter unquestionably refers to the Mosaic law, which was written. This law could not change one. It was only the ministration of death. The letter of the law, or the written law, is a ministry of condemnation, for all of us are sinners, and it pronounces death; but the Spirit of the living God makes alive. He quickens, He revives by entering the sinner's heart. Even as the Spirit of God quickened the Lord Jesus Christ, so also He quickens us. Whether we look at God's method of salvation in the Old Testament or the New, it makes no difference. The written Word was the word of death, but the living Spirit was the means of life. Anyone who tried to win the promise of salvation by the written Word failed and was condemned, and those who believed the promise are quickened by the Spirit of God because of the Christ who was to come and make atonement for their sins.

Thus we can see the great and deadly error of modernism, which proclaims that the Spirit means the spiritual meaning and the letter means the literal word. By this means the modernists set aside what the written Word actually says and try to adhere to some spiritual meaning. This can never be, for the teaching of the written Word and the testimony of the Spirit of God is the same, except that the written Word condemns and the Spirit makes alive.

The third instrument in this letter is Christ who has written the epistle, namely, the Christ of the new covenant. The Corinthians are called "the epistle of Christ," that is, Christ's redemptive work is manifested in them before the public. All of the promises of the old covenant were fulfilled in Christ, and whosoever is a minister of the new covenant is a minister of Christ, writing Christ upon human hearts. Even the confidence of such a servant as Paul as to the nature of this work being from God is through Christ. We can believe that our work is acceptable to God and commendatory only if it exalts Christ. It would be profitable for us to contrast the ministration of death in the written Word and the ministration of life in the Christ through His Spirit, for this Scripture declares that as Moses stands ministering death both at Sinai and unto the present time, for the law has never lost its power, his purpose is to turn men unto the promise given to Abraham and fulfilled in Christ. Whenever that law is preached it ought to point men to the promise, which is able to save. Then the ministry of the law is concluded and the ministry of the Spirit begins, for life succeeds death and the living law the written law, and thus God, through His servant the apostle, through the living Spirit of God and through Christ, has written this epistle in your hearts.

III. THE CHRISTIAN CHARACTER IS THE GLORIOUS IMAGE OF CHRIST WROUGHT BY THE SPIRIT

It is necessary for us to skip over the wonderful teaching concerning the two covenants in this chapter and to which we shall return, God willing, but one thing we cannot pass over, and that is the glory which bathed the face of Moses and which is now to bathe the face of the Christian. We are told that the ministry of Moses was glorious, so that the children of Israel could not steadfastly behold the face of Moses for the glory of his countenance, which glory was to be done away. What God did for Moses in the communion which Moses enjoyed on Mount Sinai He is able to work in all believers by the indwelling Spirit of God. That glory on the countenance of Moses was so great that the people of Israel would not come near him, but hid themselves from him until Moses took a veil to cover his face while he talked with them. Those sinful men could not look upon the glory of God reflected in the face of Moses and they needed a veil to separate them from it. Paul said that that veil still remains on the heart of Israel and upon the hearts of all men who do not turn unto the Lord unto this day.

But "we all with open face beholding as in a glass the glory of the Lord, are changed into the same image, from glory to glory, even as by the spirit of the Lord." This describes the glory which comes to the believer in Christ. The believer, with unveiled or open face turned to Christ the Lord by means of real repentance and faith, enters into a communion which results in a transformed character. The word "beholding" means to attend, and as we attend to God and God's things we ourselves become a reflection or a mirror in which the glory of Christ is revealed to men. Usually men tell us that this text means that we behold in a mirror the glory of the Lord, that is, God reflected in nature and life, etc. But the meaning is clearly that we ourselves are the mirror reflecting the glory of Christ in our countenances and our actions. Because of the Spirit living within our lives we are to become a Divine reflection greater than that of Moses, because the message and the Person of Christ are greater than Moses. Moses reflected judgment in the ministry of death, but we reflect mercy in the ministry of life. What higher privilege could there be in the whole world than to have a life and faith and mind which reflect the Divine glory in salvation!

Yet there is even a greater matter than a reflection. That is that we have the image of Christ wrought in us by the Holy Spirit. In other words, we become transformed in nature, changed from glory to glory, from new light to new light, until we actually bear the image of our Lord Jesus Christ. This is the metamorphosis from the glory of a reflection to the glory of the image of the Son of God. "Now are we the sons of God, but it doth not yet appear what we shall be, but we know that we shall be like him, for we shall see him as he is." More and more we shall bear His image, His likeness, His form, that which is derived from the original.

The Scripture makes it plain that this transformation is wrought by the Holy Spirit in sanctification. The Spirit of God gradually renews, changes, transforms, by regeneration and sanctification in a continuous growth from glory to glory, from faith to faith and from grace to grace. The infinite reaches of this (for Christ is infinite) are appropriated in proportion to our search, for we are told to ask for the Holy Ghost, and in proportion to our obedience the Holy Ghost is given to those who obey Him. We may go on and on and on in this transformation until we shall be like Him. The more Christlike we become in every thought, word and action, the more we will reflect His glory and light to men. This is the work of God by the

Holy Spirit. You, then, are our epistles known and read of all men. Yea, you are the epistles of Christ, ministered by us.

What light, what message, what testimony, what glory do you give to men? It is true that you cannot see your own glory, but everybody else will see it. It may be secret to you, but it is not secret to others. God has done this great work for you in order that you may be His messenger to men, as Moses was His messenger to the Israelites. Therefore, let your light so shine before men, that they may see your good works and glorify the Father who is in heaven, for ye are the light of the world.

X

THE OLD AND THE NEW TESTAMENTS

TEXT: *"God . . . hath made us able ministers of the new testament; not of the letter, but of the spirit: for the letter killeth, but the spirit giveth life."*—II COR. 3:6-11.

WHAT A PHRASE! "Able ministers of the new testament!" Some day I shall preach an ordination sermon on that title. Now we must confine our attention to the contrast of this New Testament with the Old Testament.

Is this New Testament or new covenant, spoken of here in contrast with the old, the same division as that made in the Bible between the Old and the New Testament and that made in Christian theology between what is called the old and the new covenant and that made by the writers of the New Testament between the law and the Gospel? We are forever meeting these groups of twos in our thinking, both in theology and in Bible exposition. Although others may declare differently we unquestionably answer yes, for we believe that any other answer will bring unending confusion to the mind of the Christian. We shall try to present the evidence for this affirmation.

The first covenant was the covenant of works. It is largely the covenant expounded in the Old Testament, and it is summarized under what is called "the law." This does not mean that grace and the new covenant were excluded from the Old Testament times and writings. Rather, these times and writings were saturated with grace, and without grace there could have been no salvation; but we may very correctly summarize these as the old covenant. In contrast with it the Bible presents what is called the better covenant, the better tabernacle, the better priesthood and the better way. Read Hebrews 8:6-8. By means of this better covenant Christ obtained eternal redemption for us.

A large part of the understanding of Christianity comes from the practice of the Apostles to compare and contrast these two covenants. Our Scripture lesson speaks about the old covenant and the new covenant, the ministration of death and the ministration of the Spirit, condemnation and righteousness. The two are always intermingled. The Old Testament or covenant could never exist without the New Testament or covenant and the New Testament cannot be understood without the Old Testament or covenant. I firmly declare that Christianity is as old as creation, that is, the creation of man. That which is fully revealed in the New Testament concerning the Lord Jesus Christ was implicit in the history of redemption. Thus the two covenants, the two Testaments, those underlying the law and grace, are essentially one, representing the same Lord, the same teaching, the same need and the same means of redemption. For anyone to proclaim that the law was foolishly accepted by the Israelites is to fail to grasp the plan of redemption. In this passage of Scripture before us the wonderful relation between the law and grace or the two covenants is brought out by Paul. The glory, beauty and wonder of the first is revealed in contrast with the surpassing and indescribable glory of the second.

In the face of this wonderful plan of redemption, is there any sufficiency for us as ministers of this new covenant? For man to press in to these holy things is to intrude where angels fear to tread. Without Christ, the sufficiency of God, as our Mediator, we would forever be excluded. Thus Paul says, "Not that we are sufficient of ourselves to think anything as of ourselves; but our sufficiency is of God; who also hath made us able ministers of the new testament." Augustine and Calvin vigorously declared that in this Scripture the total inability of man is declared. Perhaps such inability is taught here, but it is our opinion that the reference is not so much to whether we are able to do spiritually good ourselves, but whether we can be competent for ministering life and death unto others. This alone is the subject at issue. It is God who makes us the sufficient ones or the empowered ones to minister the new covenant, salvation.

Burden makes me pause here to say a word to the numerous young men facing toward the ministry. Here is the greatest privilege ever given to a human being, namely, the liberty to handle the things of glory every day, to minister life, to impart spirit, to instill hope and to be a mediator of redemption for the souls of men. These are the things of eternity, of the invisible world, of permanence, in contrast with the froth and flux of daily, material life. Let him who assumes this ministry remember that no preparation is too complete, no consecration is too deep and no sacrifice too great to be an able minister of the new covenant, to bring about as the result of one's ministry the glorious transformation of character and of status for men in the presence of God. Contrast this ministry of dispensing forgiveness and salvation through Calvary's Cross with the ministry of those who know nothing about this New Testament of blood for the forgiveness of sins. Think of the limitation, the impotence, the conceit, the folly of men who instead of preaching the new covenant made by God are willing to rest in the doctrines of men and in the efforts of human instruments to change character. God has given an equipment, an empowerment and a message, which is able today to make the least servant a sufficient or able minister of the new covenant. To be satisfied with less in one's own ministry or in the ministry under which one sits is folly.

I am one who believes in the best intellectual preparation of college, theological seminary, graduate school, a constant stream of books coming to one's desk and incessant travel as equipment for the ministry, but this is not the ultimate and the final equipment. Our sufficiency is of God, and unless we have been born again, called and anointed for this holy ministry of mediating life and death to our fellow men, we have not received the one essential equipment and preparation. Our sufficiency is of God.

In the light of this we must also declare that the popular attitude toward the Bible itself is not true. The words of this text, "The letter killeth, but the spirit giveth life," have been used over and again to declare that we cannot trust the literal, written word in the Bible, but that we must take the spirit of the Bible teaching, regardless of its faithfulness to the received and accepted text. Wherever one uses the Word of God literally, someone advances this idea. We are told that we should not carefully ascertain the meaning of the text, for that is not inspired. We must only get at the inner spiritual meaning which the writers were trying to convey. We are told that it is quite possible to have illumination of God apart from the Word of God. You may recognize this as the teaching of a fair portion of Protestants today. You may also recognize it as one of the principles of an enthusiastic group working on an international scale for what they call changed characters. Whatever these people take the word to mean, though it very often is contrary to the plain meaning of the accepted text, is said to quicken, to make alive and to be the source of spiritual life. Such teaching is absurd, for the Bible means exactly what it says, and those who do not wish to accept the teaching of the Bible can get no comfort from this particular passage in order to support their views. But beyond this, our text is not referring to the Bible as a whole at all, but only to the law, to the written thing, to the grammar. It is the law. It is the old covenant, namely, the covenant of works which kills and it is the Spirit, namely, the Holy Spirit, who makes alive, as this whole passage and every similar passage in the Bible clearly declares. Therefore, let us look at these two Testaments, two ministrations and two glories.

I. The Two Testaments

That there are two Testaments is clearly implied by the statement, "of the new testament." A man never makes out a new will unless he has had an old will which it is to supersede. The purpose of the new covenant and the new testament was to supersede the old. The word "covenant" has been used by the American Revisers in this translation, but we believe that it is correctly understood when the word "testament" defines it. A covenant is usually made between two parties in the form of an agreement, but in no sense were the two major covenants of God made with man. Therefore, they were called Testaments. Let us illustrate this first. The covenant of promise or of grace was declared to have been made with Abraham. According to Paul:

"And the Scripture, foreseeing that God would justify the heathen through faith, preached before the gospel unto Abraham, saying, In thee shall all nations be blessed. So then they which be of faith are blessed with faithful Abraham . . . that the blessing of Abraham might come on the Gentiles through Jesus Christ; that we might receive the promise of the Spirit through faith."

Whatever the new covenant is we know at least that it is of promise, of faith and of redemption. All this was made with Abraham. Let us look back to see how it was made. This is told in Genesis 15. God commanded Abraham to take a heifer, a she goat, a ram, a turtle dove and a young pigeon, to divide them in two and to lay each piece against the other, with the exception of the birds. Then a deep sleep fell upon Abraham and a great darkness came over him in which God renewed his covenant with Abraham. Following it, Abraham in his dream saw a smoking furnace and a burning lamp pass between those pieces. The Scripture says, "In the same day the Lord made a covenant with Abraham." The irrevocable covenant was not made between Abraham and God, for Abraham did not pass between the two parts of an animal, which was the sign of an irrevocable covenant. Rather, that which symbolized God the Father and God the Son passed between the parts. The covenant was made within the Trinity, and the Testament was made to Abraham in promise. Neither the covenant of redemption, whereby God, the Father, Son and Spirit assumed the division of labor in reference to man's redemption, nor the covenant of grace was made with man, but God made testaments with men.

A testament is an established order sealed by blood. Namely, it is of value after the death of the testator,

"for a testament is of force after men are dead: otherwise it is of no strength at all while the testator liveth. Whereupon neither the first testament was dedicated without blood. For when Moses had spoken every precept to all the people according to the law, he took the blood of calves and of goats, with water, and scarlet wool, and hyssop, and sprinkled both the book and all the people, saying, This is the blood of the testament which God hath enjoined unto you."

The Old Testament, or the means of God's relation with His people, was sealed by blood, symbolized in the death of the animals slain. The New Testament was sealed in the blood of Christ, as He Himself said, "This is my blood of the new covenant, which is shed for many for the remission of sins."

God has sealed two ways of dealing with men. One is by works and one is by grace. In public manifestation the covenant of works, revealed in the giving of the law upon Mount Sinai, came before what is called the covenant of grace, established in the death of Christ upon the Cross, but in God's great plan, faith, grace and redemption came first. They came in promise, in the prophecy of a Messiah who was to be a suffering Messiah and to take away our transgressions by the shedding of His blood, but, nevertheless, they were given first. Therefore, the reason for the giving of the law as a covenant is explained by Paul: "The law was our schoolmaster to bring us unto Christ, that we might be justified by faith." Yet he adds that the law which came four hundred and thirty years after the promise to Abraham could not disannul that covenant of promise and hence of life. The law was added merely in order to show the transgression, to make it manifest.

Glance, then, at this first Testament or covenant which was made for Israel under Moses. The Sinaitic code was given in the midst of thunderings and lightnings and of a glory which necessitated a protecting veil for the Israelites. That glory was the glory of God's justice, holiness and righteousness. Whatever glimpse we get of God is glorious, but when we see His ineffable holiness and moral perfections, the vision is beyond the power of mortal man. Hence, without holiness no man shall see the Lord. The revelation given on Sinai was a revelation of law, of perfection by moral and ethical living, and for this reason the law is merely an instrument of condemnation, a limitation on men before and behind, showing unto them their sin. Paul said, "I was alive without the law once: but when the commandment came, sin revived, and I died. And the commandment, which was ordained to life, I found to be unto death." The purpose of this law was to turn men unto the promise of Christ the Redeemer. "What things soever the law saith, it saith to them who are under the law: that every mouth may be stopped, and all the world may become guilty before God. Therefore by the deeds of the law there shall no flesh be justified in His sight: for by the law is the knowledge of sin." The law of Moses is nothing but the ministration of death.

But law was not new on Mount Sinai. Law was first given by God in the Garden of Eden and it was there that the covenant of works was revealed. God said, "This do, and thou shalt live." Man was placed under a certain period of probation on the principle of works and obedience. Had he terminated that probation by perfect obedience and holiness he could have made the transition into the state which God purposes for man's ultimate redemption. What God laid down as a covenant of works in the Garden of Eden he merely enlarged in the Mosaic Law and further amplified in the Sermon on the Mount given by Jesus. That Sermon on the Mount is law, and if you think you know what holiness is just reread it and ask yourself if you are a sinner or not. We hold this law of God to be absolutely permanent, changeless and in force over all mankind. It is as permanent and changeless as the nature of God, for it is the revelation of His own holiness and justice. The law tells us the kind of God with whom we must deal. Justice and law are at the heart of the universe.

The New Testament was made with the believers under Christ.

For this we must glance at Calvary. There, according to Jesus, the blood of the new covenant for the remission of sins was shed. There, according to the interpretation which He placed upon his own death, we are to believe that the means of pardon and of righteousness were made available to those who will believe. There,

> "Christ being come a high priest of good things to come, . . . neither by the blood of goats and calves, but by his own blood he entered in once into the holy place, having obtained eternal redemption for us. . . . How much more shall the blood of Christ, who through the eternal Spirit offered himself without spot to God, purge your conscience from dead works to serve the living God? And for this cause he is the mediator of the new testament, that by means of death, for the redemption of the transgressions that were under the first testament, they which are called might receive the promise of eternal inheritance."

By means of this death of the Son of God not only our sins are forgiven and righteousness in standing is imputed to us before God, but we are constituted the sons of God, the heirs of God and the partakers of the Divine nature. Hereby the Spirit of the living God brings new life, eternal life, unto those who participate under the testament.

This promise was not new, however, at Calvary. It had been made to Abraham, and long before it was ever made to Abraham it was made to Adam and Eve in the Garden of Eden. God had promised that the seed of the woman would bruise the head of the serpent. For this reason He began immediately to clothe man and woman with the skins of animals, in obtaining which blood was shed, and He soon demonstrated that He would accept in worship that which typified the ultimate sacrifice of Christ on the Cross. Therefore, Abel's sacrifice was accepted and Cain's was rejected. Hence, whether men lived in the days of Paul or whether they lived in the days of David, if they were saved at all it was by the covenant of grace and not by the covenant of works. Though they lived before the confirmation of this covenant by the blood of Christ, they entered into the benefits of that covenant by faith in the promise of the coming Messiah. The symbol of their faith in this was the performing of blood sacrifices in accordance with the command of the Lord, for without the shedding of blood there was no remission of sins. For this reason we unhesitatingly declare that Adam, Abel, Enoch, Noah, Abraham, Moses, David, Hezekiah, John the Baptist, Paul and every Christian since that day have been saved by God's grace and the new covenant rather than by the old. Christianity is as old as creation.

II. THE TWO MINISTRATIONS

Paul talks about the letter as killing and calls it the ministration of death, written and engraven in stone. This was the first covenant or testament, and, without a doubt, it is from this that the first section of our Bible receives its name. Let me repeat that the first testament or covenant still remains. It has never been abrogated. It is as eternal as the nature of God, but it always condemns. It never gives life. "By the law is the knowledge of sin." It is the law which says, "Thou shalt not," and as soon as this command arises in one form or another, man's liberty is abridged and all which does not conform brings guilt. The law says nothing of condemnation until we break it. Just so long as a man keeps the law he'll know nothing of its penalties, but who is there who has kept the law? If there can be no lessening of the standard of righteousness and no one is able to reach that standard of righteousness, then no flesh can be justified and all are condemned by the law.

Moreover, we are told that guilt and condemnation bring judgment. If, according to the holiness of God, absolute righteousness and perfection are demanded by Him, then anything less than absolute righteousness will be punished by God with its correct penalty. That penalty is declared to be death. Death is the ultimate penalty, but all transgressions, even in the incipient stage, lead on to that ultimate penalty. In the day that Adam ate of the forbidden fruit he began to die, and in the day that we transgress the commandments of God the dying process has begun. It is this death which is other than physical about which the Bible speaks most and which is contrasted with life.

Does this, then, make the law to be sin, the first covenant to be evil, because it takes a man and brings to him condemnation and death? The law is holy and just and good. It does a useful service in that it brings to man the realization that he is not able to fulfill God's holiness and righteousness. It reveals his sin. It is his schoolmaster to bring him unto Christ, or to the promise, that he might be justified by faith. The law, the covenant of works, the first testament, were not given by God as an end in themselves. They were given to be the ministers of condemnation in order that the ultimate purpose in the covenant of grace, the ministration of the Spirit, of righteousness and life, might ensue.

Therefore, our Scripture tells us that the second testament ministers righteousness. Just as the law brought nothing but condemnation, so the testament of grace brings nothing but righteousness. Whoever turns to Jesus Christ finds the burden and guilt of his sins lifted, an infusion of new life and a sense of acceptability by God. God gives him the witness of the Spirit to this end. Being no longer under law, but now under grace, the condemnation of the law is removed and as a result justification ensues. "As by the offense of one judgment came upon all men to condemnation; even so by the righteousness of one the free gift came upon all men unto justification of life. For as by one man's disobedience many were made sinners, so by the obedience of one shall many be made righteous." The Lord Jesus Christ in the second covenant did all that could never have been done for us in the first covenant. By the redemption which is in Him, whom God hath set forth to be a propitiation through faith in His blood, we are able to be freely justified and to be declared righteous before a righteous God and a righteous universe. This is the doctrine of justification by faith. "By grace are ye saved through faith; and that not of yourselves: it is the gift of God: Not of works, lest any man should boast." The result of justification is spiritual life ministered unto us by the Holy Spirit. It is even called by Paul in our Scripture "the ministration of the spirit." Being justified, a new Spirit is given unto the believer who mediates, supplies and enables the believer to appropriate the life of the eternal God.

We have already emphasized that both ministrations existed in the entire Bible, that both exist at the present time and that the division between the Old and New Testaments is the division between the historic manifestation of the two covenants or ministrations. In the Old Testament there were many promises, invitations and pleas for men to accept God's means of redemption. Certainly this is not law, "Come now, and let us reason together, saith the Lord: though your sins be as scarlet, they shall be as white as snow; though they be red like crimson, they shall be as wool." Nor is this, "Let the wicked forsake his way, and the unrighteous man his thoughts: and let him return unto the Lord, and he will have mercy upon him; and to our God, for he will abundantly pardon." Neither is this, "Turn ye, turn ye . . . Why will ye die?" If this promise of a Redeemer, of a Messiah, of the Christ, of a Savior, was given to Adam, to Abel, to Abraham and to the saints of the Old Testament, then it reached glorious fulfillment in the Lord Jesus Christ. Then the old covenant was turned into the New Testament. Then the letter of Sinai still threatened death, but the fulfilled Gospel, which is pure Spirit, bestowed life on all who turned away from that death. God, who promised to make a new covenant with the house of Israel and with the house of Judah, has fulfilled that promise in a covenant written in the hearts and in the minds of the people of God. Yes, life reigns among true believers in the old as well as in the new dispensation, but it always reigned in the same manner through what is called the New Testament or the new covenant or the grace of God in the Lord Jesus Christ. The promise is of faith in Christ. Just so each one of us stands under one or the other covenant this day. If we are attempting to be saved by works and character we are under the ministration of death, but if we are attempting to be saved by faith in the Lord Jesus Christ we are in the ministration of life.

III. THE TWO GLORIES

Now, we are told:

"If the ministration of death, written and engraven in stones, was glorious, so that the children of Israel could not steadfastly behold the face of Moses for the glory of his countenance; which glory was to be done away; how shall not the ministration of the spirit be rather glorious? For if the ministration of condemnation be glory, much more doth the ministration of righteousness exceed in glory."

These glories differed in reference to the person of the mediator, in reference to the permanence of the covenant, in reference to the purpose thereof. We cannot forget that the law came by Moses. In his face the Israelites beheld the reflected glory of an infinite God, His holiness and His perfection. This was so great that the Israelites could not look upon Moses until he covered his face. But grace and truth have come by the Lord Jesus Christ. In Him the fulness of the godhead bodily dwelt. "The Word was made flesh, and dwelt among us, (and we beheld his glory, the glory as of the only begotten of the Father,) full of grace and truth. . . . No man hath seen God at any time; the only-begotten Son, which is in the bosom of the Father, he hath declared him." The contrast drawn is between the glory of Moses and the glory of Jesus Christ, who perfectly reflected the glory of the Father. "God, who commanded the light to shine out of darkness, hath shined in our hearts, to give the light of the knowledge of the glory of God in the face of Jesus Christ." Now, we must face God in one of these two individuals. If we face Him in the glory of holiness and justice, it is under the law with judgment and death, with trembling and fear, with terror and abhorence, but if we face God in Jesus Christ, then the glory of that image will be restored within our own lives and we shall be able to look upon Him because we shall be like Him.

The contrast is also drawn in reference to permanence. Though the first covenant and the law are as permanent as the nature of God, nevertheless, they are transitory in their control over us. Once we have come out from under the law into grace, the law as a schoolmaster, or a taskmaster, or an authority, ceases to exist so far as we are concerned. Its task is done when it has turned us to Jesus Christ. Then it is that the Holy Spirit begins to work the permanent life and glory in the life of the believer. So that we are changed into the same image from glory to glory by the Spirit of the Lord. Faith, then, does not make void the law, but rather establishes the law, for what the law could not do, in that it was weak through the flesh, God, sending His own Son in the likeness of sinful flesh, condemned sin in the flesh, that we might be the righteousness of God. Walking after the Spirit, the glory which once overwhelmed and amazed and condemned us, now will be reflected in us.

The final contrast of glory is connected with the purpose of these two instruments. The law could never give life, and thus it could not be final in the Divine purpose. It has no regenerating or even fully reforming power. It merely condemned, spoke of vengeance and judgment, but the Gospel melts the human heart. It bespeaks mercy and love, and it saves by the glory of the Cross. Here, then, we have two glories contrasted. One is Sinai, which in many ways is the most striking and terror-inspiring. The other is Calvary, which also had its light and its darkness, its earthquake and its thunder, but this time they were the thunders of judgment beating upon our substitute, even Christ. Therefore, if the one speaks of righteousness as a standard of judgment, the other speaks of righteousness as a means of mercy. Sinai, the law's glory, was overshadowed by the Gospel, for it reaches unto heaven rather than to hell. Without Calvary, without the new covenant, without the New Testament, the doors of heaven would be closed to every man.

Thus there must be an intermingling of both testaments, both covenants, both law and grace in the ministry. We preachers need once again to turn back to the law, to awaken men to the sense of sin, judgment and death, to what the inevitable requirements and consequences are for a life outside of Christ. Then legal preachers and moralist thinkers need to turn to Christ, who alone can save them and produce the righteousness which is necessary before God.

Therefore, attempt not to find salvation, life and heaven by the works of the law. Rather, walk in the glorious way, for surely Christ has not died in vain for you.

XI

REMOVING THE VEIL

TEXT: *"If our gospel be hid [veiled], it is hid to them who are lost."*—II COR. 3:12-4:6.

THE OCCASION of this text is an appeal by St. Paul to the commendation of truth and of conscience which he presented in refutation of a false charge against his character. The questions had been raised about his sincerity, his frankness and his forthrightness. False teachers had challenged him by insinuating themselves at Corinth. They were attempting to make converts out of his churches because of their inability to go to the world in power and make converts of the unconverted. Wherever there is a flourishing Christian work, one will find parasitic movements, those that play the parasite on the churches already established. It was because of this attack that St. Paul affirmed, "We have had our conversation in the world and more abundantly to you-ward," and again, "We are not as many, which corrupt the word of God: but as of sincerity, but as of God, in the sight of God speak we in Christ."

Paul declares unequivocally that once and for all he and his co-workers had renounced these things of darkness and of insincerity at their conversion. Said he, "We have renounced the hidden things of dishonesty, not walking in craftiness, nor handling the word of God deceitfully; but, by manifestation of the truth, commending ourselves to every man's conscience in the sight of God." Paul acknowledged that God took him and his fellow workers as poor miserable creatures and by mercy exalted them to salvation. Everything—the Christian life and ministry—was the result of a Divine mercy in their conversion. That mercy on St. Paul is evident from his constant reference to the Damascus Road experience. It was to that experience that he referred when he said that he was the least of all the saints. He had in mind his persecution activity cut short by the revelation of Christ to him on the Damascus Road.

Therefore in spite of discouragements, set-backs, opposition and rejection of this message by many, he and his fellow workers failed not. That is, they did not lose the confidence to which they referred when Paul said, "Thanks be unto God, which always causeth us to triumph in Christ." They refused to stoop to adulterating the word of God, to falsifying it to catch the crowd and in order to commend themselves. Anything false, cowardly, crafty and deceitful should be left behind a believer in the great renunciation of his conversion. Rightly, Paul implies that those who stoop to these things after their professed conversions were giving the lie to their profession.

Over against the charge made against St. Paul was his method of publishing or declaring the truth and by that means commending himself to every man's conscience. He used great plainness, openness, boldness of speech, so that he need not be misunderstood in making known the truth, the whole counsel of God.

Paul knew that when he spoke the truth it was confirmed in every man's conscience. Said he, "By manifestation of the truth commending ourselves to every man's conscience in the sight of God." Every man has a conscience, which distinguishes him from the brute. The ideas of God, duty, right, retribution, all belong to man and are connected with man's conscience. Paul claimed that by exhibiting to men the great truths of the law and the Gospel, he made his appeal to every man's conscience in a way that enforced each man's approval. No man who understood this truth could doubt its evidence and no man who understood its moral claims could dispute those claims. The human conscience and the Bible are at one, and they agree in their moral decisions and their teaching. Conscience reveals the same duty and obligation as God's law reveals. It tells us that we are to love God and love our fellow men. Conscience and the Bible agree that man has fallen from duty and that apart from grace no man can fulfill his duty. Conscience affirms all the precepts of the Bible, the need of repentance, the need of atonement, of justification by faith and of holiness of life. Never, when a conscience is thoroughly aroused by the conviction of sin and then comes to rest in the work of Christ, can you revive its sense of condemnation or fear. It then enters an experience of peace. This is a great attestation to the truth and the inspiration of the Bible.

What man, therefore, thinks of us rests upon how his conscience reacts in the sight of God to the Divine truth we publish. Truth ever commends itself to the conscience and thus recommends those who publish it.

But this raises the problem, if the truth is self-evident and our Gospel is all that it claims to be, why do so many reject it? It is true that in all times many have rejected the Gospel messages. Many consciences have not responded affirmatively. Christ asked the Jews, "If I say the truth, why do ye not believe me?" and he referred to those who "loved darkness . . . because their deeds were evil." On another occasion the Lord suggested that the great majority will reject the truth. He said, "Wide is the gate, and broad is the way, that leadeth to destruction, and many there be which go in thereat." Though the Gospel is brought to the attention of men and conscience affirms it, many still refuse to accept it. The same Gospel which saves some is rejected by others, and they perish. Paul said, "It is hid to them that are lost." Why is this?

Predestination is not the answer, but punishment is. No eternal, irrevocable decree of God doomed these perishing ones to hell and everlasting death. The Gospel was sent to save them. The answer lies in the word, "veiled," or "hidden." This gives us the key to the title of the discourse, "Removing the veil." The illustration used by St. Paul is Moses' use of the veil when he came from speaking with God upon the holy mount and spoke unto the people. Moses did not use the veil in order to hide the glory of his countenance from the people, but he used that veil to cover his countenance, to hide the diminishing glory until he went in again to speak before the Lord. The glory was seen by the Israelites and they covered their faces because of it. Moses lifted the veil from his countenance when he talked to the people. When he finished talking to the people he covered his face until he went again to speak with the Lord. This glory was of the Divine law which spoke judgment and it was given at Sinai. It was a lesser glory and was to pass away in the coming of a greater when the glory would no longer speak death but life through the Gospel of righteousness by Christ.

Because these Israelites remained in unbelief they were not permitted to see the end of this mystery of condemnation. As they did not see the end of the glory on Moses' face, so they did not see the purpose of God in the transient nature of the old covenant. The symbolism was utterly lost upon the Israelites, for they were hardened, "stonied," in considerations or thoughts. Not predestination but judgment hardened those who would not believe. This is the meaning of a quotation of Isaiah's prophecy which says:

"By hearing ye shall hear, and shall not understand; and seeing ye shall see, and shall not perceive: for this people's heart is waxed gross, and their ears are dull of hearing, and their eyes they have closed; lest at any time they should see with their eyes, and hear with their ears, and should understand with their heart, and should be converted, and I should heal them."

Self-hardening is followed by God's judicial hardening. This was the story of Israel. The veil is thus a symbol of hardness, blindness, and unbelief, both in the Jews and the Gentiles. It is mentioned eight times in our Scripture.

I. THOSE VEILED IN HEART

Historically, the eyes of the Jews are veiled. Israel has been hardened. Their "minds were blinded," which might be translated, "their considerations were made like stone." The very process is described for us in Romans 11, under the figure of a knitting of a bone. The bone itself throws forth the substance which covers the break and hardens it so that the place is stronger and harder than any other part of the bone, in spite of the break. Thus it is that the human heart throws forth a hardening substance in its resistance to the will of God, until afterward it is harder than a heart which has not heard the Gospel of Jesus Christ. The thoughts with which the Israelites considered what Moses said and did were unbelief. They refused to believe and hardened their hearts. Thus Stephen also described them in his speech before the Sanhedrin, saying, "Ye stiffnecked and uncircumsized in heart and ears, ye do always resist the Holy Ghost; as your fathers did so do ye." God hardens only a heart which rejects his truth.

The same reference brings the figure of blindness to our attention, and Israel is said to be blinded. Her stiff-necked rebellion, her spiritual adultery, her turning from God's revelation is the general story of the history of Israel. Isaiah cried, and Paul quotes it, "Lord, who hath believed our report . . . all day long I have stretched forth my hands unto a disobedient and gainsaying people." The veil of spiritual blindness remains unlifted from the eyes of Israel. Paul said, "Even unto this day, when Moses is read, the veil is upon their heart." True, the objective veil of Moses is gone. It decayed before his own body decayed, but the subjective veil on their hearts remained.

The condition of Israel today is the same—veiled. Moses is still read and attended to in the synagogue, but he has only the glory of justice and of condemnation. They have rejected the Moses who pointed in the Pentateuch to the new covenant. They do not see that this was "done away in Christ" and the righteousness of justification established in the place of the righteousness which is by the law. The Jewish unbelief which existed in Paul's day and caused his persecution at the preaching of Christ in Jerusalem, Iconium, Corinth, and Rome was the same as the unbelief which existed at Sinai. They glorified Moses and rejected Him to whom Moses pointed. Every time the Jews read their Pentateuch the same hardness and blindness exist today. If they are veiled, they are lost. No special favors of God to Israel exist today. The glory of the ministry of the law is over. The veil is removed. The Jews must be told these facts instead of being coddled in their unbelief.

The Jews, however, are not the only ones who have a veil on their spiritual eyes. The unbelieving Gentiles are also veiled. Paul said, "In whom the god of this world hath blinded the minds of them which believe not, lest the light of the glorious gospel of Christ, who is the image of God, should shine unto them." Unbelieving Gentiles are veiled, hardened and blinded if they reject Jesus Christ. The same law which operated in reference to Israel operates on the Gentiles who reject Christ. There is no difference between all those who are out of Christ, no privilege to the Jew and no privilege to the Gentile. God is no respecter of persons. Whoever faces the glory of Christ and His Gospel and rejects it is hardened by that process. All the unsaved are perishing, but not judicially hardened in this condition, until they reject the Gospel of Jesus Christ.

This blinding process is carried on by the god of this world. That is a description, of course, of Satan, who incarnates the wickedness and ungodliness of this age in contrast with that which is to come. He is the seducer, the deceiver, the accuser, the enemy of our souls. To choose him and his system rather than the blessedness of the Lord Jesus Christ is to be blinded to the glory of the Gospel. Satan works by controlling "the thoughts" of men. He has blinded the minds of them. This is the consideration which arises in hearing the Gospel and which is the suggestion of Satan. Such individuals are "taken captive by him at his will." Their thoughts become blinded or stonified to the truth. They are warped to follow falsehood. Servants of the Lord are often compelled to marvel at the blind spots in people's moral perception, even in Christians. Some people are blind to their anger, others to their envy, others to their pride, and they need to have this blindness removed by the Lord Jesus Christ to see themselves as He sees them. When one considers God's grace, the gift of Calvary, the blood of Christ, justification and new life and yet thinks nothing of them, he is blinded. Satan can never dim the Gospel light by all his attacks. He can blind our eyes to the glory of the Gospel of salvation in Christ only by our wilful consideration of thoughts suggested by him.

Unbelievers, therefore, are condemned to darkness. The dawn of light did not break on them. The Gospel day has come. It is here for multitudes, but unbelievers still continue in darkness, experiencing only the night of condemnation. What a wonderful day this Gospel era is, with the glory, the light, the freedom and the blessings to those who have experienced the sunrise in their hearts. We are no longer under law. We are now in the glorious liberty of the sons of God. Yet one's mind may become such that the greatest sunrise will never alter his darkness. He may be thoroughly blinded or hardened. God forbid it, and may we guard against it. Yet the fact remains.

If we are veiled, whether Jews or Gentiles, we are lost. All men without the Gospel are perishing, but they are in a condition to be saved. It is this lost condition of man which stirs us to action in preaching, in missions and in evangelism. Because men are lost, we need a Savior, and we need the Gospel. These lost persons may yet believe and accept, for such lostness is not final. It is uncertain and it may soon end, but when the Gospel reaches men and they reject, their perishing becomes certain, an established fact. The hardening begins when one resists and rejects the Gospel of Jesus Christ. "How shall we escape, if we neglect so great salvation?" "Today, after so long a time; as it is said, Today if ye will hear his voice, harden not your hearts." If the Gospel is hidden or veiled to you, you are perishing. Satan has blinded your thoughts and taken you captive, but that veil may be removed.

II. The Removal of the Veil

Paul hastens on to say, "Which veil is done away in Christ," and then adds, "When it shall turn to the Lord, the veil shall be taken away." The fact that the veil can be removed is the truth of the Gospel. First of all, it is removed by that very truth. Paul said, "Their minds were blinded: for until this day remaineth the same veil untaken away in the reading of the old testament; which veil is done away in Christ." The transient economy of the law of works and of condemnation is gone. The glory of God appeared in the person of the Lord Jesus Christ. John said, "He exegeted the father." That glory of Christ in all of His divine and human excellencies makes Him the focal point of light in the universe, deserving adoration and worship. In Him are found all the wonders of righteousness, justification and life. The full and permanent economy of the grace of God is in Christ, "who is the image of God." Thus He could say, "He that hath seen me hath seen the father," and Paul declared, "Who, being in the form of God, thought it not robbery to be equal with God." He is the express image of His glorious person. This glorified Christ now sheds forth the Divine love and grace for us all. Therefore, the Gospel is "Jesus Christ as Lord." There is no other. So Paul said, "We preach Jesus Christ *the* Lord." To preach one's own self is to offer one's own thoughts and doctrines and to reshape the word according to our own ideas for the sake of honor, personal return or personal advantage. The true preacher is not seeking a worldly advantage to the Gospel. He is not setting himself up in opposition to the Lord or in the place of Him, but faithfully heralds the things of Christ which are revealed. The true position is that of a *doulos,* or slave, of Jesus Christ for the progress of the Gospel. Christ is the center, the circumference and the total of the Gospel. Christ is the end of the law. Christ is incarnate God. Christ is the source of life and light and glory. We must preach Christ crucified.

The veil is taken away not only through the Gospel, but by our turning unto the Lord. Said Paul, "When it shall turn to the Lord, the veil shall be taken away." This bespeaks conversion. It is an allusion to Moses facing the Lord with the veil removed. The "it" probably refers back to the heart spoken of in the fifteenth verse, and on which the veil is said to lie. When the individual heart turns to the Lord the veil is removed. This is conversion. It is always an individual matter. Conversion means turning to Christ the Lord. The veil of unbelief, whether on Jew or Gentile, is removed when we turn to Christ. Thus it is shown to be a self-imposed veil. The wonder of transformation by conversion is a miracle of the Lord, and yet the power of converting is within every person. Christ said, "Except ye convert and become as little children ye cannot see the kingdom of God."

A remnant of Israel converted then and a remnant is converted now. Not all Israel was hardened, and the hardening of the nation is not permanent. It will ultimately be removed. This is the message of the ninth to the eleventh chapters of Romans. Though the nation has a veil, yet individuals of that nation may be saved by their turning unto the Lord.

That the nation will yet turn to the Lord in conversion and have that hardness or that veil removed is declared plainly by Paul. "Blindness in part is happened to Israel, until the fulness of the Gentiles be come in. And so all Israel shall be saved." The fall of Israel, that is, its hardening, caused great blessing to come to the Gentiles through the death and resurrection of the Lord Jesus Christ constituting the Gospel, but now, in their going away or their hardness, they are not the people of God. God will restore them to their place of privilege and of blessing, but only when the hardness is removed through their conversion.

The third means of removing the veil is by the work of the Holy Spirit. This is declared in the seventeenth and eighteenth verses:

"Now the Lord is that spirit: and where the spirit of the Lord is, there is liberty. But we all, with open face beholding as in a glass the glory of the Lord, are changed into the same image from glory to glory, even as by the Spirit of the Lord."

The work in the heart is done by the Holy Spirit when one turns to the Lord. Paul says, "The Lord is the spirit." This is not a denial of the Trinity, but an affirmation that the essence and the work of both the Holy Spirit and of God is identical. Where the Lord is, His Spirit is. Where the Spirit is, the Lord is. This is the full teaching of the doctrine of the Spirit. When Christ was glorified, He shed forth the Spirit into the hearts of believers. That Spirit is the gift of God to the converting and believing soul. It is He who removes the veil or the hardness from our hearts.

The essence of the new dispensation is spiritual. It is a dispensation of liberty. The law, bondage, condemnation and death are left behind, so that we are called into the liberty of the sons of God, no longer veiled, but in unveiled fellowship with the Father, with His Son the Lord Jesus Christ and with one another.

This Holy Spirit in us produces Christ's image in all of its glory, not a mere reflection as in a glass, but a reproduction revealing the image of the Son of God. The fruits of the Spirit are the virtues and the attributes of the Lord Jesus Christ.

III. THE UNVEILED GLORY

An unveiled countenance is described by St. Paul as "an open face." It is a permanent, inward state for all believers of unveiled attendance on beholding the things of the glory of the Lord, really an attitude of the heart. The Gospel is a matter of a changed heart, where Christianity produces its greatest effect and which ultimately shows in our external lives. For all of us who have turned to the Lord, where we behold the image of God, there is a transformation into that same image beginning at regeneration and continuing by sanctification through life. All of it is wrought by the Spirit of the Lord. We ourselves become the reflection of that glory of His image.

The reservoir or source of that glory is declared by St. Paul to be God. He said, "God, who commanded the light to shine out of darkness, hath shined in our hearts, to give the light of the knowledge of the glory of God in the face of Jesus Christ." Here is a reference, first of all, to the Divine fiat of creation, when, with a word, God created light. This is the revelation of God as light and as opposed to darkness, whereas the god of this world blinds and brings darkness to the soul. Here Paul places his sanction on the Mosaic account of the creation, not one of evolution of life, but a universe suddenly filled with life.

But now God shines in our hearts, having entered there. This is the reason why Christians are the children of light, of glory. Christ-in-us is the hope of glory. From within a radical change has occurred, bringing about that light. This illumination comes in the face of the Lord Jesus Christ. Hence, to receive Christ by the Spirit is to have the eternal and immortal light of life within us. It is the glory of God on the face of Christ reflected in us by the Spirit.

The last clause ought to be translated, "for the purpose of illumination by the knowledge of *the* Christ." That illumination is personal. It takes place within the life of the believing, converting man. God intends that these darkened, blinded, discouraged hearts of ours shall be illumined, that the god of this world shall not rule them. To this end, we have the Gospel. Such illumination comes from the knowledge of Christ. The only knowledge of God who is the light comes through Jesus Christ the mediator. "He that hath seen me hath seen the father," said Christ. Truly we come to know Christ by the historical records, but we must also come to know Him by experimental faith. Such knowledge is not a once and for all experience, but it constantly increases, and as it does, we experience the greater measure of the light of God. If then we would know God we must first know Jesus Christ.

What reigns in your heart? Darkness or light? The god of this world or Christ? Are you still veiled and hardened because you have rejected Christ and the light, or have you converted, committed your life to Him and trusted Him, that the sunrise might occur in your soul?

Sunrise has already taken place. The light is shining in Christ, historical and contemporaneous. Christ not only lived and died and rose again, but Christ lives today. Other multitudes have turned to Him and have experienced the dawn, the sunrise in their souls. Why, then, should you continue to be blinded in thought so that the light of God "will not get to dawn in you"? Turn yourself. Convert to the light of the world, which is Christ, and the veil will be removed from your heart.

XII

THE PRINCE OF DARKNESS OR THE GOD OF LIGHT

TEXT: *"The god of this world hath blinded the minds of them which believe not, lest the light of the glorious gospel of Christ, who is the image of God, should shine unto them."*—II COR. 4:1-6.

IN THIS TEXT we have a marked contrast of the source of spiritual darkness and the source of spiritual light in this world. These are called gods, one being a god of goodness and the other of evil.

One evening I walked down through a path between the pines on the shores of the Atlantic near Bar Harbor, Maine, to the coast line. The tide was out and so my companion and I decided to walk along the stones of the water front to the road some rods away. As we turned toward the west, along the Reach, a glorious sight greeted our eyes. Sunset colors beyond description meeting and being reflected in the waters of the Reach, quietness of the evening and a gentle breeze blowing off the ocean led one to a worshipful attitude and to thoughts of the great Creator and all that was good in the world. Suddenly, in the midst of these reveries we became aware of large mosquitoes and gnats, which stung us in fury for invading their breeding places, and the stench of decaying crabs and fish left by a retreating tide met our nostrils. Immediately we became conscious of what is ugly, painful and repulsive in the world. One's mind went out toward all the suffering caused by war. What a contrast! On the one hand, goodness, loveliness and beauty! On the other hand, wickedness, brutality and pain! Yes, both are in the world.

Apparently these two principles, powers or persons are in constant conflict and struggle. At times, it seems that the God of light arrests and conquers the attention of men, and at other times the god of darkness takes his turn. Surely there is hardly any time to became bored by the monotony of good, for evil supplants it too soon. This struggle is the heart of the teaching of an ancient religion called Zoroastrianism. Therein is a dualism which draws its source from two coequal and coeternal gods, one Ahura-Mazda, the god of light, goodness, beauty and truth and Angra-Mainyu, the god of darkness, evil and suffering. These two gods, according to the Zoroastrian dualism, are in eternal conflict for the dominion of the world. They account for all that is subsumed under the realm of one or the other, and their actions are reflected in men. Hence, life itself becomes a battle ground of the god of light and the god of darkness. All things for the Zoroastrians were divided in two. There were two gods, two marshalled hosts, two modes of living, two places of final destiny. Every man must choose his course. The human will is free and bound to nothing, save the necessity of choice. Bound up in this religion was a hope for the victory of the good, but there was no basis for that hope, for from the eternal struggle one or the other might snatch the ultimate victory. But this hope caused a tremendous emphasis to be placed upon the choice of the good and the pure and the hatred of evil. The comprehensive code of Zoroastrianism is very close to that of Christianity, namely, pure thoughts, pure words, pure deeds. The struggles and the difficulties of life were to be patiently endured with a profound hatred of evil.

In the Bible also a dualism is presented. There we have two princes: one, Christ, the God of light, of order, of goodness; the other, Satan, the god of darkness, of chaos and of evil. Satan is called the god of this world, the prince of darkness, the prince of this world and the prince of the power of the air. Christ is called the Prince of life, the Light of the world, the Son of God and the Lord of lords. Likewise, in Biblical theology there is a constant conflict during the history of the race between Satan and Christ over the allegiance of men. This conflict is due to the power of choice of the individual, who may give his allegiance to one or the other. Yet the divergence between the Biblical dualism and that of Zoroastrianism rests in the fact that ultimate victory is assured for the God of light. The Bible depicts a Divine foot upon the serpent's head and not a struggle of two equal titans of tremendous strength. Therefore, the Biblical view presents purpose, hope and victory upon an assured basis. Moreover, there is a subordination in the Biblical view. Satan is described as a created being who is limited in power and life, who also has already been defeated in this great conflict by the great victory of Calvary. Though sentence has been passed upon Satan, the god of darkness, it has not yet been executed. Therefore, in the history of the human race the conflict goes on.

The arena of this awful conflict is the world of mankind. The struggle is for the possession of our minds, or affections and wills in allegiance to one of these gods. Who is it that will ultimately gain dominion over humanity? Will it be the god of darkness or the God of light? The Bible has its answer, and outside of the Bible there is no possible assurance of being right in one's answer, for as one looks upon the evil which is in the world he cannot know whether right or wrong will triumph. In the Bible cosmic evil is described as the result of this spiritual struggle between the God of light and the god of darkness. Paul tells us that the whole creation awaits the victory of the God of light, who is the Lord Jesus Christ, at which time the sons of God shall be manifested and the creation shall be delivered from its bondage. Many of the prophets foretell that there is a day coming, when instead of the thorn shall come up the fir tree and instead of the brier shall come up the myrtle tree. That is, nature shall utterly change from its present state.

Many were the stages in this great spiritual struggle which have been manifested in the history of mankind. The first contest recorded is that which occurred in the Garden of Eden. The arena was the human nature of the first man. The Lord, in whose image he had been created, gave only one commandment as a sign of His lordship, to which if man had been obedient he would have yielded allegiance forever. However, this dominion of the Lord over man was contested by the god of darkness, and through the contest man gave his allegiance to the god of this world, followed the lust of his mind and body, and became by nature a child of wrath. Millenniums later this contest was again waged between the two great adversaries over the people of Israel. God gave unto the nation a law which was ethical and monotheistic. From that law Israel constantly strayed because of the temptations which came to it in many forms, but which had their origin in Satan. Once again, the god of this world won and the nation repudiated its allegiance to God. The last test which we will mention was that of the presentation of the person of the Lord Jesus Christ. Surely, in the perfections of His nature, teaching and person man should be willing to accept Him as Lord and King, but once again the god of this world won and mankind both rejected and crucified the Lord of glory. The whole struggle is that typified in the description of Satan contending against God for His servants as recorded in the book of Job. Mankind is the arena for this titanic spiritual struggle.

Apparently the conflict between evil and good is intensified in our day. History reveals periods of lull and periods of activity in this conflict. One might almost call it a war in which great battles are followed by periods for the opposing sides to consolidate their gains or to compensate for their losses, after each of which another period of activity occurs. Today there is a terrible outbreak of conflict and a resurgence of evil on a world-wide scale comparable to the famous crises of history. Moreover, there will be a culmination of activity reaching the most intense conflict in the attack of evil upon righteousness at the conclusion of this age. Surely we have such an outbreak comparable at least to that prophesied in the world-wide dislocation of the peaceful pursuits of the race and in the putting of entire humanity under a test. But even if such a holocaust did not exist and we were living in peace, life would still be the constant scene of this conflict in a minor way for every individual.

I. The Cause of this Conflict—The Free Agency of Man

When one views the conflict of evil and good, the problem arises. Why God permits such a world? The answer is just as simple as the question, namely, because man was created in the Divine image, that is, as a free agent with intelligence and yet bound by law or duty. Because he has these three elements of his nature and environment he may be subjected to a test which will confirm him eternally in the state which he chooses.

This intelligence of man is stressed in the text by Paul's emphasis upon the "manifestation of the truth." The power of rational thought inherent in man is wonderful. It brings to us a universe in which we can think and build an ever-increasing body of knowledge in science, medicine and sociology. The world and history, therefore, are not chaotic but intelligent, because an intelligent God holds the past and the future together in a reasonable law of the present. It is upon this uniformity of the rational structure of the universe and man that we construct knowledge. Some may doubt that there is a supreme intelligence back of the universe, but why they doubt it we cannot understand. This is a universe in which, wherever it is found, truth is of God, who Himself is intelligence personified. The question, Is there truth? or, which might be synonymous, What is truth? must be answered in the affirmative. There is such a thing as truth, and this fact justifies our intellectual search and our processes of knowledge.

The rationality of man is patterned after God's. God said, Let us create man in our image. For us to say that God's intelligence is different from ours is to wreck the rational structure of the universe. Some interpret Isaiah's words, "As the heavens are higher than the earth, so are my ways higher than your ways, and my thoughts than your thoughts," saith the Lord, to mean that they are of a different kind, but in this context of the Scripture God was speaking about the wicked man whose wicked ways and wicked thoughts were morally different from His. Metaphysically, our thoughts must be the same as God's. That is, qualitatively they are alike in kind, although quantitatively they are not alike in amount, for God is infinite and we are finite. But if our minds are similar to the rational structure of the universe then they must be of the same kind as God's. We must be able to recognize truth. Therefore, we conclude that God will never violate our thoughts of justice, honesty, righteousness, purity, etc. What is true for man must be true for God, for if what is false for men were true for God, then the rationality of the universe would be gone. Two times two can never equal five for God any more than for man.

It is this power of rationality in man which enables him to grasp the value of the end to be chosen and makes him guilty for choosing something other than the end which God and conscience declare he must choose. The alternative for the choice of the good is the choice of the evil, or self-gratification for the individual.

This, of course, implies that there must be a standard of duty or right. This Paul also says in his words, "By manifestation of the truth, commending ourselves to every man's conscience in the sight of God." The truth is confirmed by man's conscience. If man is to follow, to choose the truth or the right, a standard of right must be subjectively present with him, to know what is good and what is evil and then be able to choose the good. That standard we hold to be present in man in conscience, which is God's subjective law confirming His revealed law given in the Bible. Whenever the truth of the Bible is presented, the internal conscience of the individual witnesses to its correctness. Therefore, when we speak of God as a God of love and of justice, of the inevitability of judgment, of the difference between right and wrong, and of the offer of forgiveness through a Savior, man's conscience witnesses thereto. Whenever man hears the Ten Commandments his conscience agrees that they are the law of God. Thus the Bible, conscience and reason agree as to a standard of duty, but that standard of truth and right was ultimately gathered up in the person and life of Jesus Christ. Therefore, he who believes upon Christ responds affirmatively to the standard which God places before us. He meets the test as to the law of God.

To do this, of course, man must be a free agent. He must possess moral agency. With an alternative choice before him, man may accept one or the other. We hold that there is no compulsion upon the will of man. He may or he may not choose goodness and light as they are presented to him. No external compulsion makes him go wrong. To deny this freedom is to run counter to experience, reason and Scripture. Within certain limitations, this choice determines in which directon man will go. True that Jeremiah said, "The way of man is not in himself: it is not in man that walketh to direct his steps." That is a recognition of God's part in our lives, which is very great. No man can be righteous by willing to be righteous, but we hold that he can take the first step in that direction, and in taking that step God will meet him with great assistance.

There is a strong pressure upon man's mind and his affections and his will from the good and the evil which are in the world. God has made a tremendous movement toward man in the Gospel and in the persuasion of the Holy Spirit who applies this Gospel. The fact that God assumed human flesh, lived among us, carried our sins and sorrows, died for us upon the Cross and gave the gift of the Holy Ghost to inspire and carry on the great work of the Church places a tremendous pressure upon our human nature to respond to good. But, on the other hand, Satan and evil, through temptation, lure and attraction of the world, the flesh and life, press in upon the soul for allegiance to evil. The outcome of the conflict is determined by the will of the individual. If the individual is willing to choose the good, the way of salvation and deliverance is present for him. This we hold to be the clear teaching of Christianity. Not that the individual saves himself, but rather that he meets the conditions so that he can be saved.

The outcome of the choice of individuals in this great conflict results in either strengthening the movement of evil or strengthening the movement of good in the world. The choice determines whether a man shall live in darkness or light. The god of this world can not blind the eyes of any except those who will not believe the Gospel, our Scripture says. Therefore, choose you whom you will serve. The magnitude of this fact of choice is great. In the prophecy concerning the child of the virgin it was said, that before he was old enough to know to discern between the evil and the good the land should be forsaken of both her kings. There is a time in life when man arrives at the maturity and point of responsibility where he may choose for himself the God of his life. Hence man is the arena of conflict.

II. THE CASE OF ONE GIVING ALLEGIANCE TO THE PRINCE OF DARKNESS

Suppose one will not believe and rather chooses, consciously or unconsciously, to follow darkness. He may do this, of course, by merely refusing to believe, by being indifferent to the offer of salvation or by doing despite unto the spirit of grace. One need only reject the God of light in order to give allegiance to the god of darkness. When we reject the God of light, we are told that the god of this world can blind the minds of those which believe not.

Blindness is not confined to the physical eye. It is often used of spiritual perception. An individual may have perfect physical sight but very impaired spiritual vision. Physical sight may be dulled in many ways, for instance, by a cataract or a veil drawn over the eye by a growth. And thus we read that unbelievers have their spiritual eyes veiled, so that they cannot understand and cannot perceive the things of God. This veil originated with them in their wilful unbelief. There is also myopia or near-sightedness. A familiarity with the precious things of God without obedience to them breeds contempt and an inability to appreciate them. There is presbyopia, that is, inelasticity of the lense due to old age. One can grow old in looking at the things of God offered to him in the Gospel until it is too late for him to be saved. He can no longer focus upon them.

He can no longer obey the Gospel. In the physical world time does its deadly work of decay, but in the spiritual world the laws of evil accomplish it under the god of this world. The dulling, hardening process immediately begins under the agency of Satan in those who choose evil and darkness.

A blinded soul spiritually sees nothing desirable or attractive in what is the source of delight to a saved man. Paul said:

"Whatsoever things are true, whatsoever things are honest, whatsoever things are just, whatsoever things are pure, whatsoever things are lovely, whatsoever things are of good report; if there be any virtue, and if there be any praise, think of these things . . . and the God of peace shall be with you."

The blinded soul arrives at the place where these lovely, beautiful and abiding attributes have lost all attraction. No wonder Jesus said, "If therefore the light that is in thee be darkness, how great is that darkness!" One need only to take pleasure in the things which he knows are forbidden and contrary to the will of God to be given up to them by God. Paul said:

"Even as they did not like to retain God in their knowledge, God gave them over to a reprobate mind, to do those things which are not convenient; who . . . , knowing the judgment of God, that they which commit such things are worthy of death, not only do the same, but have pleasure in them that do them."

That is the description of a blind soul, a seared conscience, one taken captive by the devil.

Such a one is also described as being perverted:

"In time past ye walked according to the course of this world, according to the prince of the power of the air, the spirit that now worketh in the children of disobedience: Among whom also we had our conversation in times past in the lusts of the flesh, fulfilling the lusts of the flesh and of the mind; and were by nature the children of wrath, even as others."

Those who have given allegiance to the prince of this world walk according to the course of the evil world. They are described as being spiritually dead, as submitting to the prince of disobedience and of being conformed to the forbidden things of the world. Their practices may merely be the following of self-will in the lusts of the mind as well as of the flesh, but this constitutes them the children of wrath by nature. They are opposed to God and they are spiritually dead. Thus, like the prince of darkness, these followers of the god of this world love darkness because their deeds are evil.

It is the renunciation of these practices to which we are led by our repentance. They are, "the hidden things of dishonesty," "walking in craftiness," "handling the word of God deceitfully," etc. Hidden things of dishonesty do not speak much of righteousness, of light and of purity. Craftiness, subtlety, falsehood, hypocrisy breathe of the things of darkness. Deceitfulness suggests the father of lies, who is Satan himself, whose children Jesus said were the Jews who rejected Him.

Such a state of life followed by an individual is as abnormal as is illness in the physical body. The individual then needs a spiritual physician, a healer and a Savior, for he is tragically stumbling in the darkness because there is no light in him, having rejected the source of light. There is a tremendous need to be helped, to be rescued, to be succored, to be snatched from the way of perversion.

When one is blinded and perverted, we are told that also he is lost. For the meaning of lost we ought to turn to the parables of Jesus. First, there was the lost coin, which depicts the condition of being lost from some place or lost by some one. The good woman having lost the coin searched for it diligently. Thus we believe that sinners are lost from the Father. It was in this manner that the boy Jesus was lost from his parents on the return from Jerusalem, when he was but twelve years of age. The second illustration, given by Jesus, is that of a lost sheep that is gone astray and is in danger of the cliffs or of the wolves or lions, that is, in danger of destruction. So, to be lost means to be in great danger. The third illustration was that of the prodigal, who when he came to himself realized that he was actually lost. He was without any compensation for being away from his father's house. Those whom the god of this world hath blinded are lost, which means they are lost from God, that they have an irreparable loss in their own lives and that they are in immediate danger of destruction.

Though this is the condition of one who has given allegiance to the god of this world, he may not realize it. He may be blinded and be content in his blindness, having no desire to see the glories of the spiritual world. He may be perverted and find certain amount of pleasure in his perversion, and he may be lost without realizing the imminent danger which threatens him. Yet our trustworthy Scriptures declare all these things to be facts, and therefore we declare them unto you that you might be warned in time.

III. Choosing to Give Allegiance to Christ the God of Light

Who is the God of light? Hear the word, "For God, who commanded the light to shine out of darkness, hath shined in our hearts, to give the light of the knowledge of the glory of God in the face of Jesus Christ." The God of light is the Creator and the Redeemer of us all. He who once created physical light by the word of His power now shines spiritually unto those who are redeemed. That spiritual sun of righteousness has risen with healing in His wings. All who are not blind may see it today. Thus Jesus said, "As long as I am in the world, I am the light of the world." Again, He said, "Yet a little while is the light with you. Walk while ye have the light, lest darkness come upon you: for he that walketh in darkness knoweth not whither he goeth. While ye have light, believe in the light, that ye may be the children of the light." And again, "I am come a light into the world, that whosoever believeth on me should not abide in darkness." As the spiritual light of the world, we see in Jesus all of the elements of the Divine life as constituent parts of that Divine light. Just as the elements of light are broken up into constituent colors by a prism, so also the Divine life manifested itself in many forms in the person of Jesus Christ. There we see His kindness, love, long-suffering, purity, and loveliness, and we know that it reveals the light of the world. That light came into spiritual darkness and the darkness could not quench it so that it continues to shine today.

How may allegiance be given unto the God of light? Three things are suggested here. First, by receiving mercy; second, by accepting Christ; and third, by walking in the light. Paul said, "As we have received mercy, we faint not." Universally, the Scripture declares that God is merciful, that He is favorably disposed, that He is ready to forgive, that He will harken unto our cries, that if we will turn from our wicked ways He will have mercy and will abundantly pardon. The only need is that we will repent and convert, that is, go to receive His mercy. Just as the prodigal, who discovered that he was lost, said, "I will arise and go to my father," so we need thus to repent and to turn to the Father. Let us ask for His mercy, for what we ask He will not deny. The publican merely cried, "God be merciful to me a sinner," and he was heard by a merciful God.

Next, we must accept Christ. The Gospel is of Christ. Those who give their allegiance to the prince of darkness believe not the Gospel of Christ. This is the Gospel about Christ, namely, His person, His life, His work of redemption, as it is declared in the Scripture. Hence, "We preach not ourselves, but Jesus Christ the Lord." The Lord became incarnate in the human Jesus, and thus God gave the prepared apparatus for redemption which was wrought on Calvary. Believing the Gospel means to receive and accept Christ as Lord and Savior. He that believes on the light shall become a child of the light. Whosoever received Him to him gave He power to become the sons of God. This means the committing of one's self to God in Christ for life and destiny, the acknowledging of Christ as Lord.

Then allegiance means walking in the light as it is revealed by Christ. Jesus said, "I am the light of the world: he that followeth me shall not walk in darkness, but shall have the light of life." Have you been following Jesus? There can be no true regeneration without obedience to the Lord. He that saith, "I have fellowship with Him and walketh in darkness," lies and does not the truth, but if he walks in the light as he is in the light, he has fellowship with other believers and the blood of Jesus Christ cleanses him from all sin. This means a renunciation of the way of sin, of darkness and of evil, an obedience to the Lord Jesus Christ.

Finally, children of God become the children of light. Just as He was called the light of the world, so He called us the light of the world. We inevitably assume the characteristics of our Prince or our God. If we are children of the devil we shall be children of lies, of murders, of lust and of evil. If we are children of God we shall be children of love, of righteousness, of purity and of grace. Hence, being the children of light, every rational hope and every promise of the Scripture tells us that we shall ultimately enter the realm of light with our Lord, who is the God of light.

Hence, the determination should be ours to acknowledge Christ as Lord, to submit ourselves to Him, to declare that we have Christian faith. Every one must choose his Master and service. No man can serve two masters and no one can make your decision for you, but from this decision come all the issues of life. Hence, it is the greatest crisis of all. Will you now acknowledge Christ as Lord? Will you acknowledge Christian faith? Will you acknowledge God as Sovereign? Will you follow the way of righteousness? This is your choice and this is the hour of decision.

XIII

HIS SUFFERING AND OURS

TEXT: *"Our light affliction, which is but for a moment, worketh for us a far more exceeding and eternal weight of glory."*—II COR. 4:7-18.

THIS TREATISE on suffering begins with a description of our human nature as an earthen vessel. This body and the human life which attends it is nothing but clay, the common earthly clay from which shatterable pottery is baked.

While walking in Indiana I passed a clay kiln where yellow drainage pipe of all sizes was made. The clay of that district lends itself to such purpose. Picking up a few pieces of it, which looked brittle, I tapped them easily together, only to find that they shattered as an ordinary clay flower pot shatters when it receives a shock. Paul's description of human nature is in this terminology. We are earthen vessels, easily broken or marred or chipped, vehicles which unless preserved are too fragile to stand the shocks and blows of life's suffering. Paul even described himself as contemptible and weak. This is the ultimate in humility. One can think no less of himself than the conception of human life as dust or clay.

The astonishing thing in Biblical revelation is that such a human nature should be assumed by the Lord in His incarnation. We must not forget that the body of Christ was no different qualitatively from the contemptible clay and the despicable dust which form the life of us all. This is what the Bible means when it says, "The Word was made flesh and tabernacled among us." Also, when it says, "Though he were rich, yet for our sakes be became poor."

We as earthly vessels have been designed, in the purpose of God, to contain great treasure. "We have this treasure in earthen vessels, that the excellency of the power may be of God, and not of us." What is this treasure? In poetic language Paul has just described it: "God ... hath shined in our hearts, to give the light of the knowledge of the glory of God in the face of Jesus Christ." This treasure, then, is the illumination in the mind, heart and life of the believer who knows God through Jesus Christ. Synonymous with these poetic words would be salvation, eternal life and the Gospel. Such treasure obviously is of infinite value, yet it is housed in vessels of clay. This is contrary to human practice. Our desire is to set the precious jewel in an appropriate setting. Some time ago I bought for a friend a very beautiful white Brussels diamond. He, in turn, took the diamond to a jeweler to obtain the most appropriate and lovely setting. Then he consecrated them both to a high purpose, namely, that of sealing his affection. Not so with God. He has displayed His precious jewel of eternal life in contemptible clay. What mighty grace! The eternal God, the source of all light, shines in our hearts that the light of the knowledge of the glory of Himself may be seen in us and displayed before our fellow men.

The incongruity of such a treasure in such a vessel is used to display the Divine power, to show that it finds its source in God and not in us. This wonderful message of salvation and of life has no source or explanation in the earthen vessels which contain it. They could never have originated it, generated it or continued it. This life is God's own possession and by His power manifests itself with salvation and victory in us. The purpose in our weakness is thus to reveal God's power in saving souls and not man's power. We preachers assure you that from these common human natures, including our minds, spirits and bodies, contemptible clay, we have no help for you except what we have received (I Cor. 15:3), the help placed in us by God. In ourselves we have nothing of any value, but in us there is a life of infinite value given by God.

This contrast reveals the excellency of the power of God, that is, the superlative greatness of God's power in stooping to such human weakness in order to save, deliver, heal and bless through human vehicles of dust. That power attends the message of the Gospel given through the weakest human vehicle.

Let us note that because we are such earthen vessels suffering is an indispensable part of existence, yet when viewed in the light of the Divine purpose, it becomes understandable and profitable. Standing in the midst of the vast suffering of humanity today this treatise should give us some help to endure.

I. OUR SUFFERING IS SHARED BY CHRIST

Immediately following the definition of life as an earthen vessel, Paul describes the sufferings through which he and his colaborers were passing, concluding with the words, "Always bearing about in the body the dying of the Lord Jesus, that the life also of Jesus might be made manifest in our bodies." Here is a reference to what was done to Jesus Christ in suffering. The word "dying" is an active noun describing what was done to Jesus and not the subjective dying of Jesus. It refers to the putting to death of Jesus. This phrase thus describes and calls to our mind all which happened in His passion, involving His trial, suffering and death. That twofold trial before Caiaphas and Pilate, with the contumely of being smitten, bruised, spat upon, falsely accused by His people, deserted by His followers and utterly alone, although innocent, is unforgettable. His sufferings after the conclusion of the trial in the buffeting by the soldiers, the scourging, the enduring of the crown of thorns, the carrying of a cross, the infliction of pain in the crucifixion and the more delicate suffering of mockery reveals what He endured for us. Add to this the death in which the just satisfaction for sin was drawn out from His own heart and mind by a righteous God and you begin to understand His suffering for you. Yes, He shed the blood of the New Covenant as a remission for your sins. All this is implied in the word "dying," or the putting to death of the Lord Jesus.

This active antipathy, persecution and killing of Jesus by His enemies is being borne always by the believer. That is, it is repeated for the sake of Christ in His followers by the same evil world which put Him to death. Jesus had foretold that if they hated Him they would also hate His followers and all that wickedness was able to do to Christ it would do to His followers. We are not to think that Jesus is suffering mystically in us but we are to realize that what happened to Him is to be repeated to us for His sake. The Satanic world, in all of its forces, whether disease, decay, or death, is arrayed against us. Probably there never was a more crushing attack of evil upon that which is good and those who are good than the present world conflict. Whether it strikes all believers or not is immaterial. We are all to be martyrs for His sake.

How are these sufferings repeated in the life of the believer? Paul draws this picture:

"We are troubled on every side, yet not distressed; we are perplexed, but not in despair; Persecuted, but not forsaken; cast down, but not destroyed.... For we which live are alway delivered unto death for Jesus' sake."

This fourfold picture describes the human life of the believer under terrible pressure and yet escaping that pressure, the mind at a loss but not utterly lost, the body persecuted, but not abandoned, the spirit cast down, caught by the enemy, but not annihilated. Paul knew that death was working in him and would ultimately catch up with him and overcome him, and yet miraculously he was saved, preserved through all trials from that last menace of death. He saw that his outward man was perishing and he acknowledged that he was kept alive only by the preserving power of Christ, who was with him. What a wonder it is that these clay vessels receive such repeated shocks by disease, by stress, and perplexity and yet are not broken. In a true sense we are delivered unto death for Jesus' sake. Just as Judas delivered Jesus to death, so we are handed over to be subject to sickness, weakness, trouble, temptation and trial as martyrs for Jesus' sake, and all this works out for us a greater amount of glory in the end, as we shall see.

Therefore, remember that in suffering, which is permitted by God to come to us all, we are never alone. We forget not the sufferings in which Christ died to save us from sin. His sufferings were vicarious, expiatory and voluntary. None of these purposes is connected with ours, but another purpose is declared to be the working out of a greater heritage in us. Surely we should be ready to return His love by being willing if necessary to suffer for Him, knowing that now, since He himself hath suffered being tempted, He is able to succor them that are tried. He led the way in suffering for us.

II. OUR SUFFERING MANIFESTS HIS LIFE

In connection with these declarations, that we are delivered to death for Jesus' sake and are bearing about in the body the dying of the Lord Jesus Christ, are connected two purpose clauses explaining the reason, namely, "that the life also of Jesus might be manifested in our bodies." Paul declared that God's purpose in our sharing His suffering is that we may manifest His life. The dying of Jesus and the life of Jesus are placed as opposites. His life conquered even in His death and so it is with us. It is this life which is to be manifested publicly in our suffering. By it God intends to declare, to teach, to exhibit a truth. That truth is that life is connected with our mortal flesh or our mortal bodies. While our mortal bodies or our mortal natures are subject to death, we may yet exhibit life. This life, of course, is the Divine life given unto us, of which God desires to make a grand public advertisement in the believer, or the one who possesses the Divine life, even while his physical body is dying. The treasure of life is kept preserved in a dying body.

Consider the nature of this life in the living one. It is noticeable that the Greek uses a word, *Zoe,* which is utterly different from another word, *Psuke,* though both are translated "life." Jesus referred to his *Psuke,* or life, with a small letter when He said, "I lay down my life, that I might take it again. No man taketh it from me, but I lay it down of myself. I have power to lay it down, and I have power to take it again." This was the human life possessed by Jesus, but Jesus Himself is Life with a capital L, or *Zoe* in the Greek. That is, He is the fountain of life or the prince of life, the source of SPIRITUAL OR ETERNAL LIFE. This is the life which is given to us when we receive Christ as our Savior. All those who have *Zoe* as a possession are living beings. They are saved because the treasure of eternal life is carried in their fragile human natures. They are spiritually alive, they are passed from death to life. It is this spiritual life which is publicly exhibited as our possession in the midst of sufferings which lead unto death of the physical life, and marvelously this eternal life is manifested in reference to our physical life, subject to suffering, decay and death. Thus Paul said, "Death worketh in us, but life in you." Life is produced in others by the living ones bearing about the dying of Jesus in their own mortal bodies, that is, by their sufferings, which certainly imply voluntary self-denials and trials undergone for the sake of making known the life of Jesus. Death is hurting the believer. Death will soon end his work. It attacks the earthen vessel. It shocks the clay, which will ultimately disintegrate; but death can never affect the *Zoe,* or spiritual life, which is eternal. Do not think that this spiritual life keeps your physical life in operation, for if so you would never die. Death could and did catch up with the Apostle Paul physically, but it had no power over his eternal life. By the very labors, sufferings and process of death Paul and his colaborers were bringing spiritual life to the Corinthians and others. Like him, we must be willing to spend and be spent in imparting our great treasure to others.

The strength to suffer for Christ lies in the faith we have in His Life. Paul said:

"We having the same spirit of faith, according as it is written, I believed, and therefore have I spoken; we also believe, and therefore speak; Knowing that he which raised up the Lord Jesus shall raise up us also by Jesus, and shall present us with you."

It is because we have faith that we are willing to speak for Christ, to labor for Him, to undertake what may be the cause of our suffering. Days have existed and may be approaching again when to speak for Jesus will mean physical death. Today it may mean light and inconsequential social persecution. In the face of the greatest sacrifice, Paul could say, "We believe, therefore we speak." Let the sorrows of death compass us about. They shall never deter us from the course of service and from the pathway of the Lord Jesus.

Reason for this is the confidence that God who raised up Christ from physical death shall raise us up and shall present us with other believers. The object of faith is thus the resurrection. Not bravado or desperation caused these to hazard death for Christ's sake, but the confidence in resurrection and in immortality. The very knowledge that our *Zoe*, or eternal life, shall triumph over our *Psuke* or physical life as it did in the Lord Jesus, according to infallible proofs, is sufficient to harden our spirits to endure any kind of suffering. If we share His *Zoe*, or life, we shall share also His resurrection. It is even possible, as Paul declared in other Scriptures, that we should not see physical death but that Life will triumph over the decaying process at the Parousia of Christ or His coming. At any rate, whether by death or by translation, we know that God will present us to Christ as His bride, His church, His own inheritance. The joy and blessedness in that hour of knowing not only that He suffered for us, but that we, in turn, were willing to suffer for Him!

All this points to an end defined in these words, "For all things are for your sakes, that the abundant grace might through the thanksgiving of many redound to the glory of God." Definitely this is a reference to sufferings endured for the purpose of increasing the number of those in whom the light of the Gospel will shine through the face of Christ. We are speaking of suffering endured for Christ's sake and for the advance of the Gospel. One commentator translates this purpose clause, "In order that the grace, by being multiplied by means of a multiplied number, may cause the thanksgiving to abound to the glory of God." By multiplying the number of believers who will share in the resurrection life and glory we also multiply the great chorus of praise and thanksgiving to God's glory. All sufferings endured for this purpose will work out a far more exceeding weight of glory.

III. OUR SUFFERINGS WORK OUT GREATER GLORY

We now consider the compensation for the sufferings of the believer. Our hope is for a far more exceeding and eternal weight of glory. Because of this hope, we are enabled to suffer. By this hope, present sufferings are paled into nothingness by contrast. And for this hope we are made willing to suffer for Christ.

Paul said, "For which cause we faint not; but though our outward man perish, yet the inward man is renewed day by day." Where this hope is, there is no fainting, no drooping of hands or weakness of knees. We have endurance and this in spite of the fact that we are aware that our outward man is decaying, failing, really dying. We are not blind to what is happening physically to us. Our human nature in our external surroundings and environment is subject to the laws of destruction and death, but inwardly our regenerated spiritual nature is being constantly renewed, is maturing, is being prepared for the sharing of His great life. Consider the tragedy of having life only in the outward man, the man which is subject to destruction. When it has decayed and been destroyed, there is nothing left. No wonder women, advancing in years, cling to their transient beauty. No wonder men mourn the passing of their athletic prowess. If only this constitutes life, how poor it is. Paul could watch tribulation, affliction, persecution and disease gradually destroy that outward life with calmness and contentment because he endured it for Christ's sake, and it hastened the renewal of the inward man. This inward man may be found only in a Christian, for it is synonymous with eternal life. What a glory there is to know that this inward man is renewed, rejuvenated and strengthened. Are you conscious of such a renewal and maturing in the inward man? Are you being strengthened with might by His Spirit in the inner man?

This hope pales present suffering to nothingness in contrast with future glory. "Our light affliction, which is but for a moment, worketh for us a far more exceeding and eternal weight of glory." Our afflictions whatever they are, whether pain, trouble, disappointment or illness, contribute to eternal glory. They are not the cause, but in the purpose of God He uses these to compensate us by grace with greater glory. By our sufferings for Him we are perfected. We might rightfully say that all things work together for good to them that love God. Moreover, our afflictions are very light in comparison with the weight of glory of the heavenlies, of eternity. Afflictions are momentary, passing, transient. They belong to time. The glory, which means the image of the Lord Jesus Christ, will be eternal. Our afflictions are in time, that is, they are spread thin from one minute to the next minute, from one second to the next second, and we are thus able to bear them. If ten years of constant pain were rolled into one moment it would be unendurable because of the weight, but when we consider innumerable lifetimes of glory rolled into a moment or a present experience called eternity we begin to understand the contrast. Thus the glory is beyond measure. It exceeds all comparison and yet it is directly contingent upon the measure of affliction which we have endured for the sake of Christ in this world.

This hope makes us willing to suffer for Christ's sake. In the early Church existed what many have called the inexplainable martyr complex, that is, men like Ignatius, the church Father, directly sought martyrdom for the sake of Christ. It has been often considered an unhealthy and a morbid characteristic of the church, but here we catch something of the reason they sought it. With joy and gladness they were willing to suffer for Christ's sake because they believed their eternal glory depended upon their afflictions for the sake of the Lord. If this text be true, and of course we believe it is, then suffering, not sought for its own sake but brought upon us because of our labors and testimony for Christ is the most desirable thing in the world. This truth joined with the promise, "We are the children of God: And if children, then heirs; heirs of God, and joint heirs with Christ, if so be that we suffer with him, that we may be also glorified together. For I reckon that the sufferings of this present time are not worthy to be compared with the glory which shall be revealed," shows the inconsequential nature of our present sufferings for Him. Peter said, "If any man suffer as a Christian, let him not be ashamed; but let him glorify God on this behalf."

The secret of strength to endure suffering is then stated: "While we look not on the things which are seen, but on the things which are not seen, for the things which are seen are temporal, but the things which are not seen are eternal." The condition here advanced is that we shall keep our eyes fixed upon and attending to the more important, eternal things, which are unseen. Far too many of us have our joys and our sorrows connected with the external, material, sensuous things of life. The practice of focusing one's vision spiritually upon the unseen in life, character, salvation and glory will remove the sting from present affliction. This Scripture should be read daily, memorized, digested, until today's vanishing of material things and pleasures seem inconsequential to us. Let us pray, "Oh, God, make the invisible more real to us. Make us to know the fellowship of His sufferings and the power of His resurrection that we may be made conformable to His image, namely, to know the weight of His eternal glory."

XIV

AT HOME WITH GOD

TEXT: *"We are . . . willing rather to be absent from the body, and to be present with the Lord."*—II COR. 5:1-9.

A SMALL CONGREGATION at the Methodist Church, Old Orchard Beach, Maine, was startled at services Tuesday evening, January 13, 1942, when Henry M. Atwater, addressing the congregation, suddenly switched from the address he was making and described a vision of his own death, after which he fell dead on the platform.

"I see a light, he said. "The light is opening. I see the throne of God. There are angels on either side of the throne. I hear beautiful music. Jesus is coming down. I am dying." He fell to the platform, and when they had recovered from the shock some of the congregation went to the platform, thinking that Mr. Atwater had collapsed. They tried to give first aid, and then summoned Dr. Walter D. Mazzacane, who found that Mr. Atwater was dead.

Those present did not realize for some time that Mr. Atwater had had a vision of his death and was describing it to them. They felt quite awed when they realized what had taken place. The minister had been performing his usual duties, although he had not been in good health for some time. He died when he was seventy-seven years, ten months and twelve days old. His complete obituary notice was given in the Biddeford *Daily Journal,* with the account which I have just given. Does such a death, so similar to that of Stephen, who claimed that he saw heaven open and Jesus standing at the throne of God, correspond to the teaching of the Scriptures?

Our Scripture lesson deals with the event called death. It follows the Divine teaching in reference to suffering and affliction which we are compelled to undergo in these earthen vessels. It is always possible that such suffering may eventuate in death. Paul had described himself and his fellow disciples as bearing about in the body the dying of the Lord Jesus. Daily he was undergoing experiences which were described as being delivered unto death for Jesus' sake, so that death was constantly working in his body. It is obvious that for all of us, as for Paul, these constant afflictions which work out for us a far more exceeding and eternal weight of glory may suddenly prove too great for our physical bodies and we shall die. We may as well face the possibility of this, for it may come at any time to any one of us. There is no certainty that all of us will die, for there will be many believers living at the Parousia, or the coming of the Lord Jesus Christ, when the living saints will be transformed into the heavenly existence without death.

"If we believe that Jesus died and rose again, even so them also which sleep in Jesus will God bring with him. For this we say unto you by the word of the Lord, that we which are alive and remain unto the coming of the Lord shall not prevent them which are asleep. For the Lord himself shall descend from heaven with a shout, with the voice of the archangel, and with the trump of God: and the dead in Chrsit shall rise first: Then we which are alive and remain shall be caught up together with them in the clouds, to meet the Lord in the air: and so shall we ever be with the Lord. . . . We shall not all sleep, but we shall all be changed, in a moment, in the twinkling of an eye, at the last trump: for the trumpet shall sound, and the dead shall be raised incorruptible, and we shall be changed."

This fact of the possibility of our not dying is also implied in this Scripture, which states the dissolving of our tabernacle as hypothetical. Therefore, our sufferings may, or may not, end in death, but the only alternative to death would be the second coming of the Lord Jesus Christ.

This Scripture presents a beautiful description of death. The prominent words used are embodied in our text, namely, "to be absent from the body, and to be present with the Lord." This literally means to go abroad from the body, to depart from one's people or from one's dwelling place. There is always a natural sadness connected with such a departure and with such a leave-taking. Any one who has gone abroad, leaving his family and kindred, knows that feeling. The young men in the army who are leaving their homes with the prospect of fighting abroad are experiencing that sadness now. It constitutes leaving the familiar, the sensuous with which we have been connected, the known, and entering upon the great adventure into the unknown. It really means to be away from our earthly home, friends and loved ones. James Whitcomb Riley caught this in his little poem entitled, "Away."

> "I can not say, and I will not say,
> That he is dead! He is just away!
>
> "With a cheery smile, and a wave of the hand,
> He has wandered into an unknown land.
>
> "And left us dreaming how very fair
> It must be, since he lingers there.

"And you,—oh you, who the wildest yearn
For the old time step and the glad return,—

"Think of him faring on, as dear
In the love of There as the love of Here;

"Mild and gentle as he was brave,—
When the sweetest love of his life he gave

"To simple things:—where the violets grew
Pure as the eyes they were likened to.

"The touches of his hands have strayed
As reverently as his lips have prayed.

"Think of him still as the same, I say;
He is not dead—he is just away!" *

This Pauline statement concerning death is the clearest in the Bible. Here is the answer to the question, "What happens at death?" and to that often popularized topic, "Five Minutes After Death." Was Dwight L. Moody right when he said:

"Some day you will read in the papers that D. L. Moody, of East Northfield, is dead. Don't you believe a word of it! At that moment I shall be more alive than I am now. I shall have gone up higher, that's all —out of this old clay tenement into a house that is immortal; a body that death cannot touch, that sin cannot taint, a body fashioned like unto His glorious body. I was born of the flesh in 1837. I was born of the Spirit in 1856. That which is born of the flesh may die. That which is born of the Spirit will live forever."

This Scripture completely confirms Moody's statement. Therefore, let us learn what we can from it about death before we experience it.

I. THE DISSOLVING OF OUR EARTHLY TABERNACLE

Death is real. There are those in our day who deny that Jesus ever died and who say that there is no such thing as death. Their official glossary uses this definition of death, "An illusion, the lie of life in matter; the unreal and untrue; the opposite of life. . . . Any material evidence of death is false, for it contradicts the spiritual facts of being." Altogether too much of our sentiment and poetry has followed his idea of the unreality of death.

What the Scripture describes as the things seen and the things experienced, like pain, suffering, affliction and death, are never de-

* Quoted by permission of Bobbs-Merrill Co., Indianapolis, Ind.

clared to be error and unreal, but only declared to be transient and temporal. They are terribly real. Do you think that that physical absence is an error and an unreality? Is the tree which has been felled by the woodsman's ax still occupying its majestic place against the sky? To say so it to deny reason and sense.

Likewise, death is not annihilation, a cessation of being. Atheists like the late Clarence Darrow may accept this view and cling to it to the end, believing that the soul is nothing but the functioning of the body and that when the body disintegrates, the soul ceases to exist. But our whole Scripture declares the existence of the soul after death, either in the state of nakedness or with a heavenly habitation. Quite true that one can never prove on the basis of pure metaphysics that there is a continuance of life after death, although I believe such a belief is rational. But on the basis of revelation we have a clear teaching of this fact.

The Christian doctrine of death is contained in this statement of Scripture. It describes our present existence as an earthly tent, a temporary abiding place of the soul, that which may be struck or dissolved or shattered or destroyed, but the soul lives on. The continued existence of what is called our earthly tabernacle is largely dependent upon the work of our hands in contrast with our future habitation, which is utterly made without hands. Here our health, food, home and well-being depend largely upon the labor of our hands, and thus our temporary abode may be adequately described as a tabernacle made with hands, not, of course, in its origin, but in its continued existence. It is this house or dwelling, which is nothing but a flimsy tent, that is described as being dissolved. The suggestion is really of destruction by the separation of the elements which make up this earthly life, namely, the leaving of the body by the soul. Then inevitably the body disintegrates. Frederick Knowles put it correctly when he said,

> "This body is my house—it is not I;
> Herein I sojourn till, in some far sky,
> I lease a fairer dwelling, built to last
> Till all the carpentry of time is past . . .
> This body is my house—it is not I.
> Triumphant in this faith I live, and die." *

The earthy, transient, temporal tent of our dwelling is compared to "a building of God, a house not made with hands, eternal in

* "The Tenant." Quoted by permission of L. C. Page and Company, Boston, publishers.

the heavens." If this present body or physical life is the tabernacle referred to in the first part of our text then the house or habitation referred to in the second part of the text is unquestionably a new dwelling place for the soul.

Let us note the nature of this new "habitation." It is in strong contrast with the old. The first was temporal. This is eternal. The first was seen. This is unseen. The first was a tent. This is a building. The first was corruptible. This is incorruptible. The first was mortal. This is immortal. The first was weak. This is full of power. The suggestions made hereby are tremendous. Three separate outlooks concerning this body may be described. One, advanced by some thinkers, is that at death the soul receives what is called an ethereal or mystical body of a new element, such as fire, and that both the angels and God possess this kind of body. We find no suggestion of this in the Bible and we feel that it is taken from pagan thinking. We need no such borrowings for our interpretation of this Scripture. The second theory is that our Scripture merely refers to heavenly life which the soul assumes after death, namely, the *Zoe*, or the life of God, given to the individual soul. The fatal objection to this view is that the same Scripture in the previous chapter has announced that we already possess this *Zoe* when we are in this earthly tabernacle. It is the gift of God, namely, eternal life, and over it death has no power. Therefore, how could it be contrasted with our present tabernacle as something which we are to assume at death. Therefore, we are confined to the third interpretation, namely, that Paul is referring to the resurrection body, our future glorious body fashioned in the likeness of Christ's own resurrection body, to which the Scripture often refers as the acme of the redemptive process. "The whole creation groaneth and travaileth in pain together until now. And not only they, but ourselves also, which have the first-fruits of the spirit, even we ourselves groan within ourselves, waiting for the adoption, to wit, the redemption of our body."

This new habitation prepared for the soul is that which was spoken of by Jesus when He said, "In my father's house are many mansions: if it were not so, I would have told you. I go to prepare a place for you. And if I go and prepare a place for you, I will come again, and receive you unto myself." These mansions are not houses as Henry van Dyke pictures them in his story, *The Mansion*, saying that God builds the mansions for us out of the materials that we send on before. They are an expression of the clothing of the soul more like the sense which is given to the word by Oliver Wendell Holmes in "The Chambered Nautilus."

> "Build thee more stately mansions, O my soul,
> As the swift seasons roll!
> Leave thy low-vaulted past!
> Let each new temple, nobler than the last,
> Shut thee from heaven with a dome more vast,
> 'Till thou at length art free,
> Leaving thine outgrown shell by life's unresting sea!"

It is for these mansions of the soul, our eternal habitations, that we groan with earnest longing. We literally desire with a great desire this full redemption and deliverance which has been wrought for us by Christ but has not yet been given to us. It is in this circumstance of desiring that we groan. There is no suggestion in Christianity of a morbid desire for death or to flee this body. Christians are not weak, nor do they lack courage in facing suffering. In fact, theirs is just the opposite attitude. Yet, in the midst of our afflictions, our sufferings and our pain, we are to look up, to look forward to that which is revealed as our final habitation, which may come through the Parousia or through death.

This habitation is "from God." God has prepared it for us. God bestows it upon us. God is its source. Such an habitation of unlimited glory and wonder is given to all the saved, all who are the sons of God and, hence, the heirs of God. Of this future possession the earnest of the Spirit is the down payment, or the foretaste. To all those who have the earnest of the Spirit God has given the assurance that they will partake of the ultimate glory.

The time when this new house or habitation is to be assumed is not mentioned in this particular Scripture, although the alternatives suggested by Paul do imply the two possibilities. By the analogy of the word of God, that is the teaching in other parts of the Scripture, we find that the giving of this resurrection body is to take place at the second coming of Christ. Paul said, "The dead shall be raised incorruptible, and we shall be changed." That "we" means the living ones. "We which are alive and remain shall be caught up together with them in the clouds, and so shall we ever be with the Lord." The first resurrection of the believers and the transformation of our mortal body into the likeness of His own immortality occurs at the coming of the Lord for His church. Paul had announced in the previous chapter that "he which raised up the Lord Jesus shall raise up us also by Jesus, and shall present us with you."

Then we shall be clothed with our new spiritual, powerful, incorruptible and heavenly body. This was Paul's desire and great wish, namely, that he might possess that body and have redemption completed in his behalf. Yet he here suggests the alternate which implies that we are not assured of this body immediately on death. We must await the second coming, or the Parousia. Yet Paul and we are confident that though the bodies sleep, they shall be raised in this new form and state. Therefore, we have no need to speculate as to the exact relation of that future body to this present body. Suffice it to say that it will be a celestial body, while this is a terrestrial, and that it will resemble it as the plant comes from the essence of the seed. It may be recognizable and connected and yet it will be glorious. Hence, we may be sure that Paul in II Corinthians did not refute his teaching in I Corinthians, but confirmed it; and later yet, in his Philippian epistle, he announced, "Our conversation is in heaven; from whence also we look for the Saviour, the Lord Jesus Christ: who shall change our vile body, that it may be fashioned like unto his own glorious body, according to the working whereby he is able to subdue all things unto himself." That fullness of redemption will come at the appearance of the Lord.

II. THE STATE OF NAKEDNESS

The alternative stated by Paul is that of being "found naked" or being "unclothed." Said he, "If so be that being clothed we shall not be found naked. For we that are in this tabernacle do groan, being burdened: not for that we would be unclothed, but clothed upon, that mortality might be swallowed up of life." Does this naked or unclothed state refer to the unsaved, whereas the state of being clothed in a new body referred to the saved after death? We unhesitatingly answer No. The unsaved are not contemplated in this passage of Scripture. This refers to believers. This description is of the state of the soul between death and the resurrection of the body. No revelation is given concerning the details of that state of what is called nakedness, except that the soul is present with the Lord. We are confident that this disembodied state, as here described, is not the consummation of redemption, but in it there is nothing to fear. Of this Paul gave evidence when he said to the Philippians:

"For to me to live is Christ, and to die is gain. But if I live in the flesh, this is the fruit of my labor: yet what I shall choose I wot not. For I am in a strait betwixt two, having a desire to depart, and to be with

Christ; which is far better: Nevertheless to abide in the flesh is more needful for you."

Likewise, Jesus announced to the thief who asked him to remember him when He came into His kingdom, "To-day shalt thou be with me in Paradise." To be with Christ, my friend, is heaven, although it may not be the consummation of heaven and of our reward. To be without Christ at death is to be claimed by hell and Satan, although that is not the consummation of our judgment and punishment.

Does then this passage of "nakedness . . . unclothed" imply a sleep of the soul? There are some who declare that at death the soul enters a sleep until the time of the resurrection, at which time it will also receive the resurrected body. There are probably no grave consequences of this theory except that it would have a tendency to make the Christian fear death, to be reluctant to die because of not seeing his loved ones again until the resurrection. However, our Scripture makes this theory impossible, because it states definitely the continued existence of the soul in a disembodied state. If the soul were sleeping until the resurrection of the body there could be nothing called "nakedness" or "unclothed" state. Besides, we have the positive promises that the righteous dead go to be with Christ. Paul said, "God hath not appointed us to wrath, but to obtain salvation by our Lord Jesus Christ, who died for us that, whether we wake or sleep, we should live together with him." Here the very word "sleep" is used to describe the soul which is living with Christ. Hence, it cannot be an unconscious sleep of the soul. There is the full possibility, however, that we who are living today shall not see death, namely, the unclothed or naked state, because of the immanence of the Parousia. It was for this coming or presence of the Lord that Paul devoutly wished and for which many Christians have wished. I have known two great saints of God who were very reluctant to die because they hoped that Christ would come in glory before their death.

Does this suggestion of an unclothed state warrant a fear of death? If Jesus does not come in glory to take the church to be with Him, and if we do die as countless past generations have died, should we fear this great menace, this inevitable event, this strange visitor called the destroying angel? For the ungodly we unhesitatingly reply Yes, for only condemnation, punishment and hell await them. Jesus promised that. But for the Christian we must say No, for it means to go to be with Christ. Hence, we understand the confidence with which Paul and his companions faced it. He repeated twice the words, "We are confident," which when translated literally mean that "we have courage" or are courageous. There was no cringing fear, no wavering, no clinging to this life on the part of the Apostle and his colaborers. Their attitude, however, was not that of bravado, with which many worldly brave blindly face death and march into the face of danger, without regard for that which is to come after death. The courage and confidence of Paul and of the Christians is founded completely upon the assurance given by God, that we shall be with Christ. Thus Christians have died through the age in expectancy, confidence, joy and assurance.

The death of John Wesley occurred in his room in City Road, London. The end was very beautiful. He lingered for three days, surrounded by those who loved him. No pain, only a growing sense of weakness, and a tranquil acceptance of the inevitable. He slept much and spoke little, but sometimes the dying flame flickered up, and the inner light which had changed the face of England glowed with its old intensity. One afternoon before he died, he surprised his friends by bursting into song:

> "I'll praise my Maker, while I have breath,
> And when my voice is lost in death,
> Praise shall employ my nobler powers."

He sang two verses and then sank back exhausted. To the widow of Charles Wesley, who bent over him, he murmured, "He giveth his beloved rest." Later in the day when weakness overcame him, by a supreme effort he marshalled his ebbing strength and gave the message which was to become the watchword of Methodism, "The best of all is, God is with us." With the exception of one last word, "Farewell," this was the end of Wesley on earth.

On November 24, 1572, a sixty-seven year old Scotchman got up from his bed, and put on his hose and doublet. But he was unable to stand, and after sitting for half an hour, asked to be helped back to bed again. In the middle of the day he asked his wife to read the fifteenth chapter of the first epistle to the Corinthians, which speaks of the resurrection. "Is not that a comfortable chapter?" he said. A little later he suddenly began, "Now for the last time I commend my soul, my spirit and my body into Thy hands, O Lord." About four in the afternoon he said to his wife, "Go read where I cast my first anchor." She read the seventeenth chapter of John, then he asked for Calvin's sermons. At seven o'clock she ceased reading, for he seemed to be asleep. The time for evening prayers came, but everybody sat still, thinking he was sleeping. At half past ten, they knelt down at last. When they rose up, some one asked, "Sir, heard ye the prayers?" "I would to God that ye and all men heard them as I have heard them; and I praise God for that heavenly sound." Then he cried suddenly, "Now it is come," and gave a shuddering sound. Bannatyne sat down by his bed and urged him to remember the comforting promises given in the New Testament. "And that we may know that ye hear us," he ended, "make us some sign." John Knox's will gathered together for the last time. He lifted up one hand and immediately passed away. He went to be at home with the Lord.

III. At Home With the Lord

By a strange figure of speech, Paul says that when the Christian is in the body he is at home in the body, but when he is with the Lord he is at home with the Lord. When he is in the body, he is absent from the Lord and when he is with the Lord he is absent from the body. It simply depends upon which perspective you take of life. Viewed from this earthly side the body is the home of the soul. The body is the temporary tent or dwelling to be honored, used and kept as the temple of our earthly spirit and of the Holy Spirit. Hence, sin is to be shunned, and pain, suffering and death are not to be courted, for God uses this earthly tabernacle as the instrument of His good pleasure, but it is ours, for we can be at home only in a house which belongs to us, and this is true of our bodies.

While we are here in this body we are absent from the presence of the Lord. That is, we are abroad from our spiritual home, from God's people, the saints of the Lord and the household of our God. It is with this idea in mind, looking at our earthly existence from the heavenly view, that we are called pilgrims or strangers in a foreign land. We are away from our heavenly home. It is true that while we are here upon earth the Spirit of the living God is with us and in us, but we do not behold the face of God in the person of the Lord Jesus Christ.

Therefore, on earth our attitude must be one of faith, for we walk by faith and not by sight. Here it is by faith that we hold to the unseen and the eternal. It is faith that enables us to have courage and confidence, to endure and to overcome, to face every obstacle, whether affliction or pain, with an eye single to that future glory. In heaven we shall not do away with faith, but our faith shall be supplemented by sight, for we shall stand in His presence. We shall be with the Lord. Then fellowship will be complete, for we shall see as also we are seen. We shall look at Him face to face, whereas now we have that fellowship only by faith.

But when the Christian is with the Lord he is absent from the body and is at home with God. It is this fact which gives us the willingness, the courage and the confidence to undergo that experience called death and also to face the sufferings leading to it in the world, for it is but a portal that enters us into the presence of the redeemed. Hence, all fear of death should be removed from the Christian. Death is but glory and gain for the soul. Why should we fear it for ourselves or why should we grieve over it in a loved one, when it is better for that one to go to be with the Lord? Unchristian grief over the loss of a loved one is selfish. Who is there that understanding death would bring back his loved one to this world of suffering and woe? Think of it, he has gone to be with the Lord. Is that not enough?

"How beautiful to be with God
When earth is fading like a dream,
And from this mist-circled shore,
We launch upon the unknown stream.

"No doubt, no fear, no anxious care,
But comforted by staff and rod,
In the faith-brightened hour of death,
How beautiful to be with God.

"Then let it fade, this dream of earth,
When I have done my life work here,
Or long, or short, as seemeth best,—
What matters so God's will appears.

"I will not fear to launch my bark,
Upon the darkly rolling flood,
'Tis but to pierce the mist—and then
How beautiful to be with God."
—ANONYMOUS.

Death simply means to be everlastingly at home with the Lord. The ultimate resurrection of the body will not change but confirm and intensify this relationship of the soul at home with God. When a believer dies, simply remember that he has gone home. It was this fact that comforted Grace Coolidge and led her to write on the fifth anniversary of the death of her beloved son Calvin Coolidge, Jr., the following words:

"You, my son,
Have shown me God.
Your kiss upon my cheek
Has made me feel the gentle touch
Of Him who leads us on.
The memory of your smile, when young,
Reveals His face,
As mellowing years come on apace.
And when you went before,
You left the gates of heaven ajar
That I might glimpse,
Approaching from afar,
The glories of His grace.
Hold, son, my hand,
Guide me along the path,
That, coming,
I may stumble not
Nor roam,
Nor fail to show the way
Which leads us—Home." *

Hence, whether at home with God or abroad from God, our honor aim is to be pleasing to Him. The word called labor is actually the love of honor or an honor aim, a high goal, sometimes called "the mark of the prize of the high calling of God," or "the crown which is laid up for me," and other similar phrases. The essence of it is to be acceptable to God, to be pleasing to Him in the sum total of the actions of life. All this is necessary because we must stand before His dais or his judgment-seat to give an account of the deeds done in the body. Therefore, by being acceptable and pleasing now, while we are abroad from our heavenly home, we may be sure that we will be acceptable to Him when we are at home with the Lord.

Where is that destroying angel called death? Let him come now. Oh, there you are! I thought you would appear soon, but this is sooner than I expected. What? You are always waiting? You have been following each of these sheep committed to my care, thinking to snatch one? Yes, I have seen you often, but usually as you departed from your dread work. Now seeing you face to face, anticipating your visit, I have somewhat to say to you.

You believe that you are terrible, to be feared, able to make us cringe with doubt and in despair. You are wrong, for you are a defeated foe. Those fiery darts have lost their sting. The edge of your sword is dulled. Those chains of bondage are broken. Your keys are

---

* "The Open Door." Quoted by permission of *Good Housekeeping*.

gone. Your very body is nothing but a shadow, and that diminishing. You cannot hurt me or my flock.

We know One who broke your bonds, who pulled your sting and who made a triumph over you openly before angels, principalities and powers. We are united to Him by faith. We live in His life. We share His victory. He tasted death for every one of us, that through death He might destroy you who had the power of death and might deliver us who through fear of death were subject to bondage. Your keys are now at His girdle and you cannot touch the least of us until He says, "It is best my child. Come home."

Go then. Claim those who are still captives of your own will. As for these, they but serve and wait for Christ to take them home. You obey. You go. It is well. As for us, we say, "Thanks be to God who giveth us the victory through our Lord Jesus Christ."

XV

THE TERROR OF THE LORD

TEXT: *"Knowing therefore the terror of the Lord, we persuade men."*—II COR. 5:10-12.

THE TITLE of this sermon is really introduced by a discussion of death and the inevitable appearance of every believer before the judgment-seat of Christ to receive the things done in his body, whether they be good or bad. On the basis of this terror of the Lord Paul engaged in the main activity of his life, that of persuading men concerning Christ, salvation and the way of life.

Persuading men is an adequate description of Paul's whole life. His was a ministry of persuasion. Beginning on the Damascus Road with a light above the brightness of the sun and ending on the road leading to the Palatine gate out of Rome, that regenerated life was a life of persuasion. In fact, some people called St. Paul mad, or "beside" himself because of what he underwent in persuading men.

He who would confine the meaning of this particular verse to the persuading of men concerning his own integrity accept an entirely too limited and restricted view of the text. Paul never hesitated to persuade men concerning his own position as an Apostle and also his own integrity as a minister of the Word of God, but the main objective of his persuasion was always that we should believe upon the Lord Jesus Christ. For this cause he carried about in his body the dying of the Lord Jesus, or, as he said on another occasion, "I bear in my body the marks of the Lord Jesus."

Persuading men is the work of the ministry. There is nothing more challenging, interesting, stimulating than persuading men to accept Christ. This involves all of the resources of logic, salesmanship, diplomacy, faith and expenditure of nervous energy which a very important transaction might summon from some other profession or work. It may include testimony, writing, preaching, living and all of one's life. It has been described in the Bible by the Lord Himself as fishing for men. Every one knows what it means to fish, but when one begins to fish for men he realizes that he is undertaking a stupendous task. He who persuades men is undertaking a work similar to the work of the Holy Spirit, who, in turn, is engaged in persuading men to believe on Christ.

Holding this as the objective of the Christian ministry is an offense to some people. An outstanding business man who owns a radio station once asked me "Are you one of these evangelistic fellows who try to get every one converted?" I replied, "Yes." Then said he, "I do not believe in it. I have my own interpretation of Christianity and whenever I hear a preacher give his, it spoils mine. Don't preach to me." He went on to illustrate the fact that he had read *Robinson Crusoe* and *Treasure Island* several times and that he had created from them a picture in his own mind of the incidents in those stories. For another to tell him or for a moving picture to depict what was in his mind would spoil it for him. But this analogy does not hold for Christianity and the Bible, for it is an inexhaustible subject needing various lights thrown upon it from the minds and hearts of others. If we are believers we must go right on persuading, regardless of what men think of us, because we know the terror of the Lord.

The justification for a life of persuasion is the knowledge of the terror of the Lord. That is a description of the time when all must stand before the judgment-seat of Christ to be examined for the deeds done in the body. This text is not a reference to the final judgment, but refers to the judgment of the Christian, for only the Christian is in view in this chapter of the Scripture, and even for such there is a terror or a fear of God. Never grow casual in your contacts with God. Keep a close fellowship, but avoid casualness. Let there always be a holy awe of this tremendous personality called God. Remember that there are two motives for holiness in the life of believers. One is love and one is fear. The fear of God is the beginning of wisdom. It is the fulfilment of the law. It is the way of life. God gives the motivation of these two sanctions, love and fear, because they produce the results in human life. It was for this reason that Joseph said to the wife of Potiphar, "How then can I do this great wickedness, and sin against God?" The fear of God will be a deterrent from evil.

The text tells us that there will be rewards or compensations for the deeds of the believer at the judgment-seat of Christ. Illustrating it by the life of Paul we see clearly that he could have built great church buildings, organizations and theological schools. He could have written many books and propagated his learning, and all of his work might have been consumed in the fire spoken of in his first epistle to the Corinthians, but Paul had seen the Lord Jesus Christ on the Damascus Road and he knew that God had called him to persuade men of the reality and lordship of Christ. He also knew that he would be compelled to give an accounting of his time, his words, his energy, his life, in respect to this task. Therefore, all that Paul suffered and endured was for the sake of persuading men, and he knew that he would be rewarded at the judgment-seat of Christ. For this reason he said, "Our light affliction, which is but for a moment, worketh for us a far more exceeding and eternal weight of glory," and "henceforth there is laid up for me a crown of righteousness, which the Lord, the righteous judge shall give me." And again he said, "For necessity is laid upon me; yea, woe is unto me, if I preach not the gospel." Paul had a very realistic conception of his relationship to God and his duty toward his fellow men.

We may be sure that all accounts will be settled for the Christian as to his stewardship and what has been entrusted unto him. Just as the unbelievers will have degrees of punishment for their sins, so believers will have degrees of rewards for their deeds done in the flesh. Knowing, therefore, the terror of the Lord we had better persuade men.

Paul held before himself the ideal that whether present with the Lord and absent from the body or present in the body and absent from the Lord he would labor to be accepted of him. As we too recognize the imminence of death and then an accounting at the judgment-seat of Christ, we Christians will labor to be pleasing unto the Lord. We shall even be willing to jeopardize the accusation that a sacred madness has laid hold upon us. We will for the sake of men persuade them to salvation. If the terror of the Lord or the fear of the Lord exists for the Christian because he must answer for the deeds done in the body, what must the terror of the Lord be to the unbeliever, who also must answer for the deeds done in the body, without any hope of salvation and without a Savior who has borne the penalty of his sins. Realizing that one who is saved, one who loves Christ, one who has honored Him must fear to stand before him at the judgment-seat how much more must this be true of the unbeliever who shall stand at the judgment of the great white throne. Knowing, therefore, this terror of the Lord we do persuade men.

I. THE AIM OF PERSUASION

When St. Paul or a modern minister, whether ordained or unordained, attempts to convict men of judgment, of sin and of righteousness, it is his duty to point out that there is a life after death, that man has an immortality derived from the great source of immortality, God. This is certain to the Christian, because the Spirit beareth witness with his spirit concerning eternal life, but it as also taught in the Bible as an attribute of man. Paul, for instance, preached at Athens of Jesus and the resurrection and declared that God "hath appointed a day, in the which he will judge the world in righteousness by that man whom he hath ordained; whereof he hath given assurance unto all men, in that he hath raised him from the dead." There will be a resurrection of all men unto judgment. Jesus said, "Marvel not at this: for the hour is coming, in which all that are in the graves shall hear his voice, and shall come forth; they that have done good, unto the resurrection of life; and they that have done evil, unto the resurrection of damnation." The prophet Daniel likewise said, "Many of them that sleep in the dust of the earth shall awake, some to everlasting life, and some to shame and everlasting contempt." The great assize is established. Christ will be the judge upon that throne. He has foretold that in that day He will say to men, "I never knew you; depart from me, ye that work iniquity." In that assize revelations of our character, of our deeds, of our personal records will be made in full accordance with the facts, and justice will be pronounced by Him who knows all things and from whom nothing is hid. The same Scripture which declares this inevitability of judgment speaks of hell and of the second death. We are told that the condition of the soul is established at death, though the final judgment as to the status of this soul will not occur until the great judgment. The teaching of the Lord Himself upon this subject of a post-earthly bliss or suffering is clearly given in the story of Lazarus.

Secondly, the duty of the ministry is not only to persuade men of the inevitability of judgment, but to convince men of sin. It is necessary to persuade men that they are sinners and under the condemnation of God. This can be done from the law, from reason and from conscience. For one who is skilled in the law of God it is easy to reveal the picture of the condition of fallen men, both in nature and in action. The dreadful picture of human nature is drawn by St. Paul in Romans 3, which tells us that there is none righteous, no, not one, for all have gone astray, all have come short of the glory of God, and which describes us as sinners in our very being, possessing a nature which issues in sinful action. This ought to be sufficient to show man that he needs a Savior. But a second source of conviction or persuasion exists in conscience, for in the very heart and mind of man there is a sense of condemnation. This inner self-aversion and dissatisfaction is the cause of the search for the knowledge of salvation in the various religions of the world. He who is skilled in persuasion will deal with the consciences of men. Yet a third source of conviction is reason. Man has an innate knowledge that injustice, corruption, impurity, dishonesty and similar vices and attitudes are not right, either in the sight of God or in the sight of man. He recognizes that there must be some cause for all this evil which is in the world, and it is a very simple thing to prove unto him that he is a sinner needing a Savior and deliverer.

The aim of persuasion must also be to convict of righteousness. The first aspect of this must be negative in producing the belief in our own utter lack of righteousness as human beings. Isaiah declares our righteousness to be "filthy rags." Paul reiterates that it is not by righteousness which we have done that we are justified before God, for by the works of the law shall no flesh be justified. Therefore, when the Gospel of God's wondrous provision of righteousness through a Mediator is presented, a natural response exists in the heart of man. Convict men that "God was in Christ, reconciling the world unto himself, not imputing their trespasses unto them" and you will persuade them of the true righteousness. This righteousness is the righteousness of God in acting in conformity with His own holiness and law, while forgiving sin through an atonement,

"Being justified freely by his grace through the redemption that is in Christ Jesus: whom God hath set forth to be a propitiation through faith in his blood, to declare his righteousness for the remission of sins that are past, through the forbearance of God; to declare, I say, at this time his righteousness: that he might be just, and the justifier of him which believeth in Jesus."

This divine righteousness becomes righteousness applied by faith, for we persuade men that "he hath made him to be sin for us, who knew no sin; that we might be made the righteousness of God in him."

II. THE MEANS OF PERSUADING MEN

Persuasion is the peculiar work of the Holy Spirit of God. Jesus said, "And when he is come, he will reprove the world of sin, and of righteousness, and of judgment." The Holy Spirit is the mighty persuader of men. It is because we fail to depend upon the Holy Spirit and to realize the efficacy of His ministry in connection with our own ministry that too often we fail in our persuasion of men. We depend upon the human means of logic, argumentation and persuasion, whereas we must depend upon the means established by God. It is an old law that persuasion became effective under a twofold witness. The guilt of a man was established under two witnesses. Even Jesus was condemned because of two false witnesses. Let there be the witness of a human instrumentality and the witness of the Holy Spirit to the Word of God, and such a witness will be effective. We cannot omit the human instrumentality any more than Paul omitted it in his ministry. For this reason he was accused of being beside himself, but he did not depend upon his own efforts alone. The Holy Spirit is absolutely essential to any effective persuasion of men concerning the lordship of Jesus Christ. He alone is able to overcome the evil influences opposing such a decision.

The second means of persuasion is the Gospel. He who declares the Divine law in giving a substitute to bear our sins is declaring the Gospel. Paul said:

"For the love of God constraineth us; because we thus judge, that if one died for all, then were all dead: and that he died for all, that they which live should not henceforth live unto themselves, but unto Him which died for them and rose again."

Christ's work in the world was the reconciling of sinners to God, for God was in Christ reconciling the world unto Himself. He died for us, and our life and death unto sin are connected directly with Him. Once this fact is seen and is proclaimed with the promise that whosoever will believe may be saved, the effective means of the salvation of men is being used. This "whosoever" was announced on that day of Pentecost. It was reiterated by St. Paul in his greatest epistle, that to the Romans, and it is God's invitation to men. Under the Gospel we give an invitation to repentance, conversion, faith and prayer for salvation in order that a man might become a new creature in Christ Jesus, old things passing away and all things becoming new.

The third means of persuading men is personal choice. Paul said, "Be ye reconciled." He appealed to the intellect of men by manifesting the truth as a system in all of its beauty. The doctrines of Christianity are beautiful in their structure and their connection one with another. These doctrines center about Christ and Christ is the truth. Therefore, as we preach Christ crucified, not with human wisdom of "persuasive words" but with the power of God, we are presenting that which will also appeal to the intellect. Paul appealed to the heart of men, or shall we say, to their conscience through God's love, God's sacrifice and God's pleading. He said, "The love of Christ constraineth us." He awakened desires for fellowship, for heaven, for righteousness, for an eternal relationship with those whom we love. He let feeling flow from the realization that this was a matter of life and death, that danger existed for every soul and that an eternal status was to be obtained by the personal choice to be made. He further appealed to the will in order to obtain a decision and some action. Yes, men must either accept or reject Christ. There is no middle ground. We are either with Him or against Him. Therefore, we preach for a verdict, to persuade men, not to leave the decision hanging in the air. The time will come when the decision will be out of your hands, when we can no longer persuade you, but now our message is, be ye reconciled to God.

III. THE END OF PERSUASION—SALVATION

The end or purpose of persuasion is that men might be saved, that they should be "in Christ." "If any man be in Christ, he is a new creature: old things are passed away; behold all things are become new." Salvation comes when men accept the Savior. When Zacchaeus received Christ in to his house, salvation came into his life. The most prominent name of Jesus is "Saviour."

There is salvation in no other. Peter said, "There is none other name under heaven given among men, whereby we must be saved." Christ Himself is salvation, and He works the salvation of the believer.

When Paul says, "Now is our salvation nearer than when we believed," he refers to the coming of Christ, who is our salvation. God hath appointed us to obtain salvation by our Lord Jesus Christ. Christ, then, is the author of salvation unto all them that obey Him, and he is the Captain of our salvation. Of Him the prophets testified, searching what the Spirit of Christ which was in them did signify when it testified beforehand the sufferings of Christ and the glory that should follow.

Likewise, Christ is the way of salvation. Paul went to Philippi preaching Christ, and the damsel possessed with a spirit of divination followed him, saying, "These men are the servants of the most high God, which show unto us the way of salvation." God did not send His Son into the world to condemn the world, but that the world through Him might have life. He is the way of salvation to every one who believeth, for by grace are ye saved through faith and that not of yourselves, but it is the gift of God. He is the way of salvation to every one who repenteth. He is the way of salvation to every one who converteth. How shall we escape if we neglect so great a salvation, if we fail to lay hold upon Christ, if we miss our anchorage as a ship fails its resting place in the storm?

We must persuade men openly to confess Christ as Savior and Lord. Let there be no secret adherence to the Lord Jesus Christ, for with the heart man may believe unto righteousness, but with the mouth confession is made unto salvation. Shame upon the man who wishes a secret marriage. Shame upon the believer who does not wish to confess Christ openly before men. You have no promise that you are saved without such an open confession. Therefore, the end of our persuasion is that men shall have salvation in Christ.

That salvation includes the forgiveness of sins, the removal of condemnation, for there is now no condemnation to him who is in Christ Jesus. Our sins are buried, forgotten, blotted out. We are saved through Christ. That salvation includes freedom from the bondage of sins, the infusion of a power to break old habits, to renew the mind of man and to be transformed into the image of the Son of God. From this salvation we are enabled to live godly in this present world, looking toward the appearance of our Savior. This salvation includes the gift of eternal life. He that believeth on the Son hath everlasting life. If we have the Son we have life, and without the Son we have not life, so salvation is life.

Salvation means safety or certainty for eternity. Through Christ we are saved from the wrath of God and prepared for heaven. Too little is said these days about heaven, its glories, its rewards and its expectancy. There are no tears, no sighing, no godly sorrow in the repentance shown by men today. Let us have a re-emphasis on the terror of God, upon the salvation wrought in Christ, upon the meaning of sainthood. People ought not to be ashamed to think or to talk about heaven. We profess to believe in it. Let us act upon it. Heaven should be the greatest object of our striving in these days. Salvation is to give us a certainty of heaven. Salvation brings a sense of security in knowing that we have One who can plead for us, an interceding Savior. When we sin we are not left alone in the presence of a holy God, but He who is the mediator undertakes for us in prayer. Such a salvation, the Scripture says, is offered now. Today is the day. Now is the time. Now you must decide, choose and settle this question. There is no tomorrow with God. There is only a great now.

If the righteous shall scarcely be saved, where shall the ungodly and the sinner appear? If, therefore, the saved, such as Paul, fear the judgment and call it "the terror of the Lord," how much more should the unsaved fear such a judgment of God when they shall answer for the deeds done in the body? It is God's will that all men should be saved, but they must be righteous in the judgment or they cannot be saved. That righteousness comes through faith in Christ. Therefore, as God's ambassadors, we beseech you to be reconciled to God. Knowing the terror of the Lord, we persuade men.

XVI

THE CHANCE OF BEGINNING AGAIN

TEXT: *"Therefore if any man be in Christ, he is a new creature: old things are passed away; behold, all things are become new."*—
II COR. 5:13-19.

THE WISTFUL DESIRE for a new life and the hope for the escape from the past is a haunting undercurrent of every life. Some of you have read a snatch of biography by Francisco Nitti called *Escape*. That thrilling tale tells of the conditions during the rise of Mussolini to power and his determination to crush all opposition. Nitti was deported as a political prisoner to an island in the Mediterranean, where he was brutally beaten and treated much the same as modern political prisoners are treated in the concentration camps of Germany. After long planning he managed to escape during a dark night through waters infested with guard ships, and after numerous trials arrived in the United States, the haven of liberty. But that escape of Francisco Nitti is not any more dramatic than the battles waged in the humdrum life of every day existence by innumerable persons for escape from confining customs dominating self, from hurtful heritage and a limiting environment. This struggle for escape sometimes manifests itself in drunkenness, at other times, in sensual indulgence or outbursts of anger, and among only a few it manifests itself in creativity of one kind or another. But the struggle for escape in the realm of personal living is a constant fight of most people.

On board ship, looking out toward the gray, misty, cloud-banked horizon, stood two young people leaning on the white rail. One was a prima donna returning to the States and to her home after a tour of Europe. The other was a preacher, who had been abroad to study the social conditions in Europe. Their conversation revolved about life. The young woman seemed to have everything one could desire—an attractive person, beautiful clothes, knowledge of the affairs of the world, a career, and youth. And yet, as she spoke about her life, she suddenly said, "I wish I could escape to some isle of the sea or to some new land and begin life over again." Her wish was not hard to understand. The dead hand of the past was reaching out of her memory and making her present social environment unbearable, for she had transgressed the laws of society. Her wistful longing for a chance of beginning again is the hunger and the desire of thousands of lives.

In 1212 A.D. Christendom was amazed by a strange happening. The spirit of the Crusades awoke again in Europe. Among the shepherd folk of the Vendome fields a young boy named Stephen took to the St. Dennis road, carrying a cross, and many children followed him. They left the sheep, the farms and the hills and marched with makeshift wooden crosses, singing hymns in high voices. Down the mountains of Italy came the throngs of children from all parts of Europe, seeking the sea, where they hoped to find a way to the Holy City to aid the Seignior Christ. They were going to recover the Holy City, and after that they would have peace. When the good people asked them whither they were going, they answered, "To God." To the quays of Marseilles they came, and then down the steep alleys of Genoa, into the canals of Venice, and to the hot shores of Brindisi. Among them and behind them came the human wolves, slave seekers and girl despoilers. At Brindisi the bishop would not let them embark. Elsewhere, ships were offered them and they were taken to the Moslem slave markets of Kairowan and Cordova. The rest of them wandered among the dark quays, waifs of a vain crusade. A remnant of them turned back. Tired, they made their way home. Heavily walked the young girls who had been raped. Sad were the children when honest folk mocked them because they came back without their crosses and their songs. They did not sing, because they were lost and ill and alone. They had gone forth spontaneously, driven by hardships and sufferings from home, seeking not the distant city in Palestine, the Jerusalem of Outremer, but another city, the New Jerusalem, which is from above, because in their childish hearts they confused it the city of God, lying unknown and unseen of men beyond all scenes of the earth, with an earthly place in Palestine. The motive of the Children's Crusade was escape from the hardships of this world.

It is that motive which has made popular a song which lives after several decades:

> "I'd live to leave it all behind and go and find,
> Some place that's known to God alone,
> Just a spot to call our own.
> We'll find perfect peace,
> Where joys never cease,
> Out there beneath those kindly skies.
> We'll build a sweet little nest somewhere in the west,
> And let the rest of the world go by."

The same motive is incorporated in that Christian hymn so often sung with benefit to discouraged hearts, called "Beautiful Isle of Somewhere."

> "Somewhere the sun is shining,
> Somewhere the songbirds dwell,
> Cease, then, thy sad repining,
> God lives and all is well.
> Somewhere, somewhere, beautiful isle of somewhere,
> Land of the true where we live anew,
> Beautiful isle of somewhere."

How to reach this place of beginning again, the hope for which is deep-seated in the lives of all, is a great question. Like the children of the vain crusade, we wander through the hills and the valleys and the forests of life, with our wooden crosses and our empty songs, sometimes mocked, sometimes fed by the good people along the way, struggling to behold the City of God, where there is an escape from the turmoil of mind, the temptation of soul and the toil of life, and we believe that if only we knew the answer given in the Bible concerning the chance of beginning again, things would really be different. It was this answer that the preacher gave to the prima donna amid the undulating swell of a great ocean. Said he, "You may go to that isle of somewhere and that land of beginning again if you will. It was for this purpose that God sent His Son into the world and He says, 'If any man be in Christ, he is a new creature: Old things are passed away; behold all things are become new. And all things are of God.' The secret of this chance of beginning again lies in a change which can take place within us, whereby we become new creatures through the power of an Infinite God."

I. WHAT MAKES US WANT A CHANCE OF BEGINNING AGAIN—THE PAST

One's past may not have been evil if he experiences the desire to escape it. It may merely have been the fact that life on the natural plane is disappointing, sinful and unsatisfying. This is enough to make any one wish for a change.

Life on the natural plane is disappointing, because, though man has by common grace ideas of the good, the true and the beautiful, he, nevertheless, is fallen from this high standard. He measures life largely by these standards, and yet it falls short because of the very evil which is in the human heart. Instead of goodness he finds wickedness. Instead of the truth he finds the false and the hypocritical. Instead of the beautiful there is the deformed and the ugly. Man naturally would like to be idealistic, whether his idealism expresses itself in patriotism or in humanitarianism, but when one beholds the corruption, the inefficiency and the waste in high places of the nation, his patriotism is often shattered; and when he beholds the disloyalty, untrustworthiness and the failure of men, his humanitarianism is sometimes shattered. Cynicism often supplants faith when we behold life on the natural plane. Man grows cynical of his fellow men. Often he finds that one whom he has trusted failed him and that it was expensive to believe in man. Today a popular play recalls the tragedy of the life of Woodrow Wilson. One of the striking scenes is the picture of Wilson being smitten by the stroke which came upon him when he learned that the people in whom he had believed and whom he had trusted all of his life failed him in the hour of his greatest idealistic crisis. Henceforth, broken in health, rejected of his nation, he was a bitter and cynical old man.

Life also is disappointing because failure is written in large letters over many of our undertakings and our resolutions. We may have worked hard to bring a movement to success and then find it dwindled away to nothing. We may have resolved steadfastly never to fall into the same sinful practice again, and then in shame we are overtaken by our besetting sin, our habitual fault. The long line of suicides testifies to the disappointing phase of life. By this means many have attempted to escape from their struggle in life. Disappointment is brought upon us by some blight. Our ambitions are crushed. An artist, a writer or an inventor finds the work of years cast aside in a moment. Because of sudden sickness an athlete finds his career impaired by loss of health. Overnight, a man who has friends may become a very lonely soul. Even those who reach the heights often find them empty. We mortals set our hopes on something and when we have obtained it, it crumbles in our hands. The joys and the satisfactions we expected are not there. We are like Midas, whose very touch turned everything to gold, in accordance with his desire, until he stroked the head of his fairest daughter and in the hour of his achieved desire found himself stripped of the joy of his life.

Life on the natural plane is sinful. The whole world lieth in wickedness. Every individual realizes through the thundering of his conscience that he has sinned. Time may deaden the reverberations of conscience, but it will not remove that heavy sense of responsibility and that wistful desire for an escape from its resulting miserable state. Once committed, evil taints the thoughts. The deed laid up in memory will return to haunt one in the hour when he least desires it, until he pleads for an avenue of escape. Natural life is sinful life, and sinful life has the glory of living veiled so that existence becomes monotonous and humdrum and we cry for escape.

How keenly we are aware of this in society today. We have seen the prodigal use of resources that should have been conserved, the wasted opportunities given to us by the lavish hand of Providence, the misled confidence placed in human leaders, until suddenly we were awakened in a condition of helplessness and confusion and danger. Selfishness in politics, industry, labor and personal life, where we have lived with no thought of the national good but only with a purpose to seize for ourselves as much of the good things of this life as possible, has brought us to the brink of disaster. Trickery, lies, corruption, bribery, graft, treachery, these are the words which describe human actions today. Surely we must realize that we are gathering the harvest of sinful life and that we must rebuild the foundations of society, both in our nation and abroad, if we are to have any hope for civilization. The fact that the productive capacity of the world is devoted to destruction of life and liberty speaks just one word, *sin!*

We also want escape because our past life is unsatisfying. There is an eternal restlessness which may be discerned in the life of man. One might almost think that the one, distinguishing difference between man and the beast is not man's reason, but his eternal restlessness, which prevents him from finding any kind of peace or quietness of spirit and mind. This ceaseless activity, groping and turmoil of the human soul is likened by Isaiah to the sea. "The wicked are like the troubled sea, when it can not rest, whose waters cast up mire and dirt. There is no peace, saith my God, to the wicked." Behold the surf of the sea beating against the rock, rising and falling, lashing against the reefs, casting up the foulness of its hidden depths and attempting to escape its bounds. One need only be cognizant of the general trend of life to know that man is groping for something, that he finds no real rest in the midst of his life.

II. WHERE WE SHALL FIND THE CHANCE OF BEGINNING AGAIN—HERE

May I emphasize that the chance of beginning life again is not in some other place. Habitually, we make a practice of looking abroad for the chance to start over again. In the time of the Reformation a small group of Germans under Simon Mennon embraced certain logical precepts which were not embraced in the main Reformation. Later many of these Mennonites from Poland, Germany and Switzerland came to America and they migrated again to the mid-west, and now some of them are emigrating to South America from North America in order to build their perfect society. We must admit that their communities are much more orderly than those of many other sections of America, but by seeking merely new places of beginning they will not solve the problem of life. I know a young woman who desired to go to another town when she had a fine job in her own city, simply because she could not get along with her father. She was looking over the horizon for a new chance of beginning. But it is not in a new land or in a new place or in other new surroundings that you will have your chance of beginning again. It is in the realization of the new Jerusalem, which is above, the city that hath foundations, whose maker and builder is God, and of which you become a citizen in the kingdom of God. Your new beginnings must be made in the same locality, among the same friends and in the same environment as before. We may continue working at the same desk, living with the same family and having fellowship with the same friends and yet find that we are living an utterly different life from that we lived before. Recently I talked with a worker from one of the largest American air lines. He had fallen into sin, and so long as he resided in a certain town, the sinful temptation would continue. He asked, "Is it necessary to leave this particular city?" My reply was, "It may be, but how much better it would be for you to conquer your temptation and sin here, for if not, it will meet you in another form wherever you go. One cannot escape from his own self."

The regenerated, renewed and transfigured life is essential for a new beginning. Your new chance can come only in a new inner life. Hence, our text said, "If any man be in Christ, he is a new creature." Man must be renewed by the Spirit of God, not by the change of his environment. He himself will change his environment when he is renewed. Testimonies of this are constantly being given. A man converted here some months ago has so changed the conditions in his home that they are not even recognizable as being anything like what they were before his conversion. A man whom I knew as a drunkard and an outcast from his family over many years wandered into Paul Rader's tabernacle and was converted, thereby losing the desire for drink and being re-established in a place of responsibility in society, in the same city and in the presence of the same companions that he had before. No, the chance of beginning again is not in some far-away place.

This chance is given to us through the Lord Jesus Christ. It is "in Christ." Every man is either in Christ or not in Christ. There is no mediating position. The Bible contrasts death and life, sin and salvation, the devil and God, the household of faith and the household of sin. One must be either in or out. There is no transition state. Hence, if you are in Christ Jesus you are a new creation. Christ, then, is the provision made by God for us to be washed from our sins, to be renewed in our minds, to be strengthened in our wills and to be established in righteousness. This chance of a new life or a new beginning is offered to all men in Christ. It implies that something has been done objectively in history to make this possible. That is,

Christ made propitiation for our sins, and not for ours only but for the sins of the whole world.

Therefore, to be "in Christ" describes a state of life of an individual. When one is in Christ he is justified, is indwelt and led by the Spirit of God, and is loved by God. No man can separate him from that love of God. Whoever is in Christ is sanctified, set apart, made holy in the death of Christ. Whoever is in Christ is now resurrected from his former spiritual deadness and dwells in heavenly places with Christ. Whoever is in Christ Jesus is enabled to triumph over all difficulties. Whoever is in Christ is in grace, is saved and has life. This, you see, is a state of life described clearly in the Bible.

Entrance into this state of life is made by coming to Christ and by committing oneself to Him and by acknowledging His lordship. Jesus said, "Him that cometh to me I will in no wise cast out," and Paul added that if any man will confess Jesus as Lord and that Christ raised him from the dead, he shall be saved. This can be done, of course, only on the conditions set forth by God. That first condition is repentance, our willingness to put away sin. The second condition is our faith, our trust in the Person, claims and work of Christ. The third condition is our obedience, our willingness to make Him the Lord of our lives, for we are created in Christ Jesus unto good works, which God hath before ordained.

This chance of beginning life again becomes a reality in those who are regenerated. For them "old things are passed away; behold all things are become new." The old desires, motives, deeds, habits, dispositions and outlook give place to new ones. Such an individual who is in Christ is conscious of putting off the old man and putting on the new, of putting away wrath, malice, lust and all the fruits of the flesh and of taking on the fruits of the Spirit. We can not always say that there is an immediate delivery of a man from sin which is complete and final, but we can say that there is a clean breach made in his life at the time of conversion. That clean breach results in a progressive deliverance in some, although in others it may be complete. The entire mental, affectional and volitional nature of man is changed. The mind which was in Christ Jesus is now in him. The Spirit of Christ abides within his heart, for no man can call Him Lord, but by His Spirit. The works which Christ did He does also. This marks a mighty change.

The old struggle within one's heart then gives place to an equilibrium of duty and desire. As the prophet said, "Thou wilt keep him in perfect peace, whose mind is stayed on thee." As Paul said,

"The peace of God, which passeth all understanding shall keep your hearts and minds through Christ Jesus." As the Psalmist said, "Great peace have they which love thy law: and nothing shall offend them." The turmoil, the contention, the war and the strife which are without and mark the entire condition of the world will not affect the inner life of the believer. There the Prince of Peace reigns and is the source of peace for him.

Herein the old disharmony is displaced by a new conformity to the will of God and to God's laws. We read, "All things are of God." God is the source. God is the standard. God is the power of this new life.

This is your chance, and it is here for you, but there is always the possibility of your missing your chance in life. Hebrews says, "How shall we escape if we neglect so great salvation?" The literal meaning of neglect is to miss one's chance, to slip by the anchorage or the port, to miss out. The Bible implies that you may clearly lose out in this great opportunity.

III. How Shall We Find the Chance of Beginning Again?—
    The New Birth

Someone may say, "Yes, you have analyzed my condition. You have told me what I need and what I desire, but now please do not send me away dissatisfied and unenlightened to continue the same existence. Tell me how I may obtain the new creation that I may live anew." Very simply I shall do it, for God forbid that our pulpit should ever degrade into a lecture platform. May the old, old story be told again and again, even to those of us who know it best. The simplest way is to follow the teaching of this Scriptural passage.

There we read, first, the message of God's redemptive love revealed in Christ Jesus. Paul said, "For the love of Christ constraineth us: because we thus judge, that if one died for all, then were all dead." Here we are taught that all men were dead in trespasses and in sins. If we are spiritually dead, then we are impotent, helpless, defeated and frustrated, and there is no possible way by which we can save ourselves. In this state a Divine act of omnipotence is necessary. As we are captives of Satan and his will, slaves of evil and in bondage to habit, something must be done in us as well as for us to bring about a change in our lives. In history propitiation was made for us, a ransom was given in our behalf, but the release must come by the work of the Spirit within us, healing us, renewing us, transforming us. We would not for a moment diminish the importance of Christ dying in behalf of us, for that is the supreme work of God in our redemption. Whatever men may say about these words, we know that Christ's death on the Cross was an atonement, for He died in our behalf and not only in our behalf but in behalf of all. It was a universal atonement made by Him as our substitute.

But though Christ died for all, only some are made alive through His resurrection. "He died for all, that they which live should not henceforth live unto themselves." This death made on our behalf ended or interrupted man's bondage to sin in the flesh. His death, His resurrection and His life have an influence upon us and a meaning for us. Therefore, those who are joined to Christ by faith have ended their relationship to sin and its guilt and are living in His life. They are now in Christ Jesus. By faith we take over this position with Him, both on Calvary and in the resurrection, and as a result of it we may be sure that sin shall have no dominion over us.

This new resurrection life is not to be lived unto self, but unto Him who died for us and rose again. The whole difference between a Christian and an unbeliever, when taken in its entirety is that one lives for self-gratification and the other lives for Christ. Here is something worth living for and something worth dying for, something that is far bigger than self. It is God and God's purposes in the world as manifested through Jesus Christ. Of course, such a life can mean nothing but service, humanitarian service, missionary service, educational service, evangelistic service, service which puts others first and self secondary.

The second suggestion in answer to the question of how, made by Paul, is, "Henceforth know we no man after the flesh: yea, though we have known Christ after the flesh, yet now henceforh know we him no more." Once Paul had a carnal knowledge of Christ. We do not believe that Paul ever saw Jesus physically before the Damascus Road experience, but he had gathered knowledge from those believers whom he persecuted, so that he knew Christ after the flesh, that is, Paul had a fleshly knowledge of Jesus. Multitudes have such a carnal knowledge of Christ today. They know all the facts about Him, about His birth, life, teaching, death, resurrection and claims concerning the future. They have no spiritual knowledge, and their physical knowledge increases their condemnation rather than saves them. Thus it was with Paul. To speak of the fleshly knowledge of Christ, or to know Christ after the flesh, does not refer to Christ being in the flesh as if that were unimportant, for the incarnation of the Son of God is all-important to the Christian faith, but it refers to Paul's own fleshly way of knowledge rather than a spiritual way of knowledge.

To know Christ spiritually is the work of the Holy Spirit. The things of God are not naturally discerned, nor, indeed, can be. They are spiritually discerned. It is by being born of the Spirit of God, by being a new creation, that we can know Christ as Saviour and Lord. Do you thus know Christ? Can you say, "I know whom I have believed"? Such knowledge means communion with Christ spiritually and it means worship of Christ as the Son of God and the One who reconciled us to God. It does not mean following His example.ABother, we are to submit ourselves completely to Him as Lord and Savior, and thus know Him.

Thirdly, Paul suggests the Divine plan of reconciliation. What a wonderful word is "reconciliation." "God hath reconciled us to himself by Jesus Christ . . . to wit, that God was in Christ, reconciling the world unto himself, not imputing their trespasses unto them; and hath committed unto us the word of reconciliation."

Here is the story of the mighty reconciliation of the God and Judge of the universe and sinful, rebellious, wicked man. What joy, what overpowering emotion, what blessing this should bring in one's life. Have you forgotten the story of the Prodigal Son, with the father waiting for the prodigal's return, and the joy and rejoicing that took place in that family on that occasion? The Bible picture is not only of God who needs to be propitiated but also of man who needs to be reconciled to God. It is necessary for the wrongdoer to come to himself, to return, to confess that he has sinned against heaven and in the sight of God. Then there will be reconciliation.

The means of that reconciliation, however, is the Cross of Christ. God hath reconciled us by Christ, and that Cross forever demonstrates that God is favorably disposed toward us and will receive us if we will but come. This was not done by a third party, but God was in Christ reconciling the world unto Himself, not imputing their trespasses. You see, God made an atonement in Jesus Christ for your sins that you might be forgiven and reconciled.

It is this message of reconciliation which constitutes the Gospel and which has been committed to us as His servants and ministers. We have the ministry of reconciliation, we have the message of reconciliation, or the Word, committed to us, and we are the ministers of reconciliation, or ambassadors beseeching you to be reconciled to God. On the authoriy of God Himself we can invite you, urge you and state the ground and the basis of this reconciliation.

Therefore, seize this opportunity now to begin life over again with God. Be reconciled to God. Accept the terms of peace offered by God. Seek the peace of God which passeth all understanding. Now is the time to end dissatisfaction, turmoil and conflict and accept contentment and harmony in heart and soul. Here is the chance of escape from the past in a new outlook, a new nature and a new strength given by God. You need only submit yourself to His will by accepting His Son. You can if you only will. Surrender that will. Be ye reconciled to God. Of this we persuade you, for the love of Christ constrains us. "If any man be in Christ Jesus he is a new creature." You have the chance of beginning again.

XVII

AMBASSADORS FOR CHRIST

TEXT: *"Now then we are ambassadors for Christ, as though God did beseech you by us: we pray you in Christ's stead, be ye reconciled to God."*—II COR. 5:20.

AN AMBASSADOR is a minister of highest rank, accredited to a foreign court to reside there and represent his sovereign and country. An ambassador usually stands on his dignity. I have a friend who once was an aide to an ambassador to the United States. He described how that ambassador delivered his messages in majestic dignity, with a far-off look in his eye, as if remembering the land from which he came, giving the impression of being a part of that country set down in foreign soil. He never spoke his own words in his official capacity, but only the words of his king.

The word ambassador is derived from the root, *presbus*, meaning old or experienced. Usually ambassadors are men tried and well proved in responsible positions. A long list of notable men have occupied this position in American history. The position of ambassador is something to which to aspire. It may be the climax of a career, an exceedingly high honor given to a man of attainment. The position of ambassador is equal to the importance of the State he represents. The embassies of the great Powers are usually respected and heeded by those to whom they are sent. No less should be true of the greatest kingdom of all, and of its ambassadors.

The ambassador is an agent. He possesses authority to speak and to act for his government. He is the mouthpiece of his ruler. In his official capacity he never speaks for himself. In fact, his own person and attainments are of very little weight. His influence exists because he is the authorized agent of the state he represents. Because of this representative capacity the person and property of an ambassador are secure, even in enemy territory. In that interesting book, *The British Agent*, the author tells how guns and other contraband were taken into Russia through the diplomatic security of the person and property of British agents. Likewise, the embassy property is inviolable. It has exterritorial rights. Local authorities have nothing to do with it. Unquestionably, this privilege has been misused on many times for propaganda and subversive activity which democratic governments have been all too slow to curb, but reluctance to stop the abuse has been due to respect of the rights of an ambassador. It is to this high position and representative agency that God appoints men in His kingdom, and it is in this capacity that God's agents ought to consider themselves, even though at times they may not be so considered by others.

Interesting it is that embassy service has been called a ministry. Surely the position of ambassador for Christ and of the kingdom should be no less a ministry of service than the secular diplomatic service, yet how far below this standard the conception of Christian ministry often falls. In this Christian ministry it is evident that we ought to be doing the will of our Ruler. We ought to be serving His subjects. We ought to be protecting their interests. We ought to be instructing them as to their welfare. We ought to be messengers of our King. In this passage of Scripture a special ministry is designated, namely, the ministry of reconciliation. Sometimes our nation sends a special mission to some state to settle a misunderstanding. Our main mission deals primarily with enmity between men and God, and it may be called a ministry or reconciliation.

I. Our Appointment as Ambassadors

To become an ambassador for God's kingdom presupposes certain requisites. One is citizenship in the kingdom. Paul declares, "Our conversation [citizenship] is in heaven; from whence also we look for the Saviour, the Lord Jesus Christ." In another place we are called "a colony from heaven." How does one receive this heavenly citizenship? The context of the Scripture passage makes this clear. "If any man be in Christ, he is a new creature: old things are passed away; behold, all things are become new." To the man in Christ a new creation is given so that in a real sense he is living in a new world or realm. We are distinctly told that he enters this new realm by being born again, that is, being born of the Spirit of God. A man must not only be born of the flesh, but he must be born of the Spirit or he shall not see the kingdom of God. Here this new birth, resulting in a new creation, is described as being reconciled to God, namely, having a new standing before, and a new relationship to, God. The repentant, converted, believing individual is a citizen of the kingdom of God. He is a potential ambassador.

Yet children are never appointed ambassadors. Imagine the incongruity of appointing an adolescent to represent the multiform interests of the United States at the court of St. James's. Maturity, wisdom, strength and experience are necessary to become an ambassador. Hence, it is no less true that a child in Christ may hardly be considered an appointed ambassador of God, yet such childhood comes to those who are new converts to Christianity. Paul calls the Corinthian Christians "babes in Christ," whom he fed with milk and not with meat. Peter describes them in the same terms, saying, "As newborn babes, desire the sincere milk of the word, that ye may grow thereby." The young Christian needs instruction, experience, testing and victory, before he can be given any position of responsibility or service, much less the position of an ambassador. We must attain to maturity, to the spiritual state, before we can be ambassadors. This does not imply a long process of many years, but the complete transition from being a "natural man" to becoming a "spiritual man." It means that we must not tarry in the state of carnality or childhood in our Christian experience. We must seek the full development of the truth within our own lives, that we may assume the responsibility of citizens of the kingdom.

It is true that all Christians are witnesses of God, no matter what their state of Christian experience is. They are called "epistles known and read of all men." God has written a letter on your life and he has posted it to men. Does that letter read truly concerning Christ and God and salvation, or is it a false message? When Paul says, "We are ambassadors for Christ," he includes all Christians. He refers to himself and to his fellow workers and to those to whom he was speaking.

In a peculiar sense, however, those called to the Christian ministry are God's ambassadors. Paul said, "Necessity is laid upon me; yea, woe is unto me, if I preach not the gospel! for if I do this thing willingly, I have a reward: but if against my will, a dispensation of the gospel is committed unto me." Paul was called of God and he simply could not do anything else. Jeremiah's experience was identical with this. After his first few messages to the people of Judah, they began to persecute him. The whole population turned against him; one of the princes had him beaten and put in the stocks, and the people mocked him because of his preaching. So Jeremiah said "I will not make mention of him, nor speak any more in his Name," referring to the Lord. But soon he was preaching as fervently as ever, and why? This is his reason, "His word was in my heart as a burning fire shut up in my bones and I was weary with forbearing, and I could not stay." He began to speak for his King. Thus it is with one who has been called to be an ambassador. He has an inner urge which will prevent him from doing anything else. His life, then, becomes identified with the interests of the kingdom. He can no longer live unto himself. Assuming the office of ambassador, he assumes a responsibility of walking wisely and carefully so as to give no offense in anything, "that the ministry be not blamed." A true minister is careful not to give the slightest offense or hurt, lest the kingdom be blamed for his own foibles and foolishness. Paul realized that much harm could be done by the representatives of the kingdom in the life they lived and in the words they spoke.

Therefore, the nature of this ministerial office is described for us in what almost appears to be an unapproachable standard. Yet this must be considered as having been fulfilled in Paul's ministry and as applying to all of his followers, and certainly in a measure it ought to apply to the citizens of the kingdom as well as to its ambassadors. American citizens traveling abroad leave definite impressions on those with whom they have contact. In a lesser, and unofficial, sense they are ambassadors of their country. Instead of giving an offense which may be blamed upon the ministry, Paul calls to a life which would approve the ministry of God. I am aware of the word cutting like a sword, but the difference in the kind of ministers a kingdom has makes the difference in its effect upon others, in the progress of the kingdom, the understanding of the principles and purposes of the kingdom and in the reconciling of men to the sovereign. What terrible blunders the ministry often makes, and what awful consequences there are.

If we imitate Paul's life and ministry and hold this standard before ourselves, what is it? The descriptive categories divide themselves into classes made up of the minister's personal experience, his position and his outlook. The long list of phrases describing the minister's personal experience is divided into a series of ten and four and four.

First, we are told that the minister approves himself by perseverence in the midst of tribulations that press upon him like a burden, in the midst of necessities which are compulsions external to himself, in the midst of distressing and perplexing situations, in the midst of stripes or physical suffering, in the midst of imprisonments or loss of personal liberty in the midst of tumults like those Paul had at Corinth, in the midst of severe and trying labors, in the midst of sleepless watchings, and in the midst of fastings, which may be voluntary or compulsory. What a contrast with our ministry today. Few of us would be willing to undergo stripes. Fewer still could stand prison experience, and how many could endure to have their homes beseiged by a multitude, only to be dragged forth to answer for sedition? Yet, if these things come again, as they may, we may discover that the power of God within us will provide resources sufficient for the need, as it did for Paul.

The second four phrases describing the personal experience of a minister are active rather than passive. They are: pureness of motive under the enlightenment of knowledge, for one without the other is often voided, and long-suffering with kindness. The last four, describing Paul's personal experience are: the Holy Ghost, love unfeigned, the word of truth, and the power of God. This, of course, is the climax produced by the Spirit in the life of the ambassador.

Then the minister's position is defined. He is between the aids of righteousness on the right and on the left. All kinds of helps are afforded him. He is between honor and dishonor in the method of discharging his duty. He is in the midst of good report and bad report, between which he must walk carefully.

Paradoxically, the minister's outlook is described in a series of seven. "As deceivers and yet true," that is, called the one but actually being the other. "As unknown and yet well known," that is, called upstarts with no standing, yet taken cognizance of in heaven. "As dying and behold we live," that is, willing to carry about in our bodies the dying of the Lord Jesus so as to manifest His life. "As chastised and not killed," that is, enduring afflictions which are but for the moment as a means of chastenment from God for the purposes of greater glory. "As sorrowful yet always rejoicing," that is, being grieved by the sin and rebellion of men and yet rejoicing in the great grace of God and its accomplishments. "As poor, yet making many rich," that is, as in ourselves earthen vessels but possessing the incorruptible treasure of God, which we dispense unto others, namely, eternal life. "As having nothing and yet possessing all things," that is, remembering that the meek will inherit the earth.

Paul here has removed all inhibitions concerning himself and his ministry. Said he, "Our mouth is open unto you, our heart is enlarged." He had opened his mouth to testify. He had opened his heart in love to these people to take them into his affections. He requested now that they should release their own emotions toward him, that love might be reciprocated by love. Said he, "I speak as unto my children. Be ye also enlarged." This is the paternal voice of a father, of the Christian dealing with his children, for whose care he was responsible to God.

II. Our Message as Ambassadors

If God has appointed to us the ministry of reconciliation we should consider His message. Paul said, He hath deposited with us the word [or the message] of reconciliation. This is the greatest possible message any man could carry. It takes three forms, namely, that God hath reconciled, that God is reconciling, and that God will reconcile.

Reconciliation presupposes an estrangement between two parties. Often we hear that the estrangement between God and man is completely one-sided. Men say that God did not need to be reconciled to man, but that man needed to be reconciled to God. The essence of some weak theology is that the suffering of Christ on Calvary was merely an exhibition of Divine love to win the friendship, affection and esteem of man. That is to overlook the essence of the Pauline teaching concerning reconciliation. We are told that sin affected God as well as man, so that in a real sense God was estranged from man. Sin resulted in God's condemnation and wrath toward man. This Divine attitude has to be dealt with before there can be any reconciliation. God's fundamental attribute of righteousness, as well as His holiness and justice, had to be satisfied before God could be reconciled to man. When the Scripture says God has reconciled man it refers to a completed act, which deals first with God and has been accomplished by Him in the person of Jesus Christ. The essence, therefore, of what happened on Calvary is the reconciliation of God. The Word of reconciliation is the Gospel message of what God did in Christ to end this estrangement, that is, His putting away of sin and his ending of wrath by the sacrifice of Himself. He assumed the awful penalty of judgment and He made known His love thereby. The means is declared. "God hath reconciled us to himself by Jesus Christ . . . to wit, that God was in Christ reconciling the world unto himself, not imputing their trespasses unto them; and hath committed unto us the word of reconciliation." It was because God satisfied the demands of righteousness and justice that He remains holy and is able not to impute or reckon sin unto men, "for he hath made him to be sin for us, who knew no sin; that we might be made the righteousness of God." The meaning of Calvary is that God was in Christ, as our substitute, satisfying justice, turning away wrath and accomplishing reconciliation. Therefore, we may declare that God is reconciled.

The present enmity between man and God is wholly on man's side. Since God has been reconciled by the propitiation made in Christ for us all, He is favorably disposed toward all. He is ready to forgive and to reinstate us in fellowship with Him, but man remains in rebellion, being alienated from, and at enmity with God. He is God's enemy instead of God's friend. Therefore, what remains to be done in salvation is the reconciliation of man. The love of Calvary, the truth of the Gospel and the persuasion of the Holy Spirit are the instruments used to effect this reconciliation, but man must repent, he must turn and he must submit. To refuse to do so is to reject that reconciliation made in Christ and to face the condemnation and wrath of God.

Christians, then, are God's ambassadors of peace, of reconciliation already accomplished, of the good news of the propitiation of God, of an accomplished fact. They declared an objective fact. They exhort men to the subjective experience of this fact. First of all, then, we are messengers. Secondly, we exhort men to accept that message. Thus we may preach that God is reconciled, and this is our message.

But in our text the present tense is used—God *is* reconciling the world, not imputing men's trespasses unto them. Paul and his fellow workers were reconciled. They had experienced the objective and the subjective reconciliation. They were forgiven, they were no longer enemies of God. Reconciliation was not only a historic fact but a present experience for them. Thus they said, "God hath reconciled us." Yet this reconciling action was continuing for the world. God is constantly engaged in reconciling men by the ministry, and the word of reconciliation is deposited with His ambassadors. That is, the ambassadors of God, in preaching the Gospel and making known the good news of the reconciliation, include the whole world, but this must be brought to the world by those who represent God and do His work, namely, His ambassadors. God is ready to remit any man's sins and to reckon to him his faith as righteousness when he accepts the Gospel. "God is favorably disposed toward all men."

This leads us to the third phase of the message, which is that God will reconcile you. The message is, "Be ye reconciled to God." This is the hortatory part, the open tense in reconciliation, the unsettled factor. Think of God's mighty condescension, that He permits and even instructs His dignified ambassadors to stoop to the act of begging, or beseeching, or admonishing men to be reconciled. On behalf of God, we beseech men. We abandon our dignity and become exceeedingly humble, that we might win some. There is nothing that a divine servant will not do to turn men's will toward God. Our plea is for you to accept God's offer, to believe He has put away sin, to accept reconcilation. All the authority of heaven and of God, mediated by His ambassadors, is inherent in the plea for you to be reconciled to God. No ultimatum has been given yet. This is only a plea. Thus, as ambassadors, our passion is the winning of the wills of men, that they might be reconciled to God.

III. OUR INCENTIVE AS AMBASSADORS

We not only have a call to do this work and a message to give, but we have good reasons to discharge our duties responsibly. The first reason is that we know the terror of the Lord. We know that we must all appear before the judgment-seat of Christ to receive for the deeds done in the body and, knowing that we must stand before His dais and that we must give an accounting of our ministry but not knowing when the summons or the recall will come, we do our work effectively. If matters are so serious for us, how much more serious will they be for the unsaved. If we talk of fear for the believer of the judgment-seat of God, what terror ought hell and destruction, as the Bible calls them, to hold for the unbeliever and the disobedient. We know what other terrors of men have been, but this will go beyond all that. It is the terror of a lost soul. Hence, we persuade men. We beseech and we beg in behalf of God. We gladly stoop from the dignity of the sons of God to become the servants of men, to save them by the word of reconciliation.

Secondly, we have the constraint of love. It is the love of Christ that constrains us, "because we thus judge, that if one died for all, then were all dead: and that he died for all, that they which live should not henceforth live unto themselves, but unto him which died for them and rose again." What God did for us in Christ is far more than any nation has done for its citizens or ambassadors. We love our country and, should we be chosen as its ambassadors, we would glory in our opportunity to serve and be grateful for the honor. How much more should the love of Christ constrain us. It was this which led Paul to endure the stripes, and fastings, sleeplessness, and riots, until people said, "Thou art beside thyself." It is the love of God in Christ Jesus, having reconciled us to Him, which will move us to sacrifice and service more than any other compulsion. This is a sufficient motive.

Yet there is one more. This is the note of urgency in our message. Harken to it, "Behold now is the accepted time; behold now is the day of salvation." This is a Messianic promise to which Paul refers and, as one suggested, the whole era of grace is an answer to Christ's prayer for His people. This is the acceptable time of the Lord. It is the era of grace in which God is favorably disposed toward men and in which if they repent they shall be saved. It is called "now," but remember "now" never comes back. "Now" must be seized, held and used.

> "The clock of life is wound but once,
> And no man has the power
> To tell just when the hands will stop
> At late or early hour."

For some it is now or never. It is the acceptance of the message in this moment or its final rejection. General Percival answered the Japanese at Singapore, "Give me till tomorrow." The Japanese general replied, "My men will attack tonight unless you surrender." For the British it was too late. Now we live under grace. Now the door is open. Now the invitation goes out. Now the ambassadors are still at work, but the end time is coming. The day of the vengeance of our God is at hand. Soon it will be too late.

Therefore, we ambassadors of Christ plead with you, "Be ye reconciled to God." Though you can not reconcile yourself, you may remember that God in Christ is reconciled and favorably disposed toward you and if you will now repent and turn, He will give you power to be reconciled to Him. He will set you at peace. Therefore, "Kiss the son lest while his anger is kindled but a little, ye perish from the way."

XVIII

WHO IS YOUR SUBSTITUTE IN THIS CONFLICT?

TEXT: *"For he hath made him to be sin for us, who knew no sin; that we might be made the righteousness of God in him."*—II COR. 5:21-6:13.

SOMEWHERE I have a substitute in this great world conflict. That substitute is bearing the brunt of warfare, the danger of death, the suffering of body and soul for me and my family. He and others like him are a wall of defense from the terrible foes that beset us in this hour. Great is my gratitude and my loyalty to such a substitute. Thus, all of us should feel it our duty to provide sufficient armament, foodstuffs, equipment and money for those who are fighting our battles.

Somewhere on the mission field for those of you who are liberally giving to the kingdom program, there is a substitute preaching the Gospel of Jesus Christ to the heathen. I know where my substitute is, and I pray for him every day. I believe he has taken my place in the great commission to carry the Gospel to the heathen. By God's grace I will be faithful in his support, both with money and with prayer. Were it not for him I would feel that I ought to be in the mission field today.

But we are to think of a substitute who is greater than any of these today. This substitute is one who stepped up to the just tribunal of the universe and assumed the guilt, penalty and pain of my sin and your sin. He is one who at the bank of morality paid our debt and made up our deficiency. He is one who when we were poor gave us of His riches that we might be rich, though He was impoverished thereby. He is the great substitute for the sinner.

Substitution is the fundamental principle of Biblical Christianity, differentiating it from other religions. From the doctrine of substitution come the truths of the atonement, forgiveness, righteousness, salvation and assurance. Hear the Word of God as it is written for your instruction. "Who his own self bare our sins in his own body on the tree, that we, being dead to sins, should live unto righteousness: by whose stripes ye were healed." "All we like sheep have gone astray; we have turned every one to his own way; and the Lord hath laid on him the iniquity of us all." "Christ hath redeemed us from the curse of the law, being made a curse for us: for it is written, Cursed is every one that hangeth on a tree." "For he hath made him to be sin for us who knew no sin; that we might be made the righteousness of God in him." Whatever you may think of this doctrine of substitution, remember that Christianity is the message of the great substitute:

"For when we were yet without strength, in due time Christ died for the ungodly. For scarcely for a righteous man will one die: yet peradventure for a good man some would even dare to die. But God commended His love toward us, in that, while we were yet sinners, Christ died for us."

I. THE PERSON IN SUBSTITUTION

The text describes our substitute as one "who knew no sin." This is sufficient to identify the person of the substitute. We have in Arlington Cemetery a tomb which has been visited by many notables from all over the world. Wreaths of gratitude and honor and glory have been laid there by grateful hearts. It is the expression of the appreciation of a nation for its soldiers, but we do not know what soldier was buried in that tomb. He is an unknown substitute for those of us who had no part in World War I. Many will be the unknown substitutes and the unknown soldiers buried in the far-flung battle line of this great war, but there is one substitute whom we know and to whom we may express our gratitude and honor.

This person is the only one who ever lived without sin. Perhaps you like to read biography and are acquainted with the great of history. The minds of most boys learn early to set George Washington on a pedestal. Never shall I forget the shock which came to me in reading the life of Mad Anthony Wayne. In the early stages of the Revolutionary War the Americans had proved themselves the equals of the British soldiers at Germantown, Brandywine and other important battles, but because of the scantiness of his troops and his scantier provisions, Washington was compelled to retreat from Philadelphia and allow Sir Henry Clinton and Cornwallis to occupy that city. The winter was spent in Valley Forge, with its terrible suffering. Then, at the close, the British started for New York and the American army, now well trained and anxious for battle, followed. Time and again, Washington had been frustrated by incompetent generals. Now, at Monmouth, came the opportunity to crush the British. Anthony Wayne, Dickey Butler and other generals made a strong attack. According to the plan of battle, they were to be reenforced by the men of Major General Charles Lee. Just as Anthony Wayne and Dickey Butler were leading their troops to victory, Lee, instead of coming to their succor, as had been planned, retreated rapidly, because he believed the American soldiers were incompetent to meet the British army. As he fell back from Monmouth, General Washington approached and encountered the flower of the American army retreating. To Lee he shouted, "What is the meaning of all this, sir? I desire to know the meaning of all this disorder and confusion." General Lee rasped back, "By God, sir, the American soldiers cannot fight the British grenadiers." Said Washington, "By God, they can fight any upon the face of the earth. You're a blankety blank poltroon," which, according to Charles Scott, who had joined the column and was standing by, was only the beginning of what General Lee had become in the estimation of General Washington, "for the commander-in-chief swore on that day till the leaves shook on the trees, charmingly, and delightfully." Never before or since did Brigadier General Scott enjoy such swearing, for the general "swore like an angel from heaven." It is quite evident that George Washington was not without sin.

Lincoln also has been placed on a pedestal and well he deserves to be, but Lincoln was not without sin. In his book, *Lincoln and His Generals*, Clarence E. Macartney tells how McClellan saved the Union after the second great disaster at Bull Run. As the troops came stumbling into Washington in panic and the archives were being shipped away, Lincoln went to the home of General McClellan, whom he had summarily dismissed on a former occasion, and asked him to save the army. McClellan said he would and took command again. When Lincoln faced his Cabinet that day there was a hurricane of anger. Chase and Stanton and other anti-McClellan men raged at Lincoln, but Lincoln said, "McClellan has the army. We need him now. I am sorry to be in disagreement with you and I am perfectly willing to resign my place and give it to another if you want." McClellan did not disappoint him. He rode out that night to meet the retreating army. A New England officer lying by a fence with another officer saw a man riding in the moonlight on his horse, and said, "If I did not know McClellan had been retired, I would say that that was General McClellan." Then another cried, "It is McClellan, McClellan is here." And that cry rolled through the army from regiment to regiment, from brigade to brigade, from division to division.

Lincoln was not mistaken. McClellan had the army, and on the march into Maryland, following Lee, he reorganized his army on the banks of the Rappahannock and then fought the battle of Antietam, the bloodiest single day's battle of the war, and, because of its political aftermath, the emancipation proclamation, declared to be the decisive battle of the war. Lincoln came to see McClellan after the battle, and sitting on a hill overlooking the army of the Potomac, with his great knees under his chin, he said, "General, you have saved the country twice," referring to what he had done after the first and second Bull Run. "You must see us through to the end." But Lincoln was hardly back in Washington before he removed McClellan from command and sent him to Trenton to await other orders, which never came. Whatever reasons may have been back of this extraordinary action by Lincoln, it is obvious that in this one instance Lincoln did not keep his promise. He did not tell the truth. No, Lincoln was not without sin.

How easy it would be for us to do today what the Bible does, that is, take the greatest characters and reveal their sins. One thing the Bible never camouflages or covers over, and that is the sins of its heroes. Abraham in Egypt became a despicable coward, willing to sacrifice his beautiful wife to save his own skin. David, a man after God's own heart, fell to such sin that he is called an adulterer, a liar and a murderer. Peter, even after his great Pentecostal experience, dissembled in hypocrisy at Antioch and had to be rebuked to the face by the Apostle Paul. Paul himself showed a streak of stubbornness and unforgivingness in relationship to John Mark that caused him to fall out with Barnabas his friend and to disrupt the first evangelistic and missionary team sent out by the Early Church. No, there is no character in sacred or secular history who was without sin, save Jesus.

Contrast with this story the sinlessness of Jesus of Nazareth. Here was one who was "tempted in all points like as we are and yet without sin." He could stand in the presence of His very enemies, who were trying to trap Him in conversation or deed so that they could condemn Him, and challenge them with the question, "Which one of you convicteth me of sin?" He was able to say to the accusers of a poor woman, "Let him who is without sin cast the first stone at her." Each one of her accusers silently slipped away. Then said Jesus, "Neither do I accuse you." This sinless being suffered loneliness. It is clear that the higher one rises above the madding crowd, the lonelier he becomes in his majestic nobility. The great souls are the lonely souls. Hence Jesus Christ must have been one of the most lonely men that ever walked the earth. Yet loneliness did not lead Him to a sin condoned for the sake of comfort in some illicit relationship. Perhaps one of the most oft repeated excuses by sinners is, "I was so lonely."

Jesus was often misunderstood. He had to rebuke His own mother because she misunderstood His work. We read that His brethren did not believe on Him. When He uttered difficult sayings most of His disciples abandoned Him, until He said to the twelve, "Will ye also go away?" Likewise, the masses would repeat, What meaneth he? "Whither I go, ye cannot come?" But though Jesus was misunderstood day in and day out, no irritability appeared upon His countenance or in His actions and words. Yet misunderstanding and lack of appreciation has led many of us to condone some sinful indulgence.

Jesus lived and worked and died under opposition. The Pharisees opposed His healings because they said He made Himself the son of God. They opposed His good works on the Sabbath because they said He violated His law. They opposed His claims and tried to stone Him because He identified Himself with the great "I AM," yet He had no hatred, no sense of personal abuse and no self-pity. There was no retiring to His tent to sulk because He was not appreciated, because there were those who opposed His progress.

Jesus suffered probably more than any other man who ever lived and yet in the midst of His sufferings there was no bitterness. He was able to say, "Father, thy will be done," and also, "Father, forgive them for they know not what they do."

Such sinlessness declares Jesus Christ to be the Son of God. Paul said, He was "declared to be the Son of God with power, according to the Spirit of holiness, by the resurrection from the dead." That Spirit of holiness motivated His life. That was His Divine nature, but it also revealed Him in His perfection of holiness to be God's Son. It is true that Jesus revealed God the Father as He is in heaven, and thus the perfections of God morally were made known by the Son. He was able to say, "He that hath seen me hath seen the Father." It was written of Him, "The word was made flesh, and dwelt among us, and we beheld his glory, the glory as of the only begotten of the Father, . . . No man hath seen the Father at any time; the only begotten Son, which is in the bosom of the Father he hath declared him." And His apostle Peter later could write, "Ye were redeemed . . . with the precious blood of Christ, as of a lamb without blemish and without spot." Morally, Jesus Christ was the most majestic man of the ages. He came into the world with one purpose expressed by the words, "I come to do thy will, O God." It was written of Him, "Though he were a Son, yet learned he obedience by the things which he suffered; and being made perfect, he became the author of eternal salvation unto all them that obey him." To His disciples He said, "My meat is to do the will of him that sent me." Yes, Jesus of Nazareth wove a garment of righteousness in His perfect obedience to God, which may be reckoned to the believer by faith. This garment is utilized in the Bible as a symbol of the righteousness of Christ given to the believer. It is a positive thing. It is formed of the life which He lived, and, therefore, we are declared to be saved not only by the death of God's Son but much more, being reconciled, shall we be saved by His life.

Victory over sin in His life enables Him to sympathize with us, for He was tempted in all points like as we are; it enables Him to succor us, for He was conqueror of these temptations, and it enables Him to save us, for He ever liveth to make intercession for us. Therefore, the life of Christ constitutes the perfect example for the life of the Christian. Let us never derogate from this great fact by holding up Christ as a Savior. He is primarily a Savior, but He is also an example. His life constitutes the prefect standard for our lives. He said, "Follow me." Nevertheless, the fact of the sinlessness of Christ showed the impossibility of our salvation by following His example. We are sinners and we are conscious of the fact. Therefore we ought logically to be conscious of the fact that we need a Savior before we can ever follow His great sinless example. It is to this mighty work of redeeming us from sin, of removing our guilt and penalty, of reconciling us to the Father, that we now turn. Without this salvation we are hopeless.

II. The Place of Substitution

Our text says, "He hath made him to be sin for us." Consider that fact, that this sinless being now became sin for us through the will of God, because by that act He was able to save us. This involved His humiliation, His identification with sin and the propitiation which He made for sin.

The humiliation of the Lord Jesus Christ began at the Incarnation, when He assumed human flesh. He whose goings forth have been from of old, even from everlasting, was born of a virgin in a manger at Bethlehem. When the second Person of the Trinity was born under the law, born of a virgin woman, He emptied Himself of His glory and humbled Himself to the place where He actually assumed flesh itself as the first step in His humiliation.

The second major step in the humiliation of Christ was His baptism. Therein the sinful position of mankind was imputed to Him. The meaning of the rite of baptism was that of repentance for sin. John's message was, "Repent for the kingdom of heaven is at hand." Let him who hath two coats give to him that hath none. Let him who is guilty of violence be violent no more. Let him who was a thief steal no more. Yet Jesus, who knew no sin, submitted Himself to that baptism. John recognized the incongruity of this fact, and he said to Jesus, in forbidding Him to be baptized, "I have need to be baptized of thee, and comest thou to me?" Jesus said, "Suffer it to be so now: for thus it becometh us to fulfill all righteousness." This was a necessary step in the further humiliation of Christ and the identification of Him with sinful man.

The final step in His humiliation was the bearing of the fruitage of sin, namely, death. He tasted death for those who all their lifetime were subject to the bondage of the fear of death. Voluntarily He yielded His body to death as the final state in His humiliation. Yes, He came from glory and by means of humbling Himself He became sin for us.

The text, however, goes farther than declaring the humiliation of Christ, which many who miss the heart of the Bible teaching are willing to accept. The Bible declares that He became sin, was made sin for us, that it, was identified with us. There was a time in history when our sin actually was identified with Jesus Christ and when He was identified with our sin. This means not only that He endured sin's penalty but that He became sin itself. It is true that He bore our sins in His body on the tree, that He became the curse of the law for us, that God placed upon Him the iniquity of us all. He was metaphysically identified with sin which was to be condemned. I say this is worse than donning clothes that have been worn by a diseased person. It is taking the disease into himself. Isaiah tells of the suffering Messiah. "Surely he hath borne our griefs and carried our sorrows," namely, our sins. It was this which Father Damian did in the leper colony of the Philippines, first tending the lepers and then, when he found that he had contracted the dread disease, having himself admitted to the colony that he might the better minister to them. Thus it was that the research physician discovered the cure for malaria by allowing the disease to enter his own body. Christ identified Himself with sin.

The place of identification was Calvary. As when the moon obscures the sun, on Calvary sin totally eclipsed the holiness, beauty and perfection of the Son of God. His identification with sin became complete. There before God this sinless One took into Himself the world's rebellion, guilt, hate of the Father, wickedness, until it all actually coincided with His Person. The gradual process which had begun at His humiliation and birth was now complete on Calvary. It is no wonder that the elements darkened their glow and that God turned away His Face during those hours on Calvary. There sin was identified with His Son.

That moment was expressed by the Lord Jesus in His terrible cry, "My God, my God why hast thou forsaken me?" That forsakenness was the expression of His experience of hell, of wrath and judgment against sin, of that which it was necessary to bear to reconcile man to God. Sin was judged in that hour and was condemned. Therefore, God remains righteous and the just ruler of the universe.

By being made sin for us Jesus Christ made a propitiation for our sin and not for ours only but for the sins of the whole world. Here on Calvary satisfaction was made to the righteousness, holiness and justice of God. There was given a moral demonstration that the government of God still continues in this moral universe. There a public demonstration was made of the condemnation of sin. Now God may forgive sin and still remain righteous. Here reconciliation was effected. That in the nature of God which is opposed to sin and which was estranged from man because of sin was now satisfied and reconciled. As soon as the words, "It is finished," were spoken on Calvary God was enabled morally and metaphysically to be favorably disposed toward men. Thereby God could open the acceptable era of grace, the offer of God for salvation. Now, only man needs to be reconciled and not God. God has even provided the means for such reconciliation of man. Here, then, God was in Christ bearing the sin of the world, reconciling the world to Himself, not imputing their trespasses unto them but unto Himself upon the Cross, thereby establishing the mercy seat of forgiveness. Fear not, then, to go to that holy throne. It is no longer the thunderings of righteousness and justice and judgment. It now is known as the mercy seat. It is the dwelling place of holiness and to it we have access. Sin has been judged and if you will meet the conditions you may be forgiven.

III. THE PURPOSE OF SUBSTITUTION

Our text tell us that all this was done, "that we might be made the righteousness of God in him." This states that we shall be constituted righteous. Here we have evidence that we may be right with God, which is the most important consideration of our lives. The possibility of righteousness is here shown and the assurance of righteousness is here offered. Ask yourself, "Am I right with God?" Do you know that you are right with God? Have you been constituted righteous in His sight through Jesus Christ? The Pauline doctrine of righteousness takes three steps: first, there is a righteousness of God as applied to Him whereby all of His actions, both in judging and in forgiving sin, are self-consistent with His nature of holiness. Next, there is the righteousness of God as revealed concretely in Jesus Christ. Christ on the Cross is declared to be the exhibition and manifestation of God's righteousness, for in Christ on the Cross the two great strains meet, namely, judgment of sin and forgiveness of sin. The third phase in the righteousness of God is that applied to the individual, so that he may be called the righteousness of God. This is given to those who are justified by faith, those who commit themselves unto God, believe what He has said and trust Him for their salvation. They are declared to be righteous before God. Therefore, objectively Christ became sin for us though He knew no sin, that in principle the justified ones may have a righteous standing in Christ. This is applied righteousness.

But righteousness must also be subjective. We, in turn, must be changed into righteous lives and thus manifest the righteousness of God. Surely, each of us will confess that he has been anything and everything but God's righteousness. This is what God has said of us. He has clearly told that the fruit of the flesh is all kinds of unrighteousness, such as adultery, fornication, uncleanness, lasciviousness, idolatry, hatred, wrath, strife, heresies, envyings, drunkenness and such like. Yet we must confess that some of us were guilty of these before our conversion. Our history is anything but that of righteousness. Now, however, in Him we are to put off the old man and put on the new, to doff the old garments and don the new garments, to be transformed by the renewing of our minds, that we might prove what is that good and perfect and acceptable work of God, to be transformed from glory to glory until we bear His very image. Therefore, God expects us to be holy, blameless, perfect in love. We are commanded to be holy as He is holy, to be perfect as our Father which is in heaven is perfect. We are told that the will of God is our sactification and that therefore it is necessary to exercise the means of grace to put off all filthiness of the flesh and to perfect holiness in the fear of the Lord. This righteousness of God which is objective must become subjective in experience; our practice must reach our principle. Our state must gradually rise to our standing before God.

All this is possible "in him." The text says, that we are made the righteousness of God in Him. This calls to our minds Paul's teaching, that if any man be in Christ Jesus he is a new creature. Old things are passed away and all things have become new. All things are of God. Here we could review the entire teaching of the new birth, the new creation, that which is supernatural and which occurs when man meets the conditions which God has laid down of repentance, confession, faith and obedience. By being such a new creature, it may be said he is created in Christ Jesus unto good works which God hath before ordained that he should walk in them. Everything, therefore, which is done for us and in us is done by Christ Jesus. It is He who sends His Holy Spirit to us as the Comforter to bless and empower, to teach and to help us. Without becoming such a new creature in Christ Jesus and possessing His Divine life and power in the Holy Spirit we have no hope to become the righteousness of God. Therefore, if we are ready to be saved at all, it is wisdom to accept the great substitute offered by God. Let us receive Jesus Christ as Savior. Let us submit to Him as Lord and let us utterly trust Him as God. This means that salvation is quite sufficient for us.

By such an acceptance of the appointed Substitute, such a relegation of your hope for safety and salvation to Him, you may in assurance let your voice join the chorus of the living creatures, of the four and twenty elders who represent the redeemed and of the great angelic host, singing His praise around the throne because of redemption and saying, "Thou art worthy to take the book, and to open the seals thereof: for thou wast slain, and hast redeemed us to God by thy blood out of every kindred, and tongue, and people, and nation; and hast made us unto our God kings and priests: and we shall reign on the earth." Thank God for The Great Substitute.

XIX

PERFECTING HOLINESS IN THE FEAR OF GOD

TEXT: *"Having therefore these promises, dearly beloved, let us cleanse ourselves from all filthiness of the flesh and spirit, perfecting holiness in the fear of God."*—II COR. 6:14-7:1.

THIS TEACHING deals with how far a Christian who lives in the world is of the world. Many extremes have been based upon these words asking for separation of the Christian from the world. We have many separationist movements in Protestantism and conflicts caused by them. Some good people think that they must separate themselves from every church in which there is any kind of error or sinfulness and form some new organization, so we have had division *ad infinitum* in Protestant history.

Likewise, there are good people who are narrow and bigoted in their judgment of other people who do not see as they do in reference to moral things. Great is the distress which they cause in Christian groups. A certain woman in great distress of mind recently wrote of the conflict which she endured because of the pressure, placed upon her by relatives and people with whom she lived, to compel her to conform her standard of life to theirs. She did not see that she was doing anything wrong. She did not see that they had anything to do with Christ, and yet these relatives and friends were almost willing to declare that she was unsaved because she participated in certain innocent practices.

The separatist idea expressed itself in history in asceticism, mainly in the monkish movement of the Middle Ages. Then people thought that it was impossible to live in daily contact with a sinful world. Therefore, they withdrew themselves from the world, constructed little communities of a self-sufficient nature, where all the defilements of flesh and spirit were to be absent. The history of this movement, however, proved that defilement followed the individuals in the communities where they sought refuge from the world.

Separatism has led also to a self-imposed persecution and ostracism for those who applied the principle. It is one thing to be persecuted for the sake of Christ, for which one is rewarded, and it is another thing to be persecuted for one's own foolishness in separating from persons and things from which he need not separate.

The essentials of Christianity, however, involve some separation from sinful things. How are we to reconcile this passage commanding us to come out from among sinful people and things with the general body of Paul's teaching concerning liberty? Because there seems to be something of a conflict here, some have declared that this passage is an interpolation, that it is unPauline, and they attack it because of the Puritanical elements and prohibitions involved in it. They say that Paul allowed all things and that this is not like Paul. But it is perfectly natural that Paul should urge such separation, for he had just been pleading with these Corinthian Christians to receive him and his associates with open heart. Obviously, if they would do that, it would be impossible for them also to receive those who were false teachers. This separation was enjoined by Paul as necessary to prove the sincerity of their love and the consistency of their convictions, for they were gradually turning away from the true apostles and the teaching of God toward that which would destroy the Church. From this it was necessary to separate. If the teaching of separation has a permanent place in New Testament Christianity, it must be applied not only to the Corinthians but to ourselves. However, we must limit it by the great example of Christ as to the kind of separation we are to practice. The Pharisees accused Him of violating His Nazarite vow because He was found in the company of publicans and sinners. Yet Christ rose to such moral heights, even in the midst of unclean surroundings, that no man was able to convince Him of sin.

The failure to go on to holiness in the Christian life is to receive the grace of God in vain, against which Paul warned these people in the beginning of this chapter. No doubt this accounts for the transition in the narrative from Paul's own kind of life to this teaching on separation, to which he urged the Corinthians. Salvation in a practical sense is not only to submit to the pleas of God's ambassadors and theoretically to receive a message of reconciliation, but to translate it into fact. We must actually become saved from the sins which formerly dominated us and from all the errors which engulfed us.

Every believer at justification is made holy before God. This, in truth, is the meaning of the righteousness of God applied to the believer. That believer is declared to be God's righteousness. That is, he is no longer considered to be a sinner, guilty of condemnation and death in the presence of God, but he is declared, by his faith in what Christ has done for him as substitute, to be not only reconciled to God but to be righteous in the presence of God. He is justified by faith. This wonderful truth declares that our past sins are forgiven, blotted out and forgotten and, with the exception of those things for which we need to make restitution, we ourselves need remember them no more. The only responsibility for one's past sin after he is justified by faith is the discharging of righteous debts and righting wrongs against individuals. This standing of holiness given to the individual, through his Savior must now become perfected in him in experience. He may be declared holy by faith and may be forgiven his sins, but still may be no better in practice than he was before his conversion. Therefore, it is necessary for him to receive the injunction of this text, "Let us cleanse ourselves from all filthiness of the flesh and spirit, perfecting holiness in the fear of God."

I. THE MORAL STANDARD OF HOLINESS

The kind of holiness required for us is here revealed in several ways. First, we are forbidden to take upon ourselves any yoke of unbelief. Just what does it mean to "be not unequally yoked together with unbelievers"? This unquestionably is a law taken from the Old Testament and spiritualized. There it was forbidden to plow with an ox and an ass under the same yoke and also to breed hybrid animals. Paul, with the insight of inspiration, took this law and applied it to moral matters. In these things he held that we should be utterly separated from all which was unclean. We should not be yoked together with unbelief, with darkness, with children of Belial and with infidelity. By one this is defined to mean "anything which unites a child of God and an unbeliever in a common purpose." Another definition is "any kind of union in which the separate character and influence of a Christian lose anything of their distinctness and energy." We feel the former definition to be a bit too stringent, for it shuts out all union for common good. Under such a law we could not become citizens of a nation, members of a political party, or adherents of anything which involve a work larger than that of mere Christians. The latter is a better definition because it permits association with the unregenerate in life in a common cause in all things where the Christian does not lose his distinctive qualities and characteristics. Were this latter not the

case, asceticism would be the necessary means of normal existence.
Sometimes this teaching has been pressed to absurd ends in applying what is a general principle. But Paul distinctly shows that we are to have no communion or agreement or yoke with the things of unrighteousness, of darkness, of Satan, of infidelity and idolatry. These are the things with which God can have nothing to do, for they are just the opposite of everything which pertains to Him, but one never finds that God is opposed to anything which is good and upright, and we conclude that the Christian should be found behind all such humanitarian and moral movements in the world. In so far as unbelievers are willing to abandon their enmity to God and to support what is good, there is nothing to prevent us from associating with them in such enterprises.

It is forbidden of God to be under the yoke with an unbeliever, because when we take such a yoke it is usually the yoke of unbelief and not the yoke of faith, for since the unbeliever cannot rise to faith we must stoop to his unbelief. We, in turn, would thereby join with him in his refusal to trust God. Apply this to business if you will. Suppose a believer and an unbeliever form a partnership. How can the believer, in time of extremity or stringency, turn to God and ask Him to help his business? He has formed a mixed relationship which must be run entirely upon a basis in which the unbeliever can join. Apply it to marriage, which is one of the most common and serious infringements of this principle. Here, in the very closest relationship of life, arise most serious matters, such as training the children, the choice of schools, and religious instruction. If one is a believer and the other an unbeliever, there cannot possibly be agreement on these matters, and there can be no blessing of God upon such union. Because of difference in ideals and purposes in life, husband and wife are always in disagreement, which leads to innumerable sorrows. The principle applies also to fraternal organizations. If your money, your name, your influence are to be used to support anything which is un-Christian you have violated the principle of separation. You have no right to be in such an organization.

The logical basis of this principle of separation rests in the conflict of Christ and Belial, which is another name for Satan. In the questions asked there are several contrasts. "Be ye not unequally yoked together with unbelievers: for what fellowship hath righteousness with unrighteousness? and what communion hath light with darkness? and what concord hath Christ with Belial? or what part hath he that believeth with an infidel?" Here two great realms are contrasted: first, in the qualities of life, second, in the powers producing those qualities, and, third, in the rulers of the realms themselves. On the one hand, the believer has in him the principle of righteousness. He is declared to be righteous by God; he has recieved the gift of the Holy Spirit, who now will produce righteousness in his life, or obedience to the will of God, and his desire and purpose are to possess such righteousness. On the other hand, the unbeliever is lawless, and lawlessness, or disobedience, is the principle underlying and governing his life. These inner qualities reveal a world of difference between the two kinds of people. How incongruous to try to bring both under the same yoke! In the second question Paul suggests the powers which produce these qualities in the individual, namely, light and darkness. We are told that God Himself is light and in Him is no darkness at all, that Christ is the true light, the light which lighteth every man that cometh into the world, and the light of the world. This light is the Divine saving truth, which has its source in God and is revealed in the Word. A righteous individual is a child of the light, walks in the light and manifests the light. Darkness, however, speaks of Satan, of error and of evil. They who do evil love darkness because their deeds are evil. Therefore, the lawless are the children of darkness. Paul said, "Ye were sometimes darkness, but now are ye light in the Lord." We are to have no fellowship with the unfruitful works of darkness. Third, Paul mentioned those persons who are the princes of these two realms, Christ and Belial. There are actually two world systems, that which is of Christ, righteous and spiritual, and that which is of Satan, evil and corrupt.

These two realms are in constant conflict. This conflict is not evidenced in the midst of the common amenities of life, but it is, nevertheless, deep, terrible and abiding. The world is at enmity to God. The time will come when this conflict will be out in the open and evident to all. Then it will become a war to the death. Those who hate God will persecute believers even to death. Many are the passages in the Bible which foretell this terrible conflict, called the tribulation. Meanwhile, because of the limiting and hindering power of The Holy Spirit, this conflict breaks out only sporadically in the open. Under which power or ruler do you live? Are you regenerate or unregenerate? Are you of light or darkness? Are you of righteousness or lawlessness? You may be a regenerate man born of the light and yet temporarily give your allegiance to evil, which is what is referred to in this passage of Scripture.

The rational action of a believer in relation to evil, either of person or of thing, is to separate himself from it. We must not forget that this teaching is to believers, to those who are already children, who comprise what is called the spiritual temple of God. In the exhortation Paul includes himself and his associates by saying, "Let us cleanse ourselves" and "we are the temple of the living God." Such believers are not to go out of the world. They are to remain in the world but not be of the world. They may have daily association and contact with the world and yet be different from that world. We have said that the term "world" means the scheme of things which is under Satan and which is opposed to God. This scheme of things is upheld by brute force, and quarrels in relation to it are decided only by force. It is true that there is a common ground of association with unbelievers and believers, though they need not be yoked together. They may do business with one another. They may sit side by side in many meetings. They may enjoy all the ordinary amenities of life together, but they must not be yoked together in the common purpose of life. The Bible teaching is that men are good or bad fundamentally and not that they are both good and bad with no one able to tell the exact proportion of either. The popular attitude represents all men as good and bad, but the Biblical teaching says that the tendency of a man's life is either good or bad and it depends upon his attitude toward God.

Separation, therefore, means that we are to come out from unclean organizations and we are not to touch that which is unclean. The Bible does not give us a list of the things which are unclean, but we are led to believe that everything contrary to the righteousness of Christ, to the faith and to the light of the Word is unclean. People often write and ask if it is necessary for them to leave a church in which the teaching is unbelieving. Personally, I cannot see how any one can support a program which is dedicated to that which is contrary to God's Word. John the Beloved declared, "he that biddeth Godspeed" to such teachers partaketh of their iniquities. When a church or an organization has gone irreparably to that which is anti-Christian it is time for the believer to separate himself from it. Whenever a lesser question arises, range it on one side or the other of the Cross according to its correct position, whether it is on Christ's side or Satan's side, and then choose between. This may cost one much in the way of sorrow, disappointment and tears, but he ought to be willing to do it for the sake of his Lord.

II. THE MOTIVE OF HOLINESS

The motive of obtaining a standard of holiness in life consists of the promises which God hath given to us. He said that He would dwell with us, that He would receive us and that He would be a Father to us.

The first consists of an incentive to holiness under the teaching of the new temple. There is a progressive promise of God's dwelling with men in the Bible. When we first see God's presence among men it is in the meeting place with Adam in the garden of Eden, but this was lost by sin. Later God appeared to and visited the patriarchs at intermittent seasons. Then He traveled with His people Israel in a symbolic Divine Presence in the pillars of fire and cloud. Later yet, God manifested Himself in the tabernacle and temple with the Shekinah of glory. Finally, God tabernacled among men in the presence of Jesus Christ, but Jesus died and ascended into heaven. Now God tabernacles in His Church, in His people, by means of the Spirit given and shed abroad on the day of Pentecost. Paul attributes this promise to God Himself, although Moses wrote it, saying, "I will set my tabernacle among you: and my soul shall not abhor you. And I will walk among you, and will be your God, and ye shall be my people." Thus it is that God walks in the midst of His people today and will continue so to do until that vision seen of John, when the tabernacle of God will be among men and He shall walk with them and He shall be their God and they shall be His people. Therefore, it is absolutely incongruous that evil, either of flesh or of Spirit, should be permitted in this temple. "Know ye not that ye are the temple of the living God, ye are not your own, but have been bought with a price?" As the temple of Israel and even the temples of the heathen were zealously preserved holy, so we should zealously preserve the holiness of our own bodies and spirits.

This promise is an incentive to separation, for it holds forth the ideal of a new fellowship. God said, "I will receive you." We are not only to separate from something, but unto something. It is from sin and unto God. Let us not think of the negative, namely, what we give up and what we renounce for the sake of God. If we center our attention upon these things, we will think only of what we do. Let us center our attention upon the positive, namely, that which we are to receive. God tells us that He will receive us. We shall be acceptable unto Him and all the promises of grace shall be bestowed upon us. This means sonship with God. He said, "I will be a Father unto you, and ye shall be my sons and daughters." Sonship with God means more than being children. It means that we are enjoying the high rights and the blessings thereof, that we are the heirs of God, that we are entering into His wonderful privileges. Nobody can enjoy such authority in the things of God unless he is acceptable to God in the life which he lives. It is for this reason that God urges us who are already children, having been born again, so to live that we may enjoy the status of sons. David said, "God hath set apart him that is holy for himself." He has a peculiar interest in a holy person. He will be a father to him, hedging him in before and behind by His presence, preserving and keeping him in the midst of all the dangers and temptations of life that he might be the child of God, that he might enter in to the glories of sonship. This is a sufficient incentive to separation.

Yet there is implied one more motive to holiness, and that is the new brotherhood. This is the incentive to service. "Ye shall be my sons and daughters." When you abandon worldly fellowship you assume the heavenly family relationship. You enter into the bond of Christian union, the brotherhood of God. There is no brotherhood, no fraternal organization, no joining of an earthly group which is comparable to being a member of the family of God and to calling the children of God brothers and sisters. With this in mind, we do not find this teaching concerning separation from sin and from the world and evil to be so difficult. Therefore, let the Christian relationship be real and vital. Cold formalism, with a lack of fellowship in a church, will drive people into union with the world, into the yoke with unbelievers, but there are joys in the household of faith which are abiding. They are based upon a relationship that transcends any blood relationship of this world.

III. THE MEANS OF PERFECTING HOLINESS

Our text suggests three things in this matter of perfecting holiness. One is, we are to cleanse ourselves. Another is, we are to complete that which has already been begun, and the last is, we are to continue in the fear of the Lord. What does it mean when it says, "Let us cleanse ourselves from all filthiness of flesh and spirit"? And again we remind you that this refers to Christians. "Let us" involved Paul, his associates, as well as the Corinthians. These people have been made holy. They have been cleansed by the blood. They are clean. Jesus said to His disciples, "Ye are clean." He also added, "Ye are clean through the word which I have spoken unto you." Yet Jesus said that they had need to be washed and to be purged of that which would not contribute toward the fruitfulness of the vine. Even Christians need to be cleansed. They are to accomplish this by co-operating in keeping themselves from sin as well as in submitting to the ordinances of God. James says, "Pure religion . . . is this . . . to keep himself unspotted from the world." John adds, "whosoever is born of God sinneth not; but . . . keepeth himself and that wicked one toucheth him not." Christians are still in the flesh and they are assailed by the contamination of sin, by defilement, by temptation, by filthiness, but they are to keep themselves from all these.

Two realms of cleansing are suggested. One is the flesh and one is the spirit. Many keep themselves outwardly separated from sin in the things of the flesh. They do not commit adultery. They do not indulge in evil. They do not keep questionable company, but they fail in the things of the spirit. To keep one's spirit from being befouled is much more difficult than keeping one's body clean. Many Christians succumb to evil thoughts who would shrink from evil deeds. It is common to find Christians guilty of jealousy, of envy, of censoriousness, of slander, of evil speaking and sometimes even of foulness of thought. Here we are sure that many fail. God is just as displeased with these sins of the spirit as He is with those of the flesh. The sins of the spirit will keep one from fellowship with God, from a true sense of brotherhood in the church and from being a purified temple of God just as effectively as will overt acts of the flesh.

To "cleanse ourselves" means that we shall refuse to touch unclean things, that we will keep separate from that which defiles. Cleansing is an act of the will. It is the using of the means which are put at our disposal and it is within the power of each of us. Just as the courageous youth will turn his glass upside down at a dinner that he may not partake of liquor, so a believer will put evil thoughts away from him that he may not be defiled.

If we are to perfect holiness, we must complete that which has already been initiated. Christ is our sanctification. Therefore, we have been made holy in our acceptance of Christ and our being accepted by Him. In Him we are set apart and declared by God to be holy. Now the experience must become subjective. The will of God is our sanctification. This means our present experience of the sanctification which we already possess in Christ. This involves our yielding, our consecration, and we believe that it begins with a decision or with a great act of surrender. Entire sanctification is making the sanctification which we potentially have in Christ ours in reality.

That holiness is completed by our separation. This means giving up or renouncing all that is evil for the sake of Christ, and it involves a great crisis, but it begins a higher life qualitatively than one we have ever lived before. God has intended that we should be holy and God has provided this means of our sanctification. Victory over sin, then, is obtained by being filled with the Spirit. Only as God's Holy Spirit fills and controls us can we live this holy life constantly, free from wilful and known sin. The means of perfecting holiness are sanctification, separation and the Spirit-filled life.

All this must be continued "in the fear of God." The word "fear" is the same as that translated "terror" in the preceding chapter, and refers to the judgment. What is a terror for an unbeliever is just fear for the believer. The believer has an honest, godly fear of the Father, who is willing to chasten, purify and even punish His children that they might be corrected and purified. We suggest that we ought not to court the chastisement of the Father, but that we ought to cleanse ourselves lest we be judged of Him. Paul continued to do this all his life after his conversion. He pressed toward the mark of the high calling of God in Christ Jesus, not as though he were already perfect, but forgetting those things which were behind, he pressed on that he might apprehend that for which he was also apprehended of Christ. This fear is the begining of wisdom. It is the beginning of salvation and it is the beginning of holiness. It is because we fear God as well as love Him that we continue to cleanse ourselves from sins and separate ourselves therefrom.

This does not suggest a perfectionist attitude or outlook, because we know that there are many sins which we do of which we are not aware, sins of omission and sins of ignorance. None of us perfectly conforms to the Divine standard of holiness, but within our ability by grace and under the power of the Spirit we may have victory over known sins and we are convinced that the Bible so teaches and demands that we are to live a holy life. To live lower than this is to deny ourselves the privilege of Divine fellowship and the blessings of Divine brotherhood.

XX

REPENTANCE UNTO SALVATION

TEXT: *"For godly sorrow worketh repentance to salvation not to be repented of: but the sorrow of the world worketh death."*—II COR. 7:2-12.

PAUL SAID, "I made you sorry with a letter." In explaining this letter we must beg your indulgence for a brief but necessary review of Paul's relationship to this particular church. Remember, he was the father of the Corinthian Church. He first preached the Gospel to them, won them from heathenism and established them by the Gospel in grace. Great were his labors, his sufferings, his love and his interest in and for them. It is evident that the relationship of Paul and this Corinthian Church was more intimate than usual. He says, "Ye are in our hearts to die and to live with." It almost appears that Paul was married to this church, for he carried the names and faces of these converts with him in his heart, praying for them and desiring God's best for them.

Yet these Corinthian Christians were not always obedient children, accepting the will of their spiritual father. Some of them challenged his authority, made accusations against him and even attempted to pervert the Corinthian Church from the doctrine and deeds taught by the Apostle. Philosophical speculations made their way into the teaching of this church and decided aberrations were manifested in their actions. We need not reiterate what these were. They were sufficient, however, to divide the church and to undermine its testimony. From these false teachers and usurpers Paul urged the Corinthians to separate themselves. From their evil practices he urged them to cleanse themselves and for their general Christian lives he desired that they should perfect holiness in the fear of the Lord. Moreover, this plea was joined with a previous invitation for them to open their hearts to him and Timothy, recognizing them as the true ministers and apostles of the Lord. Paul had thus opened his heart unto them. He had declared his love for them and had completely revealed his motives and desires in reference to the work at Corinth. Thus he begins this chapter with the words, "Receive us; we have wronged no man, we have corrupted no man, we have defrauded no man. I speak not this to condemn you: for I have said before, that ye are in our hearts to die and to live with you."

The interruption in this close fellowship was due to the necessity of Paul's disciplining the church. A number of exceedingly hideous things had occurred in the Corinthian Church which more or less were incursions of heathenism into the practice of the Christian community. One was a case of incest. To test their general obedience to the truth and to his apostolic authority Paul singled out this case and demanded that the Corinthians should exercise discipline over the individual in order to purify the church. He said, "I wrote unto you . . . not for his cause that had done the wrong, nor for his cause that suffered wrong, but that our care for you in the sight of God might appear unto you." Therefore, there is no need for our tarrying on this particular case. It was merely the means by which Paul intended to awaken the church from its indifference, to call the Christians back to their first love and to urge them on to the self-cleansing so necessary for holiness. For this purpose he wrote a severe and condemnatory letter on the basis of his apostolic authority, promising discipline and punishment unless there was reformation within the church. The whole attitude and outlook of the church was changed by this letter, as we have seen.

The Corinthian Christians repented and with great indignation and zeal excommunicated this grievously sinning member, cleansed themselves from all irregularities of conduct and worship and proceeded to put their church in order according to the word of the Apostle. But during the interim between the sending of the letter and the return of Titus bringing the news concerning the reaction of the Corinthian Christians, Paul was not without uneasiness. He awaited the results of these stringent measures on his part with considerable trepidation. He speaks about his condition in Macedonia as being one when his flesh had no rest, when he was troubled on every side, having fightings without and fears within, which state was relieved by the coming of Titus with his report. Titus had been Paul's appointed representative to initiate and superintend this reform in the Corinthian Church. Paul himself intended to come on to Corinth via Macedonia after he had strengthened and ministered to the churches along the way. Titus, in turn, was to return to him as soon as possible to report the reaction of the Corinthians to his strong measures of rebuke. The arrival of Titus after long delay brought immense consolation and comfort to the Apostle. He immediately sat down to write the second letter and began it with the words, "Blessed be God, even the Father of our Lord Jesus Christ, the Father of mercies, and the God of all comfort; who comforteth us in all our tribulation, that we may be able to comfort them which are in any trouble, by the comfort wherewith we ourselves are comforted of God." He added, "God, that comforteth those that are cast down, comforteth us by the coming of Titus." Not only the fact that Titus was safe, that no harm had fallen to him along the way, but also the news from Corinth comforted Paul's soul. He learned from the report of Titus of their earnest desire for his coming, their mourning over his criticism and their fervent attitude toward him as the father of the church. Their repentance had been complete and now it merely remained for Paul to establish the full reconciliation.

This incident of sin and repentance by the Corinthians gave Paul opportunity for some clear teaching on the question of sorrow unto repentance, which, in turn, leads to salvation. In this passage we behold the three "Rs" of sorrow. First, regret, which is sorrow according to self. Second, remorse, which is sorrow according to the world. And third, repentance which is sorrow according to God.

I. REGRET—SORROW ACCORDING TO SELF

Speaking of this letter which made them sorry, Paul said, "I do not repent [regret], though I did repent [regret]." Here is a candid admission by Paul that during the interim of silence on the part of the Corinthian Church he did regret his action in sending such a severe and condemnatory letter as the first epistle to the Corinthians. This leads us to consider an experience of the Apostle Paul which is very suggestive of many of our own experiences.

It is the keystone of Paul's later epistles concerning the central outlook of the Christian that he should be anxious in nothing, that he should be content in all things, that he should have a perfect confidence in God. We find this teaching particularly in the fourth chapter of Philippians, one of Paul's prison epistles. There we read:

"Be careful for nothing; but in everything by prayer and supplication with thanksgiving let your requests be made known unto God. And the peace of God, which passeth all understanding, shall keep your hearts and minds through Christ Jesus . . . I have learned, in whatsoever state I am, therewith to be content. I know both how to be abased, and I know how to abound: everywhere and in all things I am instructed both to be full and to be hungry, both to abound and to suffer need. I can do all things through Christ which strengtheneth me."

It is true that this teaching came at the end of Paul's life, after he had suffered exceedingly and about the time he was ready to write, "I have fought a good fight, I have finished the course, I have kept the faith: Henceforth there is laid up for me a crown of righteousness." But each of us must admit that this is a wonderful state in which to be. For one to depend only on prayer, to fasten his mind upon the things which are true, honest, just, pure, lovely and of good report, to be content whatever occurs to him in life and to be empowered by Christ to endure and to do all things is truly wonderful. This high state of life corresponds exactly with what Jesus taught in the Sermon on the Mount. There He told us that we were to take no anxious thought for the morrow, that we were to seek first the kingdom of God and His righteousness, that the evil of each day was sufficient unto itself and that we should never think of the evils of tomorrow until they come. Unquestionably this calmness is a Biblical standard for the Christian.

But here, strangely, we find in the greatest of all apostles anxiety, concern and worry clearly manifested. Paul admits that in Troas a door was open to him to preach the Gospel, but that he was so distressed and anxious because he did not find Titus his brother at Troas that he refused to enter the door which was open and left for Macedonia without preaching. How unusual such an action was for Paul. He also repeats twice that his flesh knew no rest during this time. He was agitated, anxious and worried. The cause, no doubt, was Titus' safety, and well might one be anxious in those days concerning the safety of his son in the Lord, for there were many dangers along the way, but probably Paul was just as worried concerning the condition of the Corinthian Church and their reaction to his epistle. This we could call spiritual worry or anxiety, and he had good reason for it, too. And then, finally, there was the worry or the anxiety concerning his impending visit to Corinth. Would they receive him? Would they have repented, or would great loss come to the Church of Christ through the strong hand which he had laid upon that church?

If worry of this kind is sin, then Paul sinned. He freely admitted that his fears for the results of the letter caused him to regret that he had written it. Perhaps you have never been in that condition, but I imagine that Paul first thought of one possibility, that of a favorable response by the Corinthians; then he thought of the other possibility, that of rebellion by these Corinthians, until he was in a state of utter mental distress. This immediately raises the question,

How can such an attitude on the part of the Apostle be reconciled with the teaching that Paul wrote that letter under the inspiration of the Holy Spirit? If it was the inspiration of the Holy Spirit, why did he worry? Can a man do something at the commandment of God and then regret that he has done it? We unquestionably say that he can. Paul's inspiration did not extend to all of his actions and thoughts and temptations and sufferings. The doctrine of inspiration means merely that when he wrote his epistles it was under the inspiration of the Holy Ghost. Inspiration was enjoyed by Paul as he wrote the first epistle to the Corinthians. This is unquestionable, but Paul was made of human flesh and was just like you and me. At times he was distressed and perplexed and worried. Here we see above all places in the Bible Paul's poor, human nature asserting itself and expressing itself in regret and worry. If this be sin and if this be falling below the Divine standards then in this case we unqualifiedly state that the Apostle sinned.

Is it possible then, for reasonable regrets to exist in Christian lives? Yes, it is not only possible, but probable for most of us. Think of the decisions we would make differently if we had a chance to make them over again today. Who is there among us who can say, "I have no regrets"? Such an attitude would demand perfect wisdom and perfect grace. How much more humble it is to admit candidly that we have made mistakes when we have. Such mistakes deal only with our ignorance and with our limitations, not necessarily with sin. The very fact that we can make them admits the fact of freedom. One of the greatest preachers whom I know once confided to me that in his early ministry he had made one terrible mistake. He had been a great success and had built up a congregation of two thousand members in a few years. God had wonderfully blessed his ministry and his church was strong, with great crowds every week. Then, however, he came to a disagreement with some of his officers and thought that he would force their hand by submitting his resignation. Much to his surprise, they accepted it. He, in turn, took another position, which was supposed to be a greater one, but his spirit so chafed under it that he soon had to give it up, and for two years there wasn't a door open to him to preach the Gospel anywhere. He said, "I would gladly have taken any mission had it been offered to me, but none was." This did not mean that he was permanently disapproved of the Lord, for he began again and today he has one of the most flourishing pulpits in America; but he freely admits that he made a mistake. There are things which we all regret today. As a nation we regret our unpreparedness. We regret that we listened to the pacifists. We regret Pearl Harbor. We regret the Philippines and Java, all of which might not have happened had we had a different outlook. Some of you as individuals regret changes which you have made in business, selling your home or failing to buy tires before the restriction. These things are not necessarily sins. They are merely mistakes in judgment.

Moreover, there often comes to us as individuals anxiety or worry comparable to that which Paul had in this case. Paul's anxiety dealt with the possibilities which were before him. There was the possible loss of the church. There was the possible danger to Titus. There was a possibility that he would have labored in vain. As he looked at these future possibilities he could not help but worry a bit. Who is there who is not in some measure worried over spiritual, material and personal affairs? I am not saying that you necessarily must worry. I am simply commenting on the fact that you do worry.

Thus it is obvious that Christians can, and do, both regret their past actions and worry about the future in life. They do this in face of the teaching of Romans 8:28, which says, "All things work together for good to them that love God, to them who are the called according to his purpose." Remember, Paul wrote those words some years after he wrote to the Corinthian Church. God may truly overrule our ignorance, our mistakes and our errors when they are not sins, and we think that He does; but we cannot help but think at times of what might have been. Paul showed how human, how much of mortal flesh he was, how similar to us he was. In each of us some of this remains, in spite of our Christian faith. Yet, as you glance at the narrative you recognize how unnecessary were Paul's worry and regret, as the outcome revealed. A calmness and unworried condition of the believer is far worthier than a state full of regret and misgiving.

Scripture has a great antidote for worry and fear. First, trust in God, such as Paul reveals in the Romans 8 and in Philippians 4. There he declares that all things work together for good, that no one can lay anything to the charge of God's elect, that nothing can separate him from the love of God, that the Christian should be anxious in nothing, that he himself had arrived at the place where he was content in all things. There he was not afraid of death, of physical hunger, of need. These things did not affect his contentedness, and he was even resigned to the effect of his labors on the churches. Perhaps this shows a growth in grace which came to Paul through his sufferings in Jerusalem, in the prison at Cæsarea and in Rome. Perhaps suffering is also necessary for us to produce almost supratemporal experience. For many of us the standard is far ahead, but it is there. Paul connected with it the great hope of the Lord's coming and the thought that the Lord is at hand will today be the means of buoying up our faith so that we are kept from worrying, regret and fear.

II. REMORSE—SORROW ACCORDING TO THE WORLD

The second "R" deals with something which goes beyond regret. This time it is "the sorrow of the world worketh death." We might define this sorrow called remorse as "the regret which deals with culpable sin and not with mistakes."

Remorse or sorrow, according to the world, is sorrow for the penal consequences of sin, not for the act or the motive which prompted the sin. Had the Corinthians merely manifested remorse they would have feared what Paul would do to them as an apostle. He had threatened to come to them with a rod, with the power of God, in contrast with the speech of those who are puffed up. He had delivered a decision concerning the guilty one, committing him to Satan for the destruction of the flesh, that his spirit might be saved in the day of the Lord Jesus. These were serious consequences of sin and excommunication might well be feared by the church. If the consequences of sin were happiness people would show no sorrow for sin, for worldly sorrow is based only on hurtful consequences. But even if sin were attended with happy consequences, it would still be sin to God, and because it was sin it should be followed by sorrow. Sorrow for the consequences of sin drives men to more sinful acts rather than to confession and restitution. They sin the more in order to cover up sin, to excuse themselves and to escape further consequences.

Worldly sorrow is stimulated by public exposure. If his sin did not become public the sinner would have no sorrow. His sorrow is not for his sin, but for the loss of his reputation. Many people have experienced no remorse for their misdeeds until they were exposed. Many suicides are a proof of this fact. Suicide usually follows not the wrong act but discovery of the guilt. It is also true that some people become hardened and develop into confirmed criminals through exposure who otherwise would remain tolerably happy. It is sometimes a mistake to think that an offender will repent if his error is hushed. Some blame the newspaper publicity for the fall and development of a criminal. True, remorse is caused by exposure, but if there is no exposure there would be no change of heart, but simply an untouched outward fear of loss of good reputation.

Remorse is usually caused by pride, not by true humility. Pride is of the world and when pride is humbled, worldly sorrow ensues. It is humiliating to give up one's self-esteem and confidence in the strength of his character. When the consequences of our individual and social sins become evident we often lose self-respect and sorrow over our humbling. We have had too much confidence in our ability of character. Today this confidence is being undermined by universal manifestations of depravity. Once a man has discovered that he is depraved, once his character deceives him, he is helpless to rebuild his life on a human plane. If he cannot turn to God his sorrow will be only that of remorse, and he will be confirmed in his sinfulness. Self-respect cannot be restored by merit, but only by forgiveness and transformation of character. Therefore, sorrow of remorse is only an emotional change, not a new choice. It refers to particulars and not to the entire life. It merely manifests regret for sin and not a reversal of one's moral purpose.

We are told that sorrow according to the world worketh death. This is its destiny. The nature of this death is that opposed to life or to salvation, which is the gift of God. Therefore, it is spiritual death. It is existence of the soul apart from God. It may be called punishment of hell or of the second death. This death, we are told, is the wages of sin. It is the result and the end of our wrong doing. The sorrows of remorse rather than hindering such a course work its inevitable claim. The evidence that death comes to one who has only remorseful sorrow for sin is his confirmation in sinful habits, his continuing as before. F. W. Robertson said, "The tears of pain are no sooner dry than the pleasures of ungodliness are renewed." The temporary reformation of remorse leaves the soul worse than before, but the day will come when the sorrows of death will stimulate the sorrows of remorse. They shall then become permanent. Jesus said, "There will be weeping and gnashing of teeth." The psalmist declared, "Many sorrows shall be to the wicked." Isaiah adds, "Pangs and sorrow shall lay hold of them in the day of the Lord." We may have experienced remorse here, but the remorse and sorrow to come will be permanent.

Glance at a few illustrations of such remorse given in the Scripture. These clearly reveal the sorrow for the consequences of sin which does not result in a change of life. First is Cain, who slew his brother Abel in the field. When questioned by the Lord concerning it, he answered, "Am I my brother's keeper?" When punished by the Lord because of this evil deed, his only sorrow was for the consequences of his deed. He complained, "My punishment is greater than I can bear. Behold, thou hast driven me out this day from the face of the earth; and from thy face shall I be hid; and I shall be a fugitive and a vagabond in the earth; and it shall come to pass, that every one that findeth me shall slay me." Cain did not repent. He was merely sorry for the consequences of his deed.

By the plagues Pharaoh of Egypt was again and again caused to suffer for sinful disobedience to the command of God. Finally, when most of the land had been consumed, Pharaoh sent for Moses and said, "I have sinned this time: the Lord is righteous, and I and my people are wicked. Entreat the Lord that there may be no more mighty thunderings and hail and I will let you go and ye shall stay no longer." Pharaoh admitted his sin only because of the consequences in the suffering of the land and the people. When the consequences were removed through Moses' prayer, Pharaoh continued in his oppression and rebellion.

Saul, the first king of Israel, was a man with great opportunities and splendid traits. He was quick to respond to the Divine warning, but he quickly turned to his own sins. When Samuel rebuked him for rejecting the Word of the Lord, he said, "I have sinned: Yet honor me now, I pray thee, before the elders of my people, and before Israel, and turn again with me, that I may worship the Lord thy God." But almost immediately he was disobeying the Lord again. Thrice Saul said, "I have sinned," and each time he returned to his old life of disobedience.

The case of Judas is probably the clearest illustration of remorse in the Bible. When he saw that his action had led to the condemnation of Jesus he repented, brought again the thirty pieces of silver to the chief priests, and cried, "I have sinned in that I have betrayed the innocent blood." Then he went out and hanged himself. Had Judas really repented he would not have ended in suicide. His sorrow was only according to the world, a remorse that would not save.

III. REPENTANCE—SORROW ACCORDING TO GOD

The third class of sorrow is "godly sorrow worketh repentance to salvation." Paul rejoiced that the Corinthians were made sorry after a godly manner. Such a sorrow is for the lack of sin and for the motive which caused the sin rather than for the consequences thereof. The way to produce this sorrow is to see the heinousness of sin as God sees it. This view of sin reveals it as a transgression of God's law, a defilement of the temple of the Holy Ghost and a rupture of the fellowship between God and the soul. Did not David take a man's wife, sin against her, against the husband and against his nation? Was he not guilty of murder and adultery? Yet when David confessed his sin, he cried, "Against thee and thee only have I sinned," in referring to the Lord. The Bible does not underestimate the injury and the hurt which sin causes to our fellow men, but all the social and moral obligations of life are founded on God's holy law. Because David had so sinned against humanity he had terribly sinned against God. Therefore he correctly confessed it as against God. A contrition which deals with the motive and the sin has an element of hope mixed in the bitterness of anguish. Peter had terribly failed in his loyalty to Christ. Perhaps it was the hurt look in the eyes of the Master that broke his heart. At any rate, he squarely faced his sin of denying his Lord and went out and wept bitterly. That very narration of Peter's sorrow gives us hope that Peter will be converted again. Contrition, then, is genuine in the exact proportion that God is in it. If your sorrow for your sins is caused by the word of God, is wrought in you by the Spirit of God and is according to the will of God, then it will end in the glory of God, which will be your forgiveness and restoration.

True contrition works repentance. Contrition or sorrow alone will not save. Contrition joined with faith equals repentance. It is the element of faith in God joined with your sorrow for your sins that leads you to repent and to come to life. Such repentance will cause reformation. It produces a change of life, an alteration of habits, a renewal of heart. The old man is put off and the new man is put on. Glance at the list of actions caused in the Corinthians by their godly sorrow:

"Behold this selfsame thing, that ye sorrowed after a godly sort, what carefulness it wrought in you, yea, what clearing of yourselves, yea, what indignation, yea, what fear, yea, what vehement desire, yea, what zeal, yea, what revenge! In all things ye have proved yourselves to be clear in this matter."

Their reformation was so complete that they utterly cleared themselves in the matter of condoning aberrations and heresies in the church itself. Here is an utter change of life and outlook. Remorse never produces such a reformation of life. True contrition, therefore, results in the renunciation of evil. If sorrow is genuine, it will deter us from doing evil. The cause of this sorrow may at first be corrective, but if we continue in the evil it will gradually take on more and more of a penal aspect. "In worldly sorrow the heartaches and trials come in vain. They do not change us. . . . In the proportion as repentance increases, grief diminishes." Therefore, if you wish relief from your sorrow, let it lead you to true repentance. You may experience grief for a time, but it will be repentance forever. Thus Paul could say, "I rejoice, not that you were made sorry, but that ye sorrowed to repentance." The joy which was stimulated in the heart of Paul is also declared to be stimulated among the angels of heaven over one sinner who repenteth.

This repentance is unregrettable because it works life. The Scripture says, "Godly sorrow worketh repentance to salvation not to be repented of." This last "repent" is the word "regret." Godly sorrow of repentance insures that no damage is wrought to the soul by the stringency of the Gospel message. These Corinthians received damage in no way by Paul's strong words and threats in the Gospel, because they repented. Sometimes we as individuals are tempted to comfort and dissuade those who come under the conviction and intense contrition for sin in their disturbed, sorrowful, anguished and exceedingly unbalanced condition. We want to comfort them and turn them from their anguish, but this we should not do. Let them alone. They will not receive damage by this. It will rather lead them to conversion. The deeper the sorrow, the more thorough will be the conversion. Such sorrow will do much good for the establishment of the soul.

Deep sorrow, then, leading to repentance will never be regretted. One might regret the necessity of repentance and giving up sin, but he will never regret, once he has done it, for repentance, when it is thorough, leads us to salvation or the gift of eternal life. That is why the promise of salvation in the Bible is conditioned upon repentance. Repent and be baptized and ye shall receive the gift of the Holy Ghost. The soul's sorrow for sin is forgotten in the birth of a new life. Jesus said, "Ye shall be made sorrowful, but your sorrow shall be turned into joy." Such sorrow is like that of a woman in travail who forgets her anguish in the joy that a child is born into the world.

True sorrow for sin is temporary, but for an hour, whereas the joy of salvation is eternal. Who would not subject himself to such contrition for the sake of salvation? Therefore, thank God for the sorrow and conviction wrought in your soul by the Word, by the Spirit and by the rebuke of true preaching. Take steps to relieve this sorrow by repentance and faith. Convert, confess and commit yourself to God.

A young woman wrote to me:

"I have been an unhappy person, trying for many years to be a good Christian and I even know that the Lord was with me and guided me as far as I allowed Him, but there was one sin that I did not have strength to give up. A short time ago, God let something terrible happen to me. It was like a deep operation. I almost think that my soul was dead for a few seconds. Now I have a very clear picture of the situation. It was the one and only thing that could throw me completely out of that state.

"As soon as I realized why it happened and made up my mind that from now on I am free and God is going to have every corner of my heart, I received a wonderful strength, peace and harmony and the suffering was over before I even knew it.

"I write this to you because it might help somebody else who is unhappy. May you always be a channel of the Holy Spirit to take from Him and give to others.

"A very happy girl."

You have been sorrowful. Let your sorrow lead you to repentance. Be not like the rich young ruler who when he learned the way of life, turned away sorrowfully. His sorrow was according to the world and it wrought for him death.

XXI

A MAN WHOSE PRESENCE WAS A COMFORT

TEXT: *"God, that comforteth those that are cast down, comforted us by the coming of Titus."*—II COR. 7:13-16; 8:16-24.

IN THIS SECTION of II Corinthians there are eight references by St. Paul to Titus, in most instances connected with the comfort which Titus brought to Paul. It is hardly possible for us to pass over these references without more detailed mention of Titus.

The first view we get of Titus is in Acts 15, where he is included in the phrase, "certain other of them," referring to the persons who went with Paul and Barnabas from Antioch to Jerusalem for the first apostolic conference. The last reference is made by St. Paul from the Roman prison, just before his death, revealing that Titus was his obedient servant performing a mission in Dalmatia.

Paul called Titus "mine own son after the common faith." We first read his name in Galatians 2:1. This reference may be identified with the journey taken over the Judaistic controversy to the apostolic conference at Jerusalem, which proved so important as to the fundamental nature of the Christian Gospel. Of the early life and conversion of Titus, we know very little. He was probably one of Paul's converts at Antioch in Syria during the revival which occurred under the ministry of Paul and Barnabas before the first missionary journey. It is referred to in Acts 11:26. Nothing describes that revival better than the brief word of Luke, "The disciples were first called Christians at Antioch." Out of their lewd, heathen, corrupt background, the Christians because of their worship of Christ and conformity of life unto Christ began to be called by his name. Titus was one of those converts. Tradition relates him to high-born persons of Crete, where he later became bishop. That he was a Greek of Gentile parents is clear from Paul's words, "Neither Titus, who was with me, being a Greek, was compelled to be circumcised." Titus and Timothy were often grouped together, but Timothy was a Jew and was compelled to be circumcised in conformity with the Jewish law, whereas Titus became the test case of legalism in the Early Church because he was a Gentile.

Titus was one of a number of young men gathered around St. Paul in this early work of the church. Others included Silas, Mark, Timothy, Trophimus, Tychicus, Luke, and Demas. In his epistle to Titus, Paul said, "Let no man despise thee," implying the youth of this Christian worker. The same words were used of Timothy when Paul said, "Let no man despise thy youth." Out of this large group of young men commended to the Gospel ministry, we have record of only two disappointments, one of John Mark, and the other of Demas, but Mark later proved himself to be profitable to St. Paul in the ministry, and thus redeemed his former failure. We have cause to wonder at the way in which God keeps calling young men into His service. We need not worry concerning a lack of able men to conduct the ministry of the Gospel. Wherever that Gospel is preached, the call to the ministry of the Word will be heard by young men.

When speaking of Titus, we must consider how Paul made him the test case of the Gospel. At Antioch, Judaizers disputed the way of salvation as preached by St. Paul. They added something to the Gospel of grace, saying "Except ye be circumcised, ye cannot be saved." Paul believed that this would again enslave men to the keeping of the law, whereas Christ has delivered us from the law as a means of salvation. This threatened the entire Gospel, and the controversy of salvation by grace versus salvation by works rent the church at Antioch so that an appeal had to be made to a higher authority, and the brethren decided to carry the case to Jerusalem. This error also spread throughout the mission fields of Galatia, Ephesus, Corinth, and far-away places. It necessarily had to be settled.

Paul calls this another gospel which is not another and attributed it to false brethren privily brought into the church. The same error has wrought much havoc in the history of Christianity, manifesting itself in the doctrine of salvation by works in the sacerdotal branches of Christianity and in modern tendencies toward character salvation.

We are happy at the settlement arrived at by the Jerusalem Council. It involved an agreement by all apostles that St. Paul's Gospel was their Gospel. They added nothing to his Gospel, and they extended to him the right hand of Christian fellowship, as the second chapter of Galatians reveals. Titus, the Greek, was not compelled to be circumcised. The other apostles enjoined Paul to remember the poor, which he was actually doing in this passage which we are studying. Hence, the Biblical doctrine of justification by faith alone will forever be associated with the name of Titus, which ought to make him a comfort to us as he was to St. Paul.

Paul variously calls Titus "my brother," "my partner," "my fellow helper," revealing that he is his colaborer in the Gospel. In a remarkable way we find that Titus was connected with the great conflicts and crises in St. Paul's life. We have seen that in the conflict with the Judaizers at Jerusalem he was a test case. In conflict with the elements of insubordination at Corinth, he was Paul's messenger and representative. Apparently, Timothy and Apollos both refused this disagreeable task. Paul specifically says that it was not the mind of Apollos at all to come to the Corinthians at that particular time. We have every reason to believe that Titus carried the first letter to Corinth, exercised discipline over the rebelling elements in the congregation, and then returned to St. Paul to report before taking the second letter back to the Corinthians. This may give us some insight into the character of Titus. He was a strong disciplinarian. The same fact is revealed by the connection of Titus in the conflict with undisciplined elements in the church at Crete. Cretans were unsteady, insincere, and quarrelsome. They were given to greediness, licentiousness, falsehood, and drunkenness. There were certain individuals who spoke against the Gospel who wrought confusion in the church and interjected error. Hence, Paul appointed Titus to stop the mouths of gainsayers, to set things in order, and to establish sound doctrine as against the Judaizers. It was a great comfort to Paul to have such a colaborer on whom he could depend in the great difficulties of the Early Church. By this we learn to understand the deep love which developed in St. Paul for this son and brother in the faith.

From this relationship, certain patent facts are evident to us. We learn that God comforts us by people. We learn why people like Titus are used to comfort others, and we learn how God may make you a comfort unto the brethren.

I. God Comforts Us by People

There is a time when every person needs comfort, when things are not going just right, when discouragement enters, when the old human body influences the mind and the spirit. The cause of Paul's anxieties and worries, and we must admit that he was anxious here, was the Corinthians' the deflection from the faith, manifesting itself in many aberrations in character and conduct. Paul also had passed through physical trials in which he despaired of his own life, but he did not worry over these, for he was delivered out of them by God. It must be admitted that our physical condition does have much to do with our mental balance and our spiritual outlook. It has been proved that a glandular condition sometimes creates mental unbalance and even criminal tendencies. Lombroso's studies in criminology have progressively attempted to prove that murderers are physiologically different from others, and that there is not the slightest hope of their improvement. Sickness, loneliness, perplexity, a sense of impotence, nervousness, and frustration do affect one's mental and spiritual outlook. If your prayers seem insipid, if your moral strength is low, if you have no desire to do good, it may be due to your physical condition. Exactly in the same manner one's spiritual condition often affects one's physical condition. Some exhilaration will quicken your mental powers. Our physical, mental, and spiritual condition is in a measure coinclusive. It is good to know that you are not necessarily backslidden when you are cast down in spirit. There are lights and shadows in the Christian life as in all other life.

Consider situations which call for comfort. The psalmist says, "Why art thou cast down, oh, my soul?" Perhaps that soul was cast down by trial, temptation, or defeat. When Jesus suffered temptation and won a victory over it, He needed to be ministered to by angels. Victorious or defeated, you need comfort in the hour of temptation. Paul speaks of God who comforts the lowly, that is, the humble. We are living in a time when the meek of the earth seem to be fatally wrong, in spite of the teaching of Jesus, and the lowly need comfort from God. Sinners who have been wounded by the Spirit, brought under conviction, need to find the balm of Gilead, to have their broken hearts bound, and to be comforted by the Spirit, for "the way of the transgressor is hard."

If you would give comfort to others, you must first be comforted. The fact that Titus had been encouraged, strengthened in the faith, and comforted by the Corinthians made him a source of comfort and joy to the Apostle Paul. There is a parallel between this and the means of salvation. The first principle of soul-winning is that you must be saved in order to win other men. How necessary it is for us to seek and find the comfort of God for the sake of the needy multitudes seeking comfort today.

Paul entitles God with the words "God who comforteth the lowly." Contrast this with the false sources of comfort sought by a worried world. Once men believed in a Maginot line. Then they sought refuge behind a fleet, then in money; later, in their homes; but all these things have proved to be temporal and transient and no defense for the soul. Men have learned that simply forgetting by pleasure and indulgence gives no comfort to the soul. No human philosophy, practice, or place is a permanent refuge for the soul.

The true source of comfort is God. Great is God's faithfulness. He is sovereign and sufficient. By acknowledging and recognizing His authority and law, by being on God's side, we may know that we shall prevail. God's will is to comfort His people—if they will be comforted.

The means of God's comforting us is by the Holy Spirit, whom Jesus called "the Comforter." He Himself comes to abide with us, to help us, to guide us, to enlighten us, and to deliver us. The Spirit of God is the great antidote for our discouragement, weakness, and impotence. When we have grieved the Spirit by sin, comfort must be given to us by another servant who is yielded to the Holy Spirit of God.

This comfort is given by God's people. God comforts us by the truth given from faithful preachers. Nothing can supplant the preaching of the truth. It deals with every realm of life; knowledge of the great doctrines of revelation establish one in Christ. God comforts us by a word given in due season from fellow believers. Like apples of gold in pictures of silver, such words steady, rebuke, exhort, instruct, assist, and are altogether fitting. A hand laid upon one's shoulder, a visit to a sick-room, a greeting from an acquaintance may be the means of comfort in the hour of need. There is a mutual strengthening of Christians by the faith one of another. God also comforts us by some courageous stand on a moral issue made by a single individual when others are wavering. Hence, we are told to lift up the hands that hang down and to strengthen the feeble knees. We are to be a comfort one to another.

II. Why God Used Titus as a Comfort to Paul

Titus was a comfort to Paul because of his joy. Paul said, "We were comforted in your comfort: yea, and exceedingly the more joyed we for the joy of Titus, because his spirit was refreshed by you all." Joy or depression of life is communicable and contagious. One immediately feels the difference when he passes from the presence of a friend with pessimistic outlook to the presence of a friend with optimistic outlook. The Corinthians had refreshed and comforted Titus. Titus refreshed and comforted Paul. Paul became a source of comfort to others. And thus the chain led on endlessly. The experience of joy communicated by Titus to Paul even led Paul to boast to Titus of these Corinthian Christians. We must never forget the prominent place given to joy in the Christian life. We are commanded to rejoice evermore, to be anxious in nothing, to remember that "sufficient unto the day is the evil thereof." Anxiety, regret, and worry must be far in the minority in the Christian experience. God cannot use you effectively unless your spirit is joyful. Christian cheer has an inestimable value; hence, "rejoice evermore," "In everything give thanks," and experience the joy which is the gift of the Holy Spirit.

Titus comforted Paul's heart because of his sympathy. He speaks of Titus' inward affection for the Corinthians and "the same earnest care in the heart of Titus for you." Here was a deep affection of a servant of the Lord for His people. None of us can will to have this affection. It must be God-given. It must come through our seeing with Divine eyes the good which is in His people and overlooking the evil. To have a deep affection for attractive and loving people is one thing, but to have affection for rebellious and sinful people is something quite different. Can you love the outcast with the love of Christ? This is what Christianity means. We must have the same kind of affection, compassion, and interest for men which Christ had. He was moved by the sick, the outcast, the untaught, because they were as sheep without a shepherd.

Titus had "an earnest concern" for the Corinthians. Feigned sympathy is repulsive because of its hypocrisy. When Absolom, the son of David, stood at the gate and feigned a love for the people by greeting them with a kiss, and saying, "O that I were made judge in the land, that every man which hath any suit or cause might come unto me, and I would do him justice," he was hypocritically attempting to win the hearts of men for an ulterior motive. An honest concern reveals the heart of a man. Titus' desire and purpose was for their welfare and spiritual growth. Into every child of God this earnest concern for others ought in a measure to come. Great is the contrast between this and the common attitude of each person living to himself.

Because of this affection and concern, Titus became a means of grace in the Corinthians, so that they were ready to act in accordance with God's will. Paul said, "We desired Titus, that as he had begun, so he would also finish in you the same grace also." God had stimulated their willingness to give of their substance for the poor saints at Jerusalem through Titus, so that their action became a definite means of grace.

Titus comforted Paul because of his fellowship. Paul describes him as "my brother and partner." The relationship between these two was very close. Though a younger man, Titus used that fellowship for good, for comfort and blessing of his father in the faith. Close relationships often cover up irritability, gloominess, and sulkiness. We sometimes think that we can give vent to these disagreeable emotions when we are in the presence of relatives or close friends. Here, however, is your first and greatest opportunity for service. If Christianity does not stand the test of the family, it is useless outside the family.

When partnership is enjoyed, the burdens are halved. There is what is called the fellowship of suffering, the fellowship of service, the fellowship of life, the fellowship of the Gospel, and this fellowship is precious. We are social creatures. We need one another. It is not good for us to be alone. Titus shared the difficult undertakings with St. Paul, and St. Paul shared his joys with Titus. And vice versa. That fellowship must be based upon righteousness.

This is also the standard for a good marriage. Within the unique fellowship of the family one has a peculiar opportunity to bring comfort to others. Only let it be the comfort of God.

III. How God May Make You a Comfort to the Brethren

By examining the epistle of Paul to Titus and learning what Titus did at the command of St. Paul, we see the source of his being a comfort. Three major things are apparent. He was a comfort to the brethren by setting in order the things that were wanting, by speaking things which become sound doctrine, and by setting a good example or pattern of conduct.

Titus remained in Crete after Paul departed, in order to complete what the apostle had left undone. It is difficult to place this journey of St. Paul to Crete. It certainly could not have occurred when he traveled as a prisoner to Rome. The only other time in the recorded narrative of Paul's journeys would have been on his return from the second missionary journey, postulating that one of his shipwrecks occurred at this time so as to compel him to stop at Crete and Ephesus. The most logical place is to project a journey between two imprisonments at Rome. Then Paul would have been released from his first imprisonment, have visited Crete, and have left for Miletus, and Nicopolis where he was taken prisoner and again rushed to Rome. Paul had no rest in mind while the work in Crete was left undone. Thus it was a great comfort to depend upon Titus to complete the organization of the churches in apostolic order and to ordain elders to continue the work.

That Titus fulfilled this commission is witnessed by tradition, which says he became the Bishop of Crete and was buried at Candia. In a fragment called "The Life and Acts of Titus," by Zenos, Titus is called the Bishop of Gortyna, and a ruin exists there of ancient masonry called the Church of St. Titus.

Nothing is more comforting in Christian work than for the brethren to know that when some one accepts a position or responsibility he will see it through. It may be ushering, teaching a class, conducting a boys' club, serving on a committee, or some other responsibility. But see it through. It is a comfort to the Lord to have servants who are faithful in prayer or in work, on whom He may depend. Dependability and accuracy are of much more value than brilliance and speed. When many things which are wanting in the Church are set in order, it brings comfort to the brethren. Those who walk in Titus' footsteps will be a comfort.

Titus was to speak things which become sound doctrine. There evidently was a great prevalence of error in Crete which needed refutation. The Cretians had a natural propensity for lying, laziness, gluttony, and un-control. They were a prey to the propaganda of the Judaizers. They listened to unbelieving gainsayers who contradicted the Gospel. But Crete had no monopoly on such persons.

Sound doctrine, as taught by Titus in accordance with Paul's epistle, was to call for essential piety on the part of all ages and classes of men in the church, to hold before them the incentive and hope of Christ's personal coming, called the "appearing of the Great God and our Saviour Jesus Christ," to declare the simple, substitutionary atonement as the means of redemption from all iniquity, and to expound justification by faith through the washing of regeneration and the renewal of the Holy Spirit.

Added to the duty of teaching sound doctrine was the responsibility to rebuke sharply, to refute, to exhort, and to reject heretics. Such practices are largely absent from our present church, and leave us comfortless concerning the outlook for the church.

Lastly, Titus was to show himself a pattern of good works in all things; with purity, gravity, and sincerity, he was to live so that opponents could have nothing evil to say of him. Great was the contrast between what Titus and the Cretians once were. Paul acknowledges in his letter, "We ourselves also were sometimes foolish, disobedient, deceived, serving divers lusts and pleasures, living in malice and envy, hateful, and hating one another." But he declares that from these things Christ had saved them. Thus, by example and precept, Titus was to urge all to live as becometh holiness and to be ready unto every good work. Paul affirmed, "I will that thou affirm constantly, that they which have believed in God might be careful to maintain good works."

Such was Titus, the man whose presence was a comfort to Paul. Why should such a man leave Paul in prison and go to Dalmatia? We presume that he went, as commanded, to Necopolis, where Paul had determined to winter, that he went with Paul, when arrested, to Rome, that he comforted him there for a season till duty in the church called him elsewhere, namely, to Dalmatia. Then, as a stern disciplinarian and as a faithful colaborer of St. Paul, his absence in the performance of duty became a greater comfort to him than his presence in the prison would have been. Titus will always be known as the man whose presence was a comfort to the apostle.

XXII

MOTIVATING YOUR MERCIES

TEXT: *"Show ye . . . before the churches the proof of your love, and of our boasting on your behalf."*—II COR. 8:1-15; 9:1-5.

THIS IS THE LONGEST passage in the New Testament on the subject of motivation in giving. This was called forth by a great need in the Jerusalem Church, either because of famine or because of persecution.

There are two kinds of mercies. First are the mercies of God, which are primarily spiritual. Paul said, "I beseech you, brethren, by the mercies of God . . .," by which he referred to the great truths of redemption. But there are also physical mercies. There are mercies which we manifest to others. The performance of such deeds of mercy by the believer reveals that he has caught the spirit of Christ. Once being the recipients of salvation mercies, we must take the attitude of the good Samaritan and manifest mercy. Many are these mercies to be performed by the Christian.

Today, we sit at the feet of him who thoroughly understood what God has done for us, and who did much for others, namely, St. Paul. This passage from his pen is a great plea for liberality. St. Paul here manifests that Christian converts should be educated to learn that giving is part of their Christian service. He taught the truths of stewardship to the Macedonians, the Achaians, and to the Asiatics. The Macedonian report from Philippi had been brought by Epaphroditus. They entered the fellowship of giving. Now, it was Paul's intention that the Corinthians should be forward to do God's will in this matter of stewardship. There was nothing selfish in Paul's preaching on giving. In fact, he worked as a tent-maker to support himself. He had taken nothing from Corinth, and hence he could request Corinth to give unto others.

The secret of Christian giving rests in motivation. Motivation is now a popular subject in modern education. We speak of motivated versus unmotivated learning. We kindle in the child an interest in botany, in geology, and similar subjects by a project of investigation for the child, thus motivating learning by his interest. Motivation is just as valuable in Christian service and giving. Service without desire is very difficult, tedious, and repulsive. Happy are we when the sanctions of duty and desire agree. Men can do very difficult tasks if selfish desire is present. I think of a business man not physically strong who endured great trials in exploring primitive Indian country of Central America because of his desire to learn of the Aztecs and early American civilization. The service of love is easy, as we have many times witnessed in a mother working for her children. Unless we desire to accomplish what the church is working for, we simply cannot be liberal in our giving. Paul here proves himself to be a good psychologist, in that he expounds the motives of Christian giving. As Christians, we need periodically to examine these. As preachers, we may be thankful for this passage, which gives us an inexhaustible mine of Christian teaching on the subject of stewardship.

The three dominating motives of this passage consist of Christian consecration, of communicated grace, and of common reason.

I. CHRISTIAN CONSECRATION

The motivation of liberality referred to by St. Paul illustrates the chief motive in giving, namely, consecration. Be sure that the reference to motivation is not an invidious comparison with the Corinthians, made to stimulate others into giving. To give because another gives is human, but it is not a high motivation. Paul knew only one principle in giving, and that is a free-will offering of an individual mind, and it is often emphasized in these verses. Rich and free Gospel grace alone is sufficient to accomplish this voluntary giving, if we trust that principle. Paul received his great collection from Corinth, Macedonia, and the other churches on this principle, for he later wrote of it, saying, "It pleased them of Macedonia and Achaia to make certain contributions for the poor saints which are at Jerusalem."

Some great trial of affliction had come to the Macedonians. It may be that one referred to in I. Thessalonians 2:14, namely, persecution by the Jews. Yet, in spite of this trial, these Macedonians were singleminded in their giving. History tells us that they had been taxed until they appealed to the Roman Senate to have their colony brought under the decree of the Emperor personally. This may have been their trial and the cause of their poverty. But Paul tells us that in a great trial of affliction the abundance of their joy and their deep poverty abounded unto the riches of their liberality.

The alchemy of poverty and joy produces a wealth of singleness of mind. The Macedonians knew poverty to the depth. One would never expect great collections for missions or relief to come from the poor. But they always do. Apparently, Paul tried to restrain these Macedonians in the midst of their poverty from giving so liberally, but they intreated St. Paul to receive the gift, so that they might have the fellowship of ministering to the saints. When we behold this act of giving as the grace of God on these souls, who are we to restrain or hinder them? It must be a delight to God to see men sacrifice for His work. They gave according to their ability, and then beyond their ability.

They knew joy to the full, described as "abundance of joy." The Gospel blessings and truths had come to them in a wonderful way. Paul describes it by saying, "Ye became followers of . . . the Lord, having received the word in much affliction, with the joy of the Holy Ghost." Joy also was theirs because God privileged them to enter the "communion of this ministry of giving." Through it, Divine grace was exercised in their souls, and they knew it. They passed over their own need and delighted in one thought, namely, helping others. They had a wealth of singleness of thought. Contrast this with Christians who hear of a missionary enterprise for those afar off and refuse to give because they should help only those at home.

The cause of this great liberality was the personal consecration of the Macedonians. "This they did, first gave their own selves to the Lord, and unto us by the will of God." When Paul approached this matter of the collection for the Jerusalem saints, he never expected much from the poor Macedonians. He expressed a joyful surprise not only in their liberality but in their own consecration. These Macedonians so dedicated themselves to God that all they possessed was His and belonged to His servants. They not only did as Paul hoped, contributed money, but first, they, gave their own selves to the Lord. No preacher could ask for more. God wants us, not our things. Usually self is the last thing we are willing to give. Herein we see that this collection was a means of grace. Through it, they were allowed to give themselves to God's true servants by the will of God, that is, they gave themselves in their gifts. Let a minister and a church hold up Christ and the truth, and it will surprise all what the grace of God can do for His work. There need be no fear for the future of God's work because of our trials, afflictions, and poverty, from war or other causes.

The Christian challenge to you is to give yourself to God. God wants not yours, but you. When God has *you*, a willingness beyond your ability will seize you, and when a true Christian work or need arises, you will be at the disposal of the Lord. Such a work will commend itself to you. The subsequent giving will then be "the grace of God bestowed upon you," to which we now wish to give heed.

II. COMMUNICATED GRACE

It is impossible to call a collection the grace of God, and yet grace is used five times in these fifteen verses, and apparently would refer to the collection. However, Paul speaks of abounding in this grace and of knowing the grace of our Lord Jesus Christ, and we do not believe that he would change the meaning of the word grace in the same paragraph. Otherwise, he would be an unintelligible writer. Since in the ninth verse it means the Divine grace of God, it must mean this in the other places. Thus, "this grace" was something communicated by God to the Macedonians, and not something given by them to the saints. This use of the word "grace" reveals the good works of the Christian to be the results of operative Divine grace. God puts the motivation into the heart, and gives grace for grace. The Macedonians' giving became a means of Divine grace to themselves, and by practicing it they came into the communion of ministry. Great grace is always on a liberal people.

Nevertheless, Paul exhorts the Corinthians to abound in this grace in which the Macedonians abounded. He speaks of five things in which they abounded, and exhorts them to abound in this grace also. We hardly need to explain the meaning of abounding in faith as a means of grace and of salvation. Abounding in utterance really means in the Word, or in doctrine, which is what the Christian believes. That is a means of grace. Abounding in knowledge refers to the spiritual knowledge which comes from doctrine, and was especially present in Corinth. Abounding in diligence is earnestness in Christian affairs. Abounding in love to the servants of the Lord manifests the instrument of grace. If these big five are means of grace, giving is also a means of grace, for Paul classifies it with them. New Christians should always be urged to practice this means of grace also, to be liberal, if they would mature in Christian experience.

It was Paul's desire that Titus should lead the Corinthians on to finish what they had begun in the grace of giving. Such participation in the relief of the Jerusalem poor would be the means of a spiritual enrichment in the grace of God for the Corinthians. As Titus was a minister of grace in stimulating these people to give, whoever convinces you of the Divine will in systematic, regular, liberal giving has brought a great blessing to you. He has brought the promises of Malachi 3:10, and of the Lord Jesus to open the windows of heaven and to give unto you good measure, pressed down, shaken together, and running over.

Paul then adduces the great example of giving, namely, the incarnation and humiliation of Christ, in which the grace of God was most evident. Said he, "Ye know the grace of our Lord Jesus Christ, that, though he was rich, yet for your sakes he became poor, that ye through his poverty might be rich." By means of this giving of wealth of grace until He became poor, we have the grace of salvation through Him. The passage means exactly what it says. It is confirmed by the Kenosis doctrine of Philippians 2:5, and following. The riches of Christ were pre-existent, sometimes called His glory, which He laid aside in His incarnation. Certain powers, attributes, and knowledge affirmed of God could not be affirmed of the Son of God, because of His self-emptying. All of these He laid aside in His humiliation. It is symbolized in this text as a giving away or a veiling of such powers and attributes. We hold that the Bible shows this incarnate Jesus to be very God and that He was still privileged to exercise these powers and attributes, but only through the Holy Spirit. The incarnate, but not the humble, state of Christ continues forever. He was resurrected and glorified. Glimpses of that state were given on the Mount of Transfiguration and after His resurrection, but by this self-imposed poverty the wealth of heavenly glory and dignity is imparted to us. This was a perfect analogy of the practice of the Corinthian and Macedonian giving. Such motivation finds its roots in following the example of Christ. Following that example will prove the sincerity of our professed love. Interesting is it that in certain mission fields a record is kept of the gifts of converts from heathendom to the church as an evidence of the reality of their profession.

III. COMMON REASON

Paul added to the Divine example and to the great principle of self-dedication other principles applicable to Christian giving which are highly rational and honorable. He advises perseverance, proportionate giving, and equality in responsibility.

Said Paul, "I give my advice: for this is expedient for you, who have begun before, not only to do, but also to be forward a year ago. Now therefore perform the doing of it." It is expedient to complete a task which one has commenced. There are detrimental results on one's personality in quitting in a purpose. Indecision weakens character, purpose, and work. If you set something before you and do not carry it through, irresolution and incapacity will result. Demoralization comes from launching a work with fanfare and enthusiasm and letting it come to nothing. There is also danger of letting a work lag, as the Corinthians had done with this collection. This creates disinterest and discouragement.

Completed tasks bring satisfaction. There is joy in seeing a thing through. Whether it is a missionary vision, a purposed education, or a youth work, see it through. To be willing is not sufficient. Performance by sacrifice and service is also necessary.

But we cannot always complete matters. Life itself often seems to be an unfinished task. There may be a willingness without the means, and God looks upon the heart and understands. Let the willing mind be first, whether we have the ability or not, for "if there first be a willing mind, it is accepted according to that a man hath, and not according to that he hath not." To have such a willingness is to have grace and enrichment of God. No poor person is shut out from this grace.

After perseverance, Paul emphasized proportion. "It is accepted according to that a man hath." Here is the wisdom of the ages. One can give only out of his possessions and his potentiality. The Scripture has established one-tenth as our standard, with extra offerings for those who can bring them. The tithe was required before the law was instituted, and it continues to exist after the abrogation of the law. It must be remembered, however, that a tithe for a rich man is not as much as a tithe for a poor man, and some need to consider this and to make extra offerings. Surely the widow in giving her mite gave herself, for she had no one on whom to depend other than God Himself.

Lastly, Paul speaks of an equality. He said, "I mean not that other men be eased, and ye burdened: but by an equality, that now at this time your abundance may be a supply for their want, that their abundance also may be a supply for your want." Balance or equality in the matter of giving is introduced for an understanding of the whole matter. Three principles exist: Readiness, or the willingness to give; rule, or giving according to what one has; and reciprocity, or balancing the giving. Do not misunderstand this equality. Paul is not urging communism any more than communism existed in the early Jerusalem Church. All gifts were voluntary, though some chose the way of poverty to make them. Giving to the church and to God's work is not an insurance policy against poverty. You may give now, and they may give later. But it was certain that the Jerusalem Church could never return what the Corinthians and the Macedonians were doing. There is no virtue in making paupers by relieving paupers. There must be a sense of balance.

Equality means a balancing of the ledger. A Christian's giving is not motivated by the expectation of later receiving from the Church. But abundances reaching an equality are spoken of by St. Paul as resulting in a balance. The Macedonians and the Corinthians gave of material things. The Jerusalem Christians had given of their spiritual things. Said Paul to the Romans, "If the Gentiles have been made partakers of their spiritual things, their duty is also to minister unto them in carnal things." Then he adduces the illustration of the manna in which he who gathered much had no more than he who gathered little. Give, then, of your abundance, for all that is of any value to you is your own need. God arranged to balance the manna, and He will arrange it now also. Full barns do not guarantee a saved soul. Give, then, with a cheerful purpose, for God loveth a cheerful and joyous giver.

XXIII

THE CHEERFUL GIVER WHOM GOD LOVES

TEXT: *"For God loveth a cheerful giver."*—II COR. 9:6-15.

PAUL HAD BOASTED of the Corinthian Church to the Macedonian Church in saying that he had prepared Achaia more than a year before to participate in the ministering to the saints at Jerusalem by giving money. When he was among them Paul had urged them to participate in relief of the poor at Jerusalem, which for some reason unknown to us was a terrible drain on the church at that particular time. They responded with alacrity and the first day of the week laid by a store as God had prospered them, in order that there might be no gathering when Paul should come. He refers to their forwardness of mind in this project, which, when he had begun it, foretold great things for the liberality of the Corinthians. It was on the basis of this experience with them that he boasted of them to Macedonia. Sometimes it is a beneficial thing to boast to the faces of people about what they have accomplished.

The zeal of the church in giving to others provoked other Christians to similar action. Paul was not attempting to make them compete in giving, but the very knowledge that the Macedonians were giving in the proportion to which Paul referred, and that the Corinthians were emulating the Macedonians, would provoke other Christian churches likewise to participate in the undertaking. Paul speaks of the bounty, or, literally, the blessing, which comes from this effort, in contrast with covetousness or niggardliness by the church. Whenever a church becomes niggardly or spends its money upon itself entirely, it will lose God's blessing. Park Street could have applied these tens of thousands of dollars given to missions every year to its own building activity, but had we done so, we would have shut off the great source of blessing which God has given to us.

Now, Paul exhorted the Corinthians to keep up the standard which they had set before them. It was superfluous for him to write of the need. They already were informed concerning that. Thus also many of us know of the great needs of the mission fields, and yet, on the other hand, we need stimulation, just as they needed stimulation, lest we lag in prosecuting a very worthy task. We need to have our interests stirred up, our work visualized, our emotions quickened, and for that reason, just as Paul sent special envoys to Corinth to carry through the work in that church, so also we must invite special envoys to stir up our interest at this time. We believe that by listening to these missionaries and their stories of the needs throughout the world and of the work which is being done, we, in turn, will be able intelligently to respond to that need as the servants of the Lord.

I. Giving

The passage before us presents the principles of giving which are sufficient for our guidance, and pleads that we follow them. We are told that Christian giving must be bountiful, purposeful, and cheerful, for God loveth a cheerful giver.

What is translated "bountiful" really means "on the basis of blessing." Paul speaks, "He which soweth sparingly shall reap also sparingly, and he which soweth bountifully shall reap also bountifully." The idea is that one man sows with an eye to the blessings he will receive from the harvest, whereas another sows with an eye placed on the amount of grain he is seemingly throwing away. When we speak of blessing, we think of the others who shall be blessed through this sowing, of God who shall be blessed by the praise rising from others knowing the Gospel and of ourselves who shall be blessed in turn by God, because we have acted on the principle of blessing. The suggestion is that by giving freely we open a fountain of blessing both for others and ourselves. The source of what we give is not our own works or labor, but God. Just as God gives the seed, the sunshine, the soil, the rain and the inherent power to grow, or life itself to the seed, so He also is the source of all that we are able to give in life. Christian giving is thus compared to sowing. All of us are farmers in the spiritual sense, and sowing is our chief business. Christ described Himself as a sower who went forth to sow. Preaching the Gospel is sowing the seed which is the Word of God, and thus giving for the support of the Gospel is here compared to the sowing of grain. As a farmer is seemingly prodigal in scattering his grain over the field, so there is a prodigal use of God's money or of our own money for God to enable us to expect a great harvest. Thus believing that there will be blessings, we give and give freely.

Secondly, we are to sow with a purpose. "Every man according as he purposes in his heart, so let him give; not grudgingly or of necessity." The purpose of sowing is to get a harvest. No man throws his grain into the ground to get rid of it. He expects a result from his sowing. Likewise also, in our Christian work we should produce and stop pouring money into works which do not produce. When we think of all the unfruitful churches and the unfruitful work in which souls are not converted, we realize why people cease giving to such work. We must have something of an outpouring of blessing if we are to continue to sow. Likewise also, when we consider the amount of blessing we want, we sow accordingly. If we want a very abundant and overflowing crop we sow freely, but if we want a small crop we sow sparingly. Such giving is never grudging or of grief, but always of gladness. One who considers the principle of blessings and the purposed end in view does not grieve over what he has given for the

Lord's work, but rather is glad that he has poured out his money in order that God might use it for blessing. Likewise, there is absolutely no compulsion or force about this matter of giving. There are no later regrets. The more one thinks it over, the more one rejoices in it. Voluntary giving is always the Christian way. In the Early Church the people voluntarily sold their property and gave money to the Apostles. God forbid that we should ever stoop to worldly competition and compulsion in order to get money. This is sufficient to ruin any Christian work.

We must remember that there is absolutely no other way to get a harvest than to sow our seed freely. Seed used ultimately ceases to be, but seed sown multiplies, and our opportunity is even greater than before. How else could we ever get a harvest? The only other way would be to rob and pillage others who sowed, namely, to proselytize from their works. To this we say, "No, no, no, a thousand times no." Let us sow our own rather than depend upon another.

The third principle is that of cheerfulness. We read that God loves a cheerful giver. Therefore, giving can be a blessing not only to others but also to one's self. Have you ever seen a farmer sow? It is a joyful experience, because he knows that he will have a return. This very word says that as God so loved the world that He gave His only begotten Son, so now God also loves the one who cheerfully gives. The word literally translated is "glad" or "hilarious" in contrast with the calculating, stern, and restricted kind of giving which is so often practiced. We often speak of the tithe, but this is only the standard of the beginning of our giving in Christian life. This was the necessity under the law. The Christian will give because he is glad to give. He will give on the great principle of grace, with the tithe as the minimum of his activity. The Christian has before him the greatest example of giving which is possible, namely, God's indescribable gift of His only begotten Son. Because the Christian is filled with this love of God, he, in turn, is willing to practice Christian giving.

Once this practice of liberality is begun, life becomes a time of blessing in exchange for blessing. We remember that Jesus promised that if we give, it would be given unto us, pressed down, shaken together and running over. Likewise, He advised us to lay up for ourselves treasures in heaven by giving to things on earth. By means of the manna of unrighteousness we were to make for ourselves friends who when they went to heaven would prepare a place for us. That is, by the wise use of money in this world we make friends of human beings benefited by our liberality. These precede us into heaven and later receive us there. He told us not to set our hearts on mammon but on God. The Christian should never display the spirit of covetousness or niggardliness. This breathes of selfishness, of grasping, of withholding, whereas God's standard is the standard of freely giving.

Thus Paul determined to make a plea to the Corinthians, namely, to exhort them really to give. Likewise, we also exhort. We have a time of education, of stimulation and opportunity, to stir up our minds and hearts, which, for one reason or another, may have lagged in Christian giving.

II. Receiving

The opposite of giving is receiving, and he who gives freely to God's work, as the farmer bountifully sows, will receive an abundant harvest. This is described as threefold: first, grace; second, righteousness; third, ability.

Paul said, "God is able to make all grace abound toward you; that ye, always having sufficiency in all things, may abound into every good work." The emphasis is on the ability of God. God is able. Think what the omnipotent God has at His disposal and what He is willing to use, both to save and to bless His people. If God is able to make all grace abound toward us, let us remember that, first of all, it is by grace that we are saved. This grace must come first, for it is the most essential of all kinds of grace, but, following it, every ability and every gift of our lives is of grace. Giving is only one of many of God's gifts of grace, and yet it is He who out of grace will make us to be sufficient for this work of giving. Paul added on one occasion that if God freely gave us Christ, the unspeakable gift, will He not with Him also freely give us all things? Yes, God is both able and willing to bestow grace upon us.

· God also intends that this grace which He gives to us shall be for good works. Just as we need the gift of grace in our heart to live worthily, so we need the means and strength of hand for our service. Grace enables us to be God's own, and grace likewise makes us able to do His work. It is sufficient that God gives from His unlimited resources, for He alone is able to make up every need which we have. Notice that Paul says, "all grace," "all sufficiency," "in all things," and "to every good work." If God is able to do this, it is quite sufficient.

Secondly, we receive not only grace, but also righteousness. Paul said, "His righteousness remaineth forever." Paul quotes from Psalm 112, which is a reference to the poor and needy and to the free distribution of one's possessions among them. This righteousness is the quality of life which results in the individual after the verdict of righteousness has been given to him at God's throne, that is, being justified by faith, he is declared to be righteous and righteousness now manifests itself in his life as of God. Righteous works always follow the righteousness of faith and are the results of justifying faith. This has the suggestion of quantity also. The Scripture speaks of this righteousness remaining forever. Here is a suggestion of Christ's saying, "Inasmuch as ye have done it unto one of the least of these my brethren, ye have done it unto me."

The third personal blessing or reward is the means or ability to do good. What God is able to do, He will do. "Now he that ministereth seed to the sower both minister bread for your food, and multiply your seed sown, and increase the fruits of your righteousness." What God does in the natural realm, He also will do in the spiritual realm to the bountiful sower. Just as he who sows bountifully, receives an increase, so God also will increase the ability of him who gives freely to give more freely. This, I believe, is the secret of Charles G. Finney's great revivalistic power. He believed that there was a natural law operative in the spiritual world, that if men would actually break up their fallow ground, if they would sow in righteousness and take care of their spiritual lives on the same basis as they would a physical experience, God would give a revival, and God invariably gave Finney a revival wherever he went. This is the clear statement of the natural law in the spiritual realm. Then why not recognize it in the spiritual as well as in the natural? Men always talk about natural law. God has put such a natural law to operate in the spiritual world. The souls which are saved spiritually are the fruits or the harvest of righteousness and are so called in this case. God will increase the fruits of your righteousness or the harvest of your labors. Remember that Jesus said," Herein is my father glorified that ye bear much fruit; so shall ye be my disciples." If such fruit is not present it is due not to the fact that God is not willing to bless us but to ourselves. The only purpose of our giving and denying ourselves innumerable things that we could enjoy is that we might save souls. Thus it is that Revelation says, "Blessed are the dead . . . and their works shall follow them." Only our spiritual works can follow us into heaven.

III. THANKSGIVING

First, we had the subject of giving, then receiving, and now thanksgiving. Paul speaks of this grace causing individuals to be "enriched in everything to all bountifulness, which causeth through us thanksgiving to God." There is, then, a harvest of thanksgiving to God through others who are benefited by our giving. Such a knowledge is a personal enrichment. While the crops are growing, a farmer feels that he is getting richer and richer, and while we are raising these crops of thankfulness to God in others, we ought to give God praise because we are being personally enriched. But, likewise, praise rises up to God from those who are benefited by your liberality. Think of those in the mission field who are praising God because the Gospel has been carried to them through your gift. Our two-score representatives are preaching in many of the fields of the world, and literally thousands will hear the Gospel who otherwise would never have heard it. Many others, both in the church and in distant cities or fields, are being saved and turned to God. They, in turn, thank God and praise Him day after day for what has originated in this place. Then Paul added, "For the administration of this service not only supplieth the want of the saints, but is abundant also by many thanksgivings unto God." Here we have mention of a liturgy of giving which results in many thanksgivings to God. We are told in one case that the presenting of our bodies is a liturgy to God. In another we are told that our spiritual oblations are offered by praise to God. Here, then, is a liturgy to God, or a service of worship in getting as many to praise Him as possible through the results of our work. Much charity must mean a sweet odor to God through those who are brought to praise Him. This, then, is the answer of our love to His. Our chief aim in life should be to multiply the praise given to God through those who hear the word by our instrumentality.

The second kind of harvest is spoken of, namely, that of a better feeling between the Jerusalem saints and the Gentiles. There had been considerable question among the Jerusalem saints as to whether these Gentiles were actually converted. Now, in this offering the factual substantiation of their professed conversion was given. By the evidence of material things, people hundreds of miles away saw that those who professed conversion actually were converted. There never was a greater need of a practical demonstration of Christianity than now. There never was a greater need for the missionary enterprise than for us who are Christians to show to the world that we still are Christians and that in this time of crisis we have not abandoned the things that we believe. How deeply, then, does your religion touch your prejudices, your pocket book, your time and your energy. This actually was a test or an experiment to reveal the subjection of the Corinthians to the Gospel, as also it is a test to reveal our subjection and submission to the Gospel.

They proved by their actions that they had obeyed the Gospel. Charity and sacrifice for others reveal that we ourselves are actually surrendered to the Gospel authority. Therefore, it becomes the source of thanksgiving to God. Such works foster better feeling between men, better relations between nations. They declare the fellowship of Christians with all others to be shown by what they have done.

Such liberality finds a response from intercessory prayer in behalf of the giver. Paul said, "By their prayer for you, which long after you for the exceeding grace of God in you." These who have received benefit through the Corinthians will glorify God through intercessory prayers on their behalf. I am positive that the blessing which we are now receiving in Park Street Church is in a measure the result of the prayers of the people who are being benefited by our missionary interest. We have missionaries in many parts of the world who are praying daily that God will revive us, that God will bless us and use us, and we have many of their Christians likewise who are praying for Park Street Church. Those prayers cannot help but release Divine power and benefits on our behalf, for which we, too, ought to thank God. This means the cementing of the branches of Christendom into one great family. It is the missionary vision, giving to others, whether for relief of the poor or support of other branches of Christendom which are in need, that binds us together in real fellowship.

Last of all, there should be the harvest of gratitude to God which centers in His unspeakable gift. The basis of all which has gone before, all that we have mentioned, is unquestionably God's great gift to man in the Lord Jesus Christ. Here Paul, by the very words which he uses, designates God's gift in His Son Jesus Christ, by means of the incarnation, the sinlessness, the redemptive life, the death and resurrection of our Lord Jesus Christ. This was the greatest of all gifts and beyond this there can be no other. It is on the basis of this blessing, of gratitude, of grace, of righteousness, that we give. Out of the gratitude and thanks of our heart we are willing to make the Gospel known to others. For this reason, we know that we are debtors to all men and are ready to discharge that debt of gratitude.

Here is the highest motive of all in giving. There is nothing cheap in comparing what God has done for us and what we do for Him. Cheapness comes in how little we have been willing to do. Noticeable is it also that Paul thanks God for this gift instead of the Corinthians for theirs. This is altogether proper. It is God's gift in Christ, in salvation, life, and immortality that we have the basis for what we as Christians do. His indescribe, unutterable gift, the Lord Jesus Christ, is the reason why we give. Therefore, we ought not to be thanking one another for the things that we do for God, but rather we ought to thank God that He put it in the hearts of His people to do this great and wonderful work.

Without question, God gave Himself for us. He, though rich, became poor for our sakes, that we through His poverty might be rich, and, therefore, we, in turn, give for Him and for His cause ourselves, our time, our money, our very future. Yes, thanks be unto God for His unspeakable gift.

XXIV

THE WEAPONS OF OUR WARFARE

TEXT: *"The weapons of our warfare are not carnal, but mighty through God to the pulling down of strong holds."*—II COR. 10:1-6.

A CHRISTIAN must be a warrior, for the Christian life is a struggle, a conflict, a war. John Bunyan did well when he described the Christian life as a holy war. He merely used the Scriptural terminology. Paul conceived of the Christian life as a war. He advised the Christian to put on the armor of God that he might be able to stand against the wiles of the devil. This armor consisted of the girdle of truth, the breastplate of righteousness, the sandals of the gospel of peace, the shield of faith, the helmet of salvation, the sword of the spirit, and the offensive weapon of prayer. This armor is adapted to the spiritual warfare we must wage. In writing to Timothy, Paul said, "Endure hardness, as a good soldier of Jesus Christ." "No man that warreth entangleth himself with the affairs of this life; that he may please him who has chosen him to be a soldier." Once one has enlisted in the Christian army, he cannot take his ease. He must fight the good fight of faith. Paul's final testimony was, "I have fought a good fight, I have kept the faith." The heroes of the faith are described in the honor roll as those who "waxed valiant in fight." With Bunyan and Paul we conceive of the Christian life as a war.

The personal appearance of Paul was not such as would make us think of a soldier. He described himself as weak in bodily presence and as suffering from some physical malady. But he must have had a commanding aspect which gave him great influence over others. This is quite in contrast with what the world expects from its leaders. Alexander, Hannibal, Cæsar, and other conquerors were men of imposing appearance. The strength of Paul, and of any Christian warrior, lies not in his outward life, but in the purity of his faith, the fearlessness of his spirit, and the faithfulness of his life to divine principles.

A soldier's life is full of peril. Paul said, "We wrestle not with flesh and blood but against principalities, against powers, against the rulers of the darkness of this world, against spiritual wickedness in high places." The perils of a Christian are more subtle, deceptive and deadly than those of a worldly warrior. Then, as though these were not enough, material troubles and sufferings are added to them. As an example, Paul was "in labors more abundant, in stripes above measure, in prisons more frequent, in deaths oft." Said he:

"Of the Jews five times received I forty stripes save one. Thrice was I beaten with rods, once was I stoned, thrice I suffered shipwreck, a night and a day I have been in the deep; in journeyings often, in perils of waters, in perils of robbers, in perils by mine own countrymen, in perils by the heathen, in perils in the city, in perils in the wilderness, in perils in the sea, in perils among false brethren; in weariness and painfulness, in watchings often, in hunger and thirst, in fastings often, in cold and nakedness."

These were a few of the afflictions which this soldier of the cross had to bear. Those of the Lord Jesus Christ were even greater. Ours may be expected as we enter the Christian war.

I. THE WARFARE WE WAGE

Ours is a holy warfare. It is intangible. Paul describes it as "pulling down of strong holds; casting down imaginations, and every high thing that exalteth itself against the knowledge of God, and bringing into captivity every thought to the obedience of Christ." This kind of warfare cannot broadcast its victories, for they are unseen. The imagination of man is without substance. Yet it was the evil imaginations of men which caused the flood. The record states, "And God saw that the wickedness of man was great in the earth, and that every imagination of the thoughts of his heart was only evil continually. ... And the Lord said, I will destroy man whom I have created from the face of the earth." We are told that in the descent of the human race as it fell from the knowledge of God the third step consisted of vanity in imagination. This includes the purposes and desires of one's heart. The imagination of man is the source of much of his sin. He conjures up images and desires, toys with them, and often is lead into sin by them. The imagination largely governs one's action. In the *Magnificat,* Mary sang of the Lord, "He hath scattered the proud in the imagination of their hearts." Christian warfare deals with that intangible thing called imagination. It casts down, through the exaltation of purity and honesty and Christian virtues, the evil imaginations of the heart.

Our warfare is waged against human emotions, against "every high thing that exalteth itself against the knowledge of God." Outside of human thoughts, temptation arises largely from the emotions of man, his loves, his hates, his ambitions, his hopes, his fears. These are the things which militate against one's obeying the knowledge of God. They set themselves up as dictators. They rule our lives. They are ruthless in their demands. Our warfare is to conquer these emotions and to make God and his law supreme in the inner man.

Our warfare is concerned with bringing every thought into captivity to the obedience of Christ. It seems strange to think of conducting a campaign against one's thoughts. Yet the theories of men are the greatest human enemies to the victory of Christ in the world. It is a definite effort to capture and hold one's thinking in line with the revealed truth of God. Thoughts are rebels, and many of us who attempt to be thoroughly faithful to the revealed truth of God and to its demands upon our lives harbor these rebels in our minds and thereby militate against our effectiveness as servants of our Lord. Bringing one's thought life into total obedience to Christ means allying it with beauty, purity, honesty, love, and truth. It is not an unattractive object, but it is a difficult thing to accomplish. This warfare is the hardest kind of struggle. Only the most sensitive soul is conscious of victories and defeats. It is easy to get discouraged.

The struggle is spiritual. Our enemies consist of principalities and powers. Undoubtedly, these are world systems, the spirits of fallen men and the devices of demons. This kind of battle cannot be won by legislation. The state is a lame creature. It cannot make people sober; it can only punish them for being drunk. It cannot make men honest; it can only cause them to suffer for being thieves. It cannot compel men to observe the Sabbath. If it is not kept in the soul there is no act of any legislature that can compel men to keep it. We must admit that we are living in a world system which is un-Christian and ungodly. It will never be completely controlled by a divine morality. Hence, we must recognize the futility of legislation in accomplishing the victory in this struggle.

The only way to wage this war is to deal with the depraved and fallen spirits of men. Our weapons are not carnal and neither is our warfare carnal. We are persuading, praying, pleading with men to accept the divine Gospel, which alone is able to make a difference in this great struggle. We can get at men only by getting at their souls. Little can be done with their bodies besides keeping them clothed and fed. Men are not ours until we have conquered their souls, for their souls govern the outward workings of their bodies and minds, whether for righteousness or evil. Hence, we are dealing with unseen enemies, those which are within a man. Our greatest enemies are always within us. They lie in wait for us until in a tired moment, in an unguarded hour, in an unobserved place, they seek to slay us. The first man we have to kill is our fallen self. Then and then only can Christ rule. You must conquer yourself before you can conquer others. Only then will you be able to deal with the problems which face your neighbor and fellow citizen.

This Christian war is interminable. The struggle began in the garden of Eden. Satan is a principality, a spiritual power. He is the enemy of men's souls. He tempts them, he accuses them to God, he is struggling for the control of a world which he has lost. This was the essence of his actions with the first man and woman, and it is repeated in the temptation of us all. For every life is a garden of Eden. The struggle between good and evil, Christ and Satan, right and wrong, will continue while the world lasts. Armageddon is being fought daily in the souls of men, just as certainly as it will be fought in the plain of Megiddo at the end of this age. The world, then, is a scene of a stupendous conflict, a holy war over the souls of men. The object of that war is to have men who are free, who are moral, who are upright, and who are worthy of fellowship with God.

Constant vigilance in the individual life and in society is necessary to prevent evil from triumphing. Evil is just as wily as the clever infiltration tactics which drive through advancing armies and attack them from the rear. One never knows from whence the attack will come. It is not possible to grow careless in our advance if we are to have victory. "Watch and pray, lest ye enter into temptation" is the command of Jesus. Altars of grace in the home, moral movements in society, doctrinal struggles in the church—these are the evidences of vigilance in the holy war. The church was compelled in the first century to enter the unending struggle to preserve her purity, which has marked it ever since. Let those who are everlastingly asking for peace at any price in the church remember that we belong to the church militant, not to the church triumphant.

II. THE WEAPONS OF THE WAR

The weapons of the holy war are not carnal, that is, fleshly, but are spiritual. Paul uses the word "mighty" as synonymous with spiritual. It recalls the promise to Zachariah, "Not by might, nor by power, but by my Spirit, saith the Lord." The spiritual weapons, then, are fivefold: The Bible, preaching, prayer, conversion by the Spirit, and a righteous life. All of these must be connected with the Holy Spirit to be effective as instruments in the warfare.

The Bible is the word of truth. It is the infallible teaching of God for man's salvation. Hence, it alone becomes the supreme authority for human action. Jesus said, "the Scripture cannot be broken." He, then, that is on the side of the Bible is on the winning side. Two figures are used to describe the Bible. It is the two-edged sword of God which is sharp enough to divide between the thoughts and the intents of the heart. This is the sword which is described as coming out of the mouth of the triumphant conqueror, even Christ, as He is seen in the apocalyptic vision. The Bible is also called God's hammer that breaketh the rock in pieces. No heart is so hard but that the constant beating of the Word of God upon it will ultimately break it. We know that in this spiritual warfare he who uses the Word of God can awaken men's consciences on moral deflections of character to which they were not sensible before. He can break the resistance of obdurate hearts and he can speak with authority concerning sin in any realm of human life.

The second weapon or instrument in spiritual warfare is the preaching of the Gospel. It has pleased God to save men by the foolishness of preaching. This is the only way. Paul began his statement of this struggle with the words, "Now I Paul myself beseech you by the meekness and gentleness [reasonableness] of Christ." Does that sound like a soldier? Soldiers have throats of iron, lungs of steel, and voices of thunder. But here is a man who wants to conquer human hearts and souls. He beseeches. He makes meekness His panoply and gentleness the strength of His arm. Thus it has pleased Christ to carry on the warfare of the spirit. When Christians are tempted to be rough in their warfare, it is time to remember the meekness and gentleness of Christ. By preaching His death on Calvary for our sins we have the most effective way of conquering spiritual enemies.

A third weapon is prayer. More is wrought by prayer than the world dreams of. Even Jesus prayed constantly. Whole nights were spent in prayer. If the captain of our struggle had need of this weapon in his spiritual battle, how can we discard it in our struggles? The man who prays is the man of power in the campaign for Christ. Paul defined the offensive weapon in the Christian armor as prayer. The church goes forward on her knees.

Another instrument is the conversion of men. He that winneth souls is wise. He is using the most effective method of the extending of the kingdom and for the overthrow of wickedness. The conversion of a man is a conquest of Satan in that soul. When you change a man's heart, he is won. This, of course, must be wrought by the regenerating power of the Holy Ghost, but man is made the evangel in accomplishing that divine purpose. Consequently, evangelism is a weapon of the church in spiritual warfare. The proportion in which we have abandoned it is to a large extent the proportion of our defeat by the spirit of worldliness today.

The last weapon, and the one without which all the others are fruitless, is a righteous life. "With the heart man believeth unto righteousness, but with the mouth confession is made unto salvation." Jesus said, "Ye are my witnesses." One cannot preach the Gospel if his life does not corroborate that message. Two factors enter into effective Christian witnessing. One is an upright, moral, Christian character which men are unable to criticize because it would be inconsistent. The other is the telling of the good news which produces this character in our lives. Such a weapon is mighty to the pulling down of strongholds. A life which seemed a tower of strength for wickedness will tumble before the trussing of this weapon. A good life alone cannot convert a man, but it can make him realize his own deficiencies and his need of the Gospel.

III. THE WINNING OF THE WAR

The enemy of Christ and of Christians is a defeated foe. Just before Jesus went to His death on Calvary, He said, "Now is the judgment of this world: now shall the prince of this world be cast out." On Golgotha the Son of God carried the sin of mankind, which sacrifice totally satisfied the demands of justice and holiness whereby man could not only be pardoned but acquitted, that is, declared innocent. Satan, through the fall of man, obtained control of this world. He is the prince of this world. But at the cross Jesus broke his power, not in a material way, but by a spiritual victory, not physically but morally. He ransomed men from sin and its power. That ransom is applied for everyone who believes and power is given to him to live victoriously over the temptations of Satan. Satan continues to control the present world system, and he will control it until Christ comes again. But at that time we read that he will be cast into the pit and later into the lake of fire which was prepared for him.

There is nothing to prevent believers from enjoying victory in the holy war in their personal lives. They may draw on the victorious Christ for spiritual power which will overcome all temptations, which will succor them in the hour of need, and which will make them more than conquerors. Satan has no power over those who are yielded unto Christ. Paul said, "I live; yet not I, but Christ liveth in me: and the life which I now live . . . I live by the faith of the Son of God." When John saw in his vision the saints about the throne of God, he heard the testimony, "They overcame . . . by the blood of the Lamb, and by the word of their testimony." We have been redeemed from the power of wickedness.

The Bible promises that the ultimate victory belongs to Christ. Dramatic is the action in which it is described. John said:

"I saw heaven opened, and behold a white horse; and he that sat upon him was called Faithful and True, and in righteousness he doth judge and make war. His eyes were as a flame of fire, and on his head were many crowns; and he had a name written, that no man knew, but he himself. And he was clothed with a vesture dipped in blood: and his name is called The Word of God. And the armies which were in heaven followed him upon white horses, clothed in fine linen, white and clean. And out of his mouth goeth a sharp sword, that with it he should smite the nations; and he shall rule them with a rod of iron: and he treadeth the wine press of the fierceness and wrath of Almighty God. And he hath on his vesture and on his thigh a name written, KING OF KINGS, AND LORD OF LORDS."

Regardless of the present state of the church and the world, or any temporary state of it or of any individual spiritually, remember that the ultimate victory belongs to the church. We see the poor oppressed, the righteous suffer, the church retreating, but let us remember that though

> "Careless seems the great Avenger; history's pages but record
> One death-grapple in the darkness 'twixt old systems and the Word;
> Truth forever on the scaffold, Wrong forever on the throne—
> Yet that scaffold sways the future, and, behind the dim unknown,
> Standeth God within the shadow, keeping watch above his own."

We are God's soldiers in the present conflict and the state of that struggle depends on us. God is looking to us as His instruments in this age of Gospel preaching. As soldiers of the Cross let us wage the holy war quietly, steadily, faithfully, in every day and phase of life, remembering that we will partake of His victory.

> "Am I a soldier of the cross,
> A follower of the Lamb,
> And shall I fear to own His cause,
> Or blush to speak His Name?
>
> "Must I be carried to the skies
> On flowery beds of ease,
> While others fought to win the prize,
> And sailed through bloody seas?
>
> "Sure I must fight if I would reign:
> Increase my courage, Lord;
> I'll bear the toil, endure the pain,
> Supported by Thy word.
>
> "Thy saints, in all this glorious war,
> Shall conquer, though they die;
> They view the triumph from afar,
> And seize it with their eye.
>
> "When that illustrious day shall rise,
> And all Thy armies shine
> In robes of victory through the skies,
> The glory shall be Thine."

XXV

THE COMMENDATION OF GOD

TEXT: *"For not he that commendeth himself is approved, but whom the Lord commendeth."*—II COR. 10:7-18.

PAUL INTRODUCES this matter of commendation by a brief dissertation on appearances. "Do ye look on things after the outward appearance?" Then he goes on to say that God looks upon the heart. It is inescapable that judgments are made after the outward appearance. Hence, we have been warned by the Lord Jesus Christ, "Judge not according to the appearance, but judge righteous judgment." This is one of the most difficult things for men to do, for we live largely by outward appearance. On the other hand, it gives reason for the admonition of St. Paul, "Abstain from all appearance of evil," lest we should give a false impression and foundation of judgment to others. Yet man is prone so to look and so to judge from appearances. The Lord announced this to Samuel when He was choosing a king after His own heart from the family of Jesse of Bethlehem. Said He, "Look not on his countenance, or on the height of his stature; because I have refused him: for the Lord seeth not as man seeth; for man looketh on the outward appearance, but the Lord looketh on the heart."

Inevitably mistakes are made by judging by appearances. Mistakes are made in receiving into church membership persons who ought not to be received. At best, it is only possible to have only a fragmentary knowledge of a person's character and life, and this lays us open to erroneous judgments. Great injustices are done by comparisons based upon appearances. If one wishes to start trouble, all he needs to do is to make such comparisons, whether they deal with the physical prowess of boys, the fame of artists, the success of business men, or the modes of women's clothes.

While Lincoln was President, there was much talk of McClellan, or "Little Mac," as he was called by the army, being made president, or even of the army offering him a dictatorship. This may account for Lincoln's strange behavior in promising McClellan at the second battle of Bull Run that he would lead the army on to victory, and then immediately upon his returning to the White House retiring McClellan into private life. Appearances make us do injustice by our judgments.

The Scripture says that God looks upon the heart. God knows all hearts, and thus He is addressed by Peter in the prayer meeting preceding Pentecost, when the mind of the Lord was being sought concerning who should take the place of Judas, who by transgression fell. Likewise, at the Jerusalem Council, Peter, in his speech telling of God's choice that the Gentiles should hear the Gospel by his mouth, stated: "God, which knoweth the hearts, bare them witness, giving them the Holy Ghost, even as he did unto us." Peter received this conception of God from the Lord Jesus Christ, who had said concerning the Pharisees, "Ye are they which justify yourselves before men; but God knoweth your hearts: for that which is highly esteemed among men is abomination in the sight of God." "Out of the heart are the issues of life." The heart is used as synonymous with the inner man, with one's true self, unseen and unknown of men. These secret thoughts, emotions, and intentions are open and known to God. In the heart man is justified or condemned by God. Christ spoke of an evil heart which issues in an evil life, and of a good heart which issues in a good life. He said, "Out of the abundance of the heart, a man speaketh."

For this reason, Christianity is a religion of the heart and not of appearances. In the Sermon on the Mount, Christ analyzed almsgiving, praying, fasting, thinking and feeling—whether in anger or lust—and judged according to the heart rather than according to action. Many feel because of this internal nature of Christianity that it is a "strictly private" matter, but the issues of the heart ultimately must also be seen in life.

The antidote to judging by appearances is stated by Paul: "If any man trust to himself that he is Christ's, let him of himself think this again, that, as he is Christ's, even so are we Christ's." Remember that you and your brother are Christ's, redeemed, members of the same body, and that judgment of one another is forbidden. Each one stands or falls to his own Lord. Though commendation of the brethren, that is, their approval, is important in life, it is not final. Happy is the man who has the commendation of the brethren. When Apollos was disposed to pass into Achaia, the brethren wrote, exhorting the disciples to receive him. Paul added, "He that in these things serveth Christ is acceptable to God, and approved of men." An epitaph of the

Lord Jesus, spoken by Peter, was "approved of God." This is far higher than the approval of men. In this sense, Timothy was advised to "study to shew thyself approved unto God, a workman that needeth not to be ashamed."

We are introduced to this passage relating to criticism, comparison, and commendation by some disaffected person who followed the leadership of self-recommended, false teachers, subverting the Corinthian Christians from the purity of Pauline Christianity. It is well for us to learn from this. Therefore, we must give attention to what Paul has to say about criticism, comparison, and commendation.

I. CRITICISM

The critics of Paul said, "His letters, . . . are weighty and powerful; but his bodily presence is weak, and his speech contemptible." This was an accusation of inconsistency of action. They claimed that Paul wrote letters to terrify them, but that his personal authority was nothing. This is identical to saying of a minister, "He is eloquent in the pulpit, but in personal life ineffectual." Perhaps such criticisms are sometimes true, that ministers are unable to counsel, to convert, to comfort, and to strengthen. When true, this is a terrible indictment. But when it is merely a criticism contrary to fact, it is very cruel. The essence of their attack was, "He speaks one thing, but does another." That is equivalent to the attitude, "This is what I preach, but not what I do." Inconsistency in the minister is a deadly criticism. We must let consistency drop as a plumbline, judging our own lives, and then others will not criticize us.

This is said of Paul, "His bodily presence is weak." What was Paul's appearance? Some have depicted him as small, bald, deformed, and suffering from a terrible eye disease. We recall that he told the Galatians that they would have plucked out their eyes and given them to him had it been possible. We also know that he thrice prayed to be delivered from his "thorn in the flesh." And we also know that when he came to Corinth it was "in weakness and fear and in much trembling." But this does not necessarily give us a picture of St. Paul, for his true appearance is shown by another picture. In the Acts of the Apostles, when he and Barnabas preached at Lystra, they performed a miracle, and as a result the people called Barnabas Jupiter and Paul Mercurius, and said, "The gods have come down to us in the likeness of men." Paul may have been small, but he resembled Mercury, the spokesman of the gods, whereas

Barnabas must have been a large physical specimen, hence called Jupiter. No doubt shipwrecks, beatings, fastings, and innumerable sufferings had a deteriorating effect upon Paul's body, for he carried about in his body the marks of the Lord Jesus. It is not always those physically big who get things done in life.

They criticized Paul's speech, saying it was contemptible. Paul apparently deliberately avoided the adorned phraseology and speculative philosophy in his preaching. He came not "with enticing words of man's wisdom, but in the demonstration of the Spirit and of power." Whenever we hear some one adorning the Gospel with labored phrases, we feel intuitively that he is not depending on the power of the Holy Spirit. Apollos compared favorably with Paul as to this, for he was eloquent and philosophical, great of speech. Men, however, are not saved by such artificial tactics, but by the simple Word of God, the preaching of the message of the cross. Though Paul may have been simple, we are sure that the men who entered the citadels of heathendom, Ephesus, Athens, Antioch, could not have been contemptible in speech. If he were, the power of God used a base thing to confound the mighty.

In many ways, Paul compared more favorably with these critics. He carried the scars in his body from the service of his Lord. They had no scars, yet they criticized his appearance. Sometimes Christians who have lived in ease and luxury criticize the appearance of missionaries who have suffered greatly for their Lord, having deprived themselves of many of the necessities of life to bring the message to the heathen. Such contempt is like that of these Corinthian Christians for the Apostle Paul. He had a basic determination to press on to the regions beyond. He was not willing to accept that made ready at hand. He spoke of this purpose to them, "To preach the gospel in the regions beyond you, and not to boast in another man's line of things made ready to our hand." In his Roman epistle, he described this in the following words, "Having a great desire these many years to come unto you; whensoever I take my journey into Spain, I will come. . . . Yea, so have I strived to preach the gospel, not where Christ was named, lest I should build upon another man's foundation." Yet those who took the benefit of an established work, of the labor and travail and affliction of Paul as a missionary, criticized him because of his appearance and his speech. No doubt, we pastors, evangelists, and Christians lose something of our mission when we live too comfortably. We must put every ounce of energy into this Christian work.

Let us, therefore, avoid this terrible business of criticism. We have viewed it impersonally in a third party, to see its cutting nature, but it is never an impersonal matter. Criticism hurts, cuts, wounds, and leaves one limp with sorrow. Remember that everything you build, everything you save, and everything you keep here will be destroyed by fire. Not one thing will remain. But the good you did to men will be to your credit in that day. Consider what God will have to say to two kinds of people, to the blustering success and to the humble servant of the cross. And then make your judgment in accordance with that unseen world.

II. COMPARISON

Criticism is based on the practice of making comparisons. These comparisons may be of several kinds, the comparison of others with others, the comparison of self with others, and the comparison of self with God's measure or rule.

Paul said, "We dare not make ourselves of the number, or compare ourselves with some that commend themselves: but they, measuring themselves by themselves, and comparing themselves among themselves, are not wise." The Corinthians had compared Paul with these Judaizers who used philosophical language, legal terminology, and eloquence. When such comparisons occur, they lay the groundwork for jealousies, competitions, and divisions. There is a sense in which all our judgments must be made by comparison, for the thinking process is made up of combining, comparing, and contrasting, but there is no need of speaking comparisons unto others, especially to the detriment of some soul. God has His place for every man. One vessel is to honor, and another is to dishonor, but the Potter made them all. For us to sit in judgment between two of these vessels is arrogance and spiritual pride.

The second dangerous comparison is of self with others. Paul said, "We dare not . . . compare ourselves with some." There are many things, all false, in this practice. It is the *argumentum ad hominem* in logic, or the appeal to man rather than the appeal to reason. There is a hymn which expresses this. "It is the old time religion, it is the old time religion, it was good for Father and for Mother, and it is good enough for me." Simply because something is good or bad for some one else does not logically make it good or bad for us. The danger of such comparison rests in the development of jealousy, envy, competition, derogation.

Moreover, such comparisons are "not wise." They make self the standard of judgment. It is the comparison of the scientist who rules every one else out as knowing nothing, simply because he is not a scientist. Such an attitude is made up of foolish pride, and is an abomination to God. Moreover, it makes oneself and others miserable, for it is the practice of "stretching beyond ability."

This practice is also hurtful. Paul said, "We will not boast." There are many things which are incapable of being measured, for there is no objective standard for them. Hence, if we are to measure personalities, we often thrust some down that others may rise. As Christians, our chief desire should be to help, and not to hinder. Therefore, Paul carefully avoided boasting of things without our measure. Rather, he emphasized the practice of "having hope, when your faith is increased, that we shall be enlarged by you according to our rule abundantly." Hence, the lifting up of the Corinthians will result also in enlarging of St. Paul and his coworkers.

The true means of comparison ought to be of self with God's measure or rule. Here we have something to pin to, a definite plumb-line, a set measure, a means of self-judgment. Of course, we are talking now to Christians. The Scripture reveals many of these things. First is the oft-repeated requirement of holiness of life. That sanctified living must reach our speech, our thoughts, and our deeds. Only you and God are capable of judging the quality of your holiness. This spiritual experience can never be evaluated by one for another. The second standard of living for a believer includes tithing. It is a Divine rule. Again, only you know whether you are tithing, or not, and you must judge yourself in this matter. The Lord Jesus set the standard of self-denial for His cause. Have you denied yourself and followed Him? The Scripture often repeats another standard, which is that every Christian should be a soul winner. "He that winneth souls is wise." "Ye shall be my witnesses." "Go ye into all the world, and preach the gospel to every creature." Finally, there is service as God's standard, and for this He gives gifts, to every man according to the measure of his faith. It is not for one man to try to do another man's work, or to measure and change his life according to another man's standard. Perform only that which God gives to you according to the measure of your faith.

III. COMMENDATION

Three kinds of commendation come to our attention in these verses: self-commendation, the commendation of others, and commendation of God.

Better is it never to undertake anything of moment than to be compelled to commend one's self. The prophet wrote concerning Christ what may also apply to His servants, "My servant shall not strive, nor cry, nor lift up his voice in the streets." Self-commendation is nauseating to people of Christian culture and sensitiveness. More are alienated than helped by such commendation. People have an aversion to a boastful attitude. Jesus did not even testify of Himself. He said, "If I bear witness of myself, my witness is not true. There is another that beareth witness of me; and I know that the witness which he witnesseth of me is true. . . . Search the Scriptures; for in them ye think ye have eternal life: and they are they which testify of me." It is for us to sit at the feet of Jesus, and follow His example in this matter. Better is it to let our lives, actions, and accomplishments speak for themselves. They shall speak far more sincerely and effectively. Know ye not that your life is described as "epistles known and read of all men." Better is it not to seek recommendation for advancement, if such recommendation does not come without your seeking it. If you are fitted for advancements, they will seek you rather than your seeking them. Ministers need to reiterate this lesson constantly.

A large place is given, however, for commendation of others in Christian living. Happy is the man who is approved by those among whom he lives. It is written of Timothy's father that he was "well reported of by the brethren that were at Lystra and Iconium." Many of Paul's epistles were written as recommendations which he voluntarily gave to some of his friends. The great epistle to the Romans was written to the Roman Church as a letter of recommendation of Phebe, the deaconess of the church at Cenchrea. Philemon was written as a recommendation of Onesimus, the runaway slave. Second Corinthians contained repeated recommendations of Titus. Philippians exalted Epaphroditus. Even the Early Church sent letters of commendation concerning the apostle Paul to all the churches.

History writes the true commendation of a man. Here the self-advertised are leveled, and the great become exalted. Death is the great leveler. History is rather impartial. It buries in oblivion, or it digs out, things you would rather not have known, but it may make up for the praise you did not get in life. That is what history is doing with Woodrow Wilson. That is what history did with Abraham Lincoln, who, to a great extent, has supplanted Washington in the hearts of his countrymen.

Greatest of all is the commendation of God. This may be present or future. In the present, it consists of the witness of the Spirit with our spirit that we are living pleasing to God. Without that commendation, we know that we have grieved the Spirit, and we are condemned in our hearts. But there is no condemnation to him who walks after the Spirit, and not after the flesh. Some live constantly with defiled consciences, needing cleansing. Others walk with a testimony like St. Paul's, "I have always a conscience void of offence." The future commendation of God is even more valuable. "We must all appear before the judgment seat of Christ; that every one may receive the things done in his body . . . whether . . . good or bad." Christ said, In that day I will say unto you, "Well done, good and faithful servant." Great will be the joy of having His approval. Never mind what anyone else says in comparison or criticism or commendation, so long as you have God's commendation.

With Paul, let all our boast, our glory, and our commendation rest in God. Their deposit is in His keeping for the future. Willingly, therefore, we will endure pain for future pleasure. "For not he that commendeth himself is approved, but whom the Lord commendeth."

XXVI

THE USE MEN MAKE OF THE DEVIL'S MASK

TEXT: *"Satan himself is transformed into an angel of light. Therefore it is no great thing if his ministers also be transformed as the ministers of righteousness; whose end shall be according to their works."*—II COR. 11:1-15.

MEN WEAR MASKS. A mask is anything used to cover or disguise the features. Figuratively, it is anything designed to conceal the emotions or sentiments. Its purpose is to deceive. A mask is often used in parties or masquerades. In drama a mask is used to resemble a character who is being portrayed. In real life a mask is often used to disguise a robber or murderer.

The purpose of a mask is pretense and subterfuge. It arises from the desire to disguise our features so that we will not be known for what we actually are. Since the face reveals one's emotions and intents, the mask usually covers the face. One may study to make his face conceal rather than reveal, and by the very expressions of his countenance he may become an artist in subterfuge without resorting to a material mask. His own features thereby become a mask. This simulation is the basis of hypocrisy, namely, pretending to be something one is not or acting a part which one is not, or assuming a false appearance of virtue or religion. No man can transform himself. All he can do is to conform himself to some guise or appearance which in reality he is not. For the Christian the practice of conformation is forbidden. We are told, "Be not conformed to this world: but be ye transformed by the renewing of your mind." Much deception or acting or the use of masks is practiced today. People wear masks of patriotism who are not patriotic at all. Others wear masks of religion for ulterior purposes. Some use a mask of self-sacrifice to cover up some other motive, and some use the mask of activity in business to cover up indolence and laziness. A mask permits one to appear that which he actually is not. His heart may be far from what he professes.

Protection from this practice of deception is very necessary. At this game of deception Satan is the greatest artist of the ages and it is his example which inspires innumerable deceivers to assume false forms and to accomplish fell designs. This is true in economics, in diplomatic work, in politics and in other spheres. We have an age of counterfeits. He who tells the biggest lie often gets the farthest in his purposes. In fact, some international leaders actually conduct their work on the basis of falsehood and deception. For evidence of this one need only read the diaries of foreign correspondents which record the lies which have been given with the intent deliberately to deceive other nations. But even religion is not free from deception. There are false Christs, false brethren, false apostles, false prophets against whom we have been warned from time immemorial. Not without meaning is it that we have been warned to try the spirits to see whether they be of God or not.

But, I say, this practice of deception is not new, for Satan has been a liar from the beginning. He is the father of lies and inspires all lies. Jesus said of him, "He was a murderer from the beginning, and abode not in the truth, because there is no truth in him. When he speaketh a lie, he speaketh of his own: for he is a liar, and the father of it."

These are strong words, but they designate every user of deception as a child of the devil and a user of the mask of Satan.

There is a need from time to time to strip the mask from these movements and minions of the great deceiver so as to protect God's sheep from destruction. Jesus warned that wolves would come in sheep's clothing, and Paul also warned his elders that wolves would come into the flock to destroy it. Only the true Shepherd and the faithful pastors are willing to strip this deception from these enemies of God's people. Such a faithful pastor was Paul.

I. THE MASK OF THE DEVIL—DECEPTION

According to our text, the mask which Satan uses is that of an angel of light. We read, "For Satan himself is transformed into an angel of light." That is, he assumes the form or the appearance of an angel of light. Let us not forget that Satan is the prince of darkness, the source of all evil and wickedness, otherwise called the Evil One, and yet he assumes the mask of an angel of light.

The Bible describes these great angels who have been the servants of God and the messengers to men in the Scripture. One rather dim and strange figure is called Michael, who, we are told, stands for the children of God. This archangel is mentioned only three times in the Bible, and always it is in conflict with Satan. Once when Daniel prayed for three weeks and the answer did not come until that time was ended, he saw a great vision and a hand touched him and strengthened him and announced to him:

"Fear not, Daniel: for from the first day that thou didst set thine heart to understand, and to chasten thyself before thy God, thy words were heard, and I am come for thy words. But the prince of the kingdom of Persia withstood me one and twenty days: but, lo, Michael, one of the chief princes, came to help me ... now I am come to make thee understand what shall befall thy people in the later days."

Again, Michael is represented as the archangel who shall deliver the people of God in the time of the tribulation and Michael was represented by Jude as one who contended with the devil over the body of Moses saying, "The Lord rebuke thee, Satan." This mysterious and misty figure of Scripture is unquestionably one of the chief powers of the angelic hosts of God.

Yet another such archangel is Gabriel, whom we might call the announcer. It was Gabriel who appeared to Zachariah by the altar and announced to him that Elisabeth his wife should bear him a son who would be great in the sight of the Lord and filled with the Holy Ghost and used of God to turn the children of Israel unto the Lord their God. It was Gabriel who appeared unto Mary the Virgin saying, "Fear not, Mary: for thou has found favor with God. And, behold, thou shalt conceive in thy womb, and bring forth a son, and shalt call his name Jesus. He shall be great, and shall be called the Son of the Highest . . . therefore also that holy thing which shall be born of thee shall be called the Son of God." Likewise, Gabriel is twice represented as having appeared to Daniel, revealing to him the things which were to come. It is not improbable that it was Gabriel who spoke to Joseph in a vision and also guided the wise men, that the knowledge of the birth of Jesus should not be known to Herod.

The Scripture describes hosts of other angels. We read of them singing when Christ was born, of rejoicing in heaven at the repentance of one sinner and of gathering innumerable companies about the throne of God singing His praise.

It is as one of these angels that Satan appeared. No doubt that is due to Satan's original form, for his original name was the Angel of Light or the Angel of the Morning. He was the most splendid of the creations of God, and his position in heaven was the highest of all of the archangels. But that was before he willed to be equal with God, before he was found rebellious and sin was discovered in him, so that it was necessary for God to cast him out from the place of his dwelling. Now Satan is known as the prince of darkness, the prince of death, the source of all doom to the souls of men. He is the god of this present evil world and all the suffering and wickedness and sorrow of this world are due to him.

Nevertheless, it is as an angel of light that Satan loves to make his appeal to men. This, no doubt, is his most effective means of tempting men. He even so appeared in the presence of God, according to the book of Job.

The Bible, however, tells us of other forms of Satan which he desires to hide. One is as a serpent, which form he assumed for the purpose of temptation, a temptation that brought all of sorrow into the world. Another is the form of a roaring lion or a dragon seeking those whom he may devour. Another is the form of "the accuser of the brethren," who seeks things within believers whom he might accuse before God that he might claim these servants of the Lord. Another title is "the Evil One," or the source of all evil in the world, from whom we pray to be protected.

Taking the form of an angel of light, Satan most effectively deceives men. He appeals to their better motives, their religious instincts, their altruistic tolerance, their humanitarianism and in the name of progress, good works and a better world he leads men captive to his will. This mask of an angel of light deceives men.

Paul refers to Satan's first use of this mask, namely, in the illustration of the deception of Eve in the beginning of human history. He said, "I fear, lest by any means, as the serpent beguiled Eve through his subtlety, so your minds should be corrupted from the simplicity that is in Christ." The reference to the serpent is a recognition by Paul that Satan uses masks. Here the mask is spoken of as though it were the tempter himself. It is made amply plain in the Bible that the serpent did not tempt the woman, but it was Satan using the form of a serpent. We have reason to believe that the serpent was once the most beautiful of God's creations in the Garden of Eden, and for this purpose it was assumed by Satan. We read, "The serpent was the most subtle beast of the field." In Eden we have no picture of a writhing, dusty, crawling reptile which is now the object of the antipathy and fear of every man. He was unquestionably a creature of beauty before he was cursed and compelled to crawl. Here Satan first appeared to man as the angel of light.

A careful study of the record of this first temptation will inform us as to the most common strategy and tactic of our enemy, namely, the assumption of the mask of an angel of light. Paul refers to the craftiness by which Satan deceived Eve and, later, to the wiles of the devil against which we must protect ourselves and stand. Notice how that craftiness is here revealed. First, Satan questions or raises doubt concerning God's revelation. He said, "Yea, hath God said?" There is no previous record that the woman had told the serpent that God had said certain things. How, then, did Satan know that God had so spoken unless it were a fact? Remember also that when anyone questions the Bible that there is a Bible to question. There is a body of truth already present and this body of truth can no more be broken than the original commandment given by God, when He said, to man, "Ye shall not eat of every tree in the garden."

The next attack made by Satan was a direct denial of the word of God. He said, "Ye shall not surely die." But God had said that man would die when he disobeyed that commandment. Here was the beginning of a substitution of something else for the word of God. Recently, I read a letter from a graduate student to another graduate student who had been trying to win the first one to Jesus Christ. That letter was full first of agnosticism, then atheism and then even of blasphemy, and in reading over this passage of Scripture telling of Satan's questioning, Satan's doubt, Satan's denial and Satan's aspersion upon the word of God, I noticed that that was exactly the course taken by this unbeliever in his attack upon God and God's Word. Thus it was and is that Satan always has acted.

Finally, in the garden he even cast aspersion upon the person of God. He said, "For God doth know that in the day ye eat thereof, . . . ye shall be as gods, knowing good and evil." He suggested that God is not good, that God was withholding something from man, that God was selfish, dictatorial, and wanted to keep man in subjection. Finally, Satan actively and positively suggested that by sinning, man would gain knowledge, pleasure and satisfaction of his desire, so that he impelled man to the sin which resulted in his fall. Now, wherever you see such doubt of God's revelation, such denial of His word, such aspersions on His Person and such suggestions leading to indulgence and satisfaction of the flesh, you know that you see the traces of Satan's activity and not that of an angel of light.

Just as this mask of friend, advocate, teacher and deliverer deceived Eve into sin, so it has deceived countless others into sin, and blinded the eyes and the minds of those who believe not, lest the light of the glorious Gospel of Christ who is the image of God should shine unto them. Satan leads men into darkness and into captivity at his will.

Many are the devices of Satan for the destruction of the soul. Paul said, "We are not ignorant of his devices." The prime object of the evil one is to usurp the place of God over men, to substitute evil principles of life for godly principles and to defeat the mediatorial, redemptive purposes of God in order to hold men in the kingdom of darkness under death and unto judgment. Some of Satan's devices are adapted to the character of the person whom he tempts. With the Lord Jesus Christ he just about ran the whole list of temptations. Therefore, it is always profitable and helpful to rehearse and to study those temptations of the Lord Jesus Christ.

Paul speaks of unforgivingness as a device of the devil for the destruction of our souls and advises men to forgive others lest Satan should get an advantage of them. Another device is sickness, which sometimes invites bitterness or complaints against God and thus results in the glory of Satan. Another device is to tempt some who have received the Word of God to fall away. Although God has promised succor to us in the hour of temptation, for Christ overcame every temptation such as we shall have and understands and knows them, nevertheless, some do not go to Jesus and are overcome. Another device is opposition, so that when we pray or when we undertake a good work Satan impedes our work. He hinders our prayers. He opposes our efforts and we are constantly in a spiritual struggle against principalities and powers, against demons, spiritual wickedness in high places, so that our lives demand constant watching, prayer, spiritual preparedness and union with Christ in order that we might always be able to triumph over Satan and his devices.

Undoubtedly, the greatest instrument of deception and destruction of soul is installing Satan's own ministers as the ministers of righteousness. Only this can explain the great numbers of people who embrace the error and anti-Biblical systems now so prevalent. It is only necessary for Satan to get men to believe a lie in order to get advantage over them and to hinder the work of God's servants in their hearts and minds. Sometimes I think it is more difficult to convert men from half truths than it is from outright heathenism. This is exactly what was happening at Corinth. Satan's ministers were being installed in the church as ministers of righteousness and they were turning these believers away from the truth. Yet it is happening today on a scale which is appalling throughout Christendom. It is not my purpose to name any such ministers of Satan, but we should ascertain the great principles upon which we may recognize them by what they are, what they teach and what they do. Who are these men who are using Satan's mask.

II. THE MEN USING SATAN'S MASK

Many have taken a leaf out of Satan's book, whether knowingly or ignorantly, and as deceitful workers prey upon the allegiance, the faith and even the superstitions of men. Paul calls them false apostles. He refers to them in this passage of Scripture as corrupters, superfine apostles and as ministers of Satan as well as deceitful workers. These unquestionably were his opponents who had wormed their way into authority in the Corinthian Church during his absence and with whom he was compelled to contrast himself. Because of a faulty translation in our King James version, which speaks of "the very chieftest apostle," men sometimes have thought that Paul was here comparing himself with Peter, James and John, but he is not in any way even referring to the chief apostles in this passage. He is contending only with spurious, self-assertive apostles. Notice how he describes them.

First, he calls them seducers attempting to corrupt the mind of the bride of Christ. The figure is used of a bride being betrothed to Christ and continuing in sincerity and purity of thought and devotion to her bridegroom, but these false apostles were attempting to seduce her from her betrothed. When one is converted to the Lord Jesus Christ he is engaged to Him in such a way that there must be no turning away without spiritual adultery, without sin. For this is to become disloyal, to make room for another lord, to deny the heavenly bridegroom. Therefore, any one who turns from the great Redeemer is of Satan. Any teacher who brings disloyalty to the Redeemer and Son of God may be described as an agent of Satan the great deceiver.

Secondly, Paul said of these false apostles that they snatched away true righteousness from men. He said, "His ministers also be transformed as the ministers of righteousness." Satan's ministers naturally are the opposite of God's ministers. Why it is that when they are first described as Satan's ministers, if they wish to simulate something else, they are not then called in the form of God's ministers? Here we have them described as masking as the ministers of righteousness. The fact is, the ministers of God who preach justification by faith and establishment in Christ are ministers of righteousness, for believers are thereby declared to be righteous. The righteousness of God is manifested from faith to faith. "Being justified freely by his grace through the redemption that is in Christ Jesus: Whom God hath set forth to be a propitiation through faith in his blood, to declare his righteousness for the remission of sins." Hence, the work of Satan's ministers is to keep God's saving righteousness from men or to seduce them from it by denying the Lord who bought them. The very devilishness of this is seen in that these ministers pretend to bestow righteousness but in reality bring damnation. They do this by denying the Gospel, by substituting a false gospel and by presenting a Jesus who is not the Jesus spoken of and presented in the Scripture.

Paul also says that they are false apostles because they are seeking personal gain. A large part of this passage consists of the contrast between Paul's life of self-denial, his labor with his hands and his extreme care to make the Gospel no means of gain to him, and the life of these false apostles quartered upon the Corinthians, fleecing them and draining them of their substance. Therefore, Paul was compelled to call attention of the Corinthians to what he himself had done, so that in contrast he might show them up. He did not like this boasting and he felt like a fool when he was doing it, and yet he was compelled to boast. We find in this chapter that he was being personally compared with these false apostles. Today there are many such false apostles who may be called religious racketeers. We find them in radio work, in evangelism, in established pulpits and in numerous other Christian fields. We could name them this morning if we desired—men who form new movements and make grandiose promises concerning healing or psychological development and at the same time mulct their victims of their possessions. Others of them deal only with the rich, and so are enabled to travel all over the world in groups living on the rich. Still others are organized into sects which have such an appeal and claim so many false healings that armored cars have to come for the money which they take from people. We suggest that the people of God should beware of such sects or religious pretenders assuming the guise of Christianity, whose leaders make no report or give no account of the funds which they establish. Rather, let our giving be done through established churches and responsible organizations.

These false apostles present a false gospel. The test of any preacher or any movement ought to be the question, "What Jesus, what gospel and what spirit do they bring?" That is exactly what Paul raised here. He said, "If he that cometh preacheth another Jesus, whom we have not preached, or if ye receive another spirit, which ye have not received, or another gospel, which ye have not accepted, ye might well bear with him." A false apostle never presents the true Jesus Christ, the true Gospel or the true Holy Spirit. The Christ of the Bible is very recognizable. He is the pre-existent One, virgin born, sinless, miracle-working, claiming to be the Son of God, dying for our sins, rising for our justification, ascending to the right hand of the Father for intercession and promising to come again in glory and power. Other Jesuses which may be legalistic, mystic or professed incarnations of God are different from that presented in the Bible and by the faithful servants of God. Listen carefully to the kind of Jesus presented by these professed servants of righteousness. Listen also to their gospel. Is it the gospel of God's love revealed in making an atonement for our sin? Does it proclaim the cross as the wisdom of God and the power of God? Does it declare a substitute for him who though He knew no sin yet was made sin for us that we through His righteousness might become the righteousness of God? Does that gospel present a propitiation through redemption by blood? Many other gospels are being declared today, but there is only one Gospel, that given in the Bible. What about the spirit which is received through these ministers of righteousness? Is it the Holy Spirit as the witness of our salvation, bearing the fruit of the Spirit? Do they bring love, peace, joy, long-suffering, temperance and faith, or are they divisive, contentious, critical and destructive? "By their fruits ye shall know them." Therefore, try the spirits of those who profess to be your leaders and know whether they be of God or not. Whenever any one comes bringing another Gospel than that which you have received or another Jesus than that which has been preached unto you or another spirit than that which God has promised in the Word, Paul cries out, Let him be accursed. Yet such a gospel and Jesus and spirit are being presented in many places in the name of Christianity today under what is called modernistic Christianity. The leading spokesman for modernism once said:

"Christianity according to fundamentalism is one religion. Christianity according to modernism is another religion. Which is the true religion is the question which is to be settled in all probability by our generation for future generations. . . . There is a clash here as profound and as grim as between Christianity and Confucianism. Amiable words can not hide the differences. 'Blest be the tie' may be sung till doomsday, but it can not bind these two worlds together. The God of the fundamentalist is one God; the god of the modernist is another. The Christ of the fundamentalist is one Christ; the Christ of the modernist is another. The Bible of fundamentalism is one Bible; the Bible of modernism is another. The Church, the kingdom, salvation, the consummation of all things—these are one thing to the fundamentalist and another thing to modernists. Which God is the Christian God, which Christ is the Christian Christ, which Bible is the Christian Bible, which church, which kingdom, which salvation, which consummation, are the Christian Church, the Christian kingdom, the Christian salvation, the Christian consummation? The future will tell."

But we do not agree that the future will tell. We believe that the Bible has told, and that the faith once and for all delivered unto the saints is the same today as it was in the first century. Therefore, we should know what kind of Christ and what kind of gospel and what kind of spirit are being preached to us.

Paul announces the final end of such false ministers of righteousness. He said, "Whose end shall be according to their works." What does the Bible say of Satan and his servants as to their end? Jesus made that very plain when He said to the wicked, "Depart from me, ye cursed, into everlasting fire, prepared for the devil and his angels." Revelation declares that they will be cast into the lake which burneth with fire and brimstone which is the second death and that the smoke of their torment ascendeth forever and ever. Over these we need not fret ourselves, because we know their end. They shall soon be cut down and be no more. These false teachers are described by Jude as

"spots in your feasts of charity, . . . clouds they are without water, carried about of winds; trees whose fruit withereth, without fruit, twice dead, plucked up by the roots; Raging waves of the sea, foaming out their own shame; wandering stars, to whom is reserved the blackness of darkness forever."

No, our fear should not be for them, because we know their end, but our fear and our burden are for the people whom they delude, as these Corinthians were deluded by false apostles. These sheep have been committed to our care; for them we fear and for them we labor, for them we contend that they may be saved and secure in the arms of Jesus.

III. THE MAIN PROTECTION FROM THESE DECEPTIONS

The one protection God has raised against those who use the mask of the devil to deceive and to destroy consists of faithful pastors and teachers, true servants of the living God. Look at Paul as an illustration of this. He compares himself here with a godly father who is concerned over his daughter whom he has espoused to a man and for whom he is responsible until she is joined to her bridegroom. The lovely bride unquestionably represented the Corinthians or the people of God whom Paul had won from heathenism. They were his children in the faith. He had espoused them to Jesus Christ and now he protected them until he could present them as spotless to the bridegroom. He spoke of having a zeal and a jealousy of God that he may present the Corinthian church as a chaste virgin to Christ, uncorrupted and unspoiled by the world. This was the reason for his labors, for his sacrifice, for his willingness to expose his own person to the attack of false apostles, for all that he did as a true apostle of God.

Wherever there are pastors who are full of zeal and jealousy of God for His work and His people we have those who will protect from these deceptions. Such true pastors care for, teach, labor for, and protect the people from error, especially their own converts for whom they are responsible. They are willing to count not the cost for the sake of God's flock. They are not hirelings. They are true shepherds. They are in it not to fleece the flock, but to preserve and keep the flock from the wolves, that they may present the flock to the Good Shepherd.

Perhaps such pastors have human failings. They may be slow of speech or unimpressive in presence as his enemies said of Paul. They may have many other limitations, but if they have knowledge and love of God, devotion to Christ and zeal for His cause, they will be the great bulwark against deception. It is for this reason that I joy in sending out so many young pastors from this church. They are the hope of the church of the future.

Yet Paul pled for a fair attitude from these Corinthians who represented the people of God. Judging by their excessive readiness to receive and to bear with false apostles, how much more should they have received and borne with the true. Here there is a bit of irony, showing the folly of their tolerance of false apostles who would wreck the church when they had been irritable and rebellious to the true father of their church, namely, Paul himself. Too often these people of God are magnanimous with those who are willing to destroy, to deny and to cause doubt in the church, but they are contentious and irascible with God's true servants, who are willing to correct and guide them by their own labors.

Likewise, we believe that we should plead for a full devotion to Christ from His people. Remember that in your conversion you have been espoused to the Lord Jesus Christ, who is the lovely, heavenly bridegroom. Therefore, let your thoughts contain no object of affection except Him. Let there be no disloyalty, no corruption of your thinking, but rather enthrone Him as your Lord, your King and your God. Likewise, keep yourself spotless until His coming, that you may be presented acceptable to Him. The personal knowledge of Him as your living Lord and companion will be an ample protection from false Christs. You will therefore be able to discern the counterfeits. I remember in college two young men who were brothers. They were as like as two peas in a pod. At first nobody could tell them apart. They used to play tricks on the girls by having one make an engagement with a girl and the other take her out, without the girl knowing any difference. Both had curly hair, high foreheads, blue eyes, and sharp features. Both were athletic, and could interchange in their positions on the athletic teams. They played forward in basket-ball and would shift from one side to the other without any difficulty. They were the battery on the ball team, catching and pitching, and could interchange without any difficulty. Gradually, through close fellowship and association, I became able to distinguish between the two. There was something in the eyes, something in the physical carriage, something in the walk, so that whether I was near or far away, I could tell the difference between Ernest and Earle. Others who did not know them so well could not tell the difference. I wonder if it is not the same with Christ. We have to become acquainted with Him personally and really know Him before we can discern the difference between Him and these substitutes which are being presented to us as the real Christ. Certainly we ought to repudiate with horror every one and every thing which would seduce our thoughts from our lovely Lord.

Then let there be no masking in this matter of salvation of our souls. Let us be intolerant of all insincerity, inconsistency, dishonesty and hypocrisy in religious matters, wherever they are found. Let us be wise enough to realize the end of those who follow these apostles, who hold to a false gospel and worship another Jesus than that which is given in the Scriptures. Only by unfeigned love and loyalty can we declare and retain our bethrothal to the Lord Jesus Christ, who is the object of our love and our hope and who some day will be thoroughly and perfectly joined to us.

XXVII

JUST A PLAIN FOOL FOR CHRIST'S SAKE

TEXT: *"Let no man think me a fool; if otherwise, yet as a fool receive me, that I may boast myself a little."*—II COR. 11:16-33.

PAUL ASSUMES the rôle of a fool, and repeatedly declares that he speaks as a fool in this passage. The mask for the part of a fool is not one men like to assume. Shakespeare said, "All the world's a stage, and men and women players. They have their exits and their entrances." We assume various rôles as we all act our parts. Some pretend to be good, others to be bold, others to be indifferent, and we often act a part to ourselves. But there are two times when men are themselves, when they cannot act a part. One is in prayer, and the other will be at the judgment. Some even try to act a part to God in prayer, but it is foolishness, for God knows our hearts. These rôles which we assume are surely prejudicial to ourselves.

Once, however, a character of Scripture, David, assumed the rôle of a fool, allowing his spittle to fall upon his beard, until men said that he was mad. But this was only a ruse for him to gain his own safety, and it was performed when he was in a backslidden state. The rôle of a boaster was assumed by Paul, and it made him feel as a fool. There are times we do things of which we are self-conscious and in which we feel foolish. These are entirely unlike our personality, and are incongruous with our character. For Paul such a rôle is "not after the Lord," but after the world. Christ's life and mind were utterly different from the boastful rôle which Paul assumed. The things of which Paul boasted from the viewpoint of Christ were heroic, praiseworthy, and the foundation of a great reward, but Paul knew that Christ would not boast of them. In comparison with the life receiving the sanction of worldly wisdom, the life and actions of Paul were those of a fool.

Paul was compelled to assume this rôle of a boaster, because of the detractors who had cast aspersions on his love of the Corinthians, his motives in making the great collection, his unassuming weakness in their presence, and his contemptibleness of speech in preaching. Hence, he gives us a self-revelation seen no place else in the Bible. In this chapter, we have a glimpse into the apostolic life and service. It is a narration excluded from the Book of Acts. It was a most difficult thing for a man to do.

By nature, Paul was a great fighter; he was unwilling to allow his converts and churches to be carried into error. This compelled him to meet his attackers on their own grounds, namely, that of boasting in deeds. His way was constantly threated by an all-engulfing paganism, or a perverted Judaism. He found a paganism which said that all kinds of conduct are lawful for a Christian man, a philosophy which makes Christian liberty a mere aid to pagan license. He found paganism in thought, the sublimation of the Christian doctrine of the resurrection of the body into the pagan doctrine of the immortality of the soul. He found human pride manifested in an effort to substitute merit for Divine grace as the means of salvation. All these conflicts were for the preservation of the church's life, yet one break after another came in the levee through which paganism was seeping. Not for a moment did Paul have peace. Nowhere do we see that better than in these epistles to Corinth. Though Paul seemed at times to lose, he won the great battle. History proves that to us, for though the great decline from Paulinism is evident in the writings of Irenæus, it was rediscovered in Augustinianism. It was again lost in the dark ages and recovered in the Reformation. It has been obscured in our day, but there is beginning to be a new revival of Paulinism.

What made Paul feel like a fool was his description of his own life. He declared that he had boldness sufficient to match the foremost of the apostles. He needed a holy boldness to do God's work as he faced the Jews in their synagogues, the philosophers in the school of Tyrannus and on the Areopagus, and the advances of other religions in the market places of heathendom. But Paul was not alone in this. Peter and John were endued with a holy boldness, as were the other apostles after Pentecost. Such boldness comes with the gift of the Holy Ghost. But Paul's life was abundant in labors and sufferings. He suffered more than the other apostles. When he was called, God said to Ananias, "I will show him how great things he must suffer." Five times received he thirty-nine stripes. There is no mention of those in Acts, and yet it means that Paul was scourged as Jesus was scourged, not once but five times. Thrice he was beaten with rods. We have the description of the time at Philippi when he was left with a broken, bleeding back, lying in the stocks in a dungeon. We have the record of his stoning at Lystra, when he was left for dead. We have three unrecorded shipwrecks endured by Paul, and one stretch of two and a half days he spent in the water. Many were the perils he enumerated—the weariness, the hunger, the thirst, the cold, the nakedness, the fasting, and the watchings he endured.

Yet Paul, in the midst of it all, had a burning heart of compassion for the souls of men and for the care of the churches. Such is the one who seven times calls himself a fool as he enumerates these deeds. He evaluated this life by saying, "If in this life only we have hope in Christ, we are of all men most miserable," and all the world would agree that he was just a plain fool. If this life were all, such deeds would be foolishness. They would justify the charge of madness, of being beside himself, of being inexplicable. Even as we read this narrative, we realize that unless some tremendous motive lay behind such a life, only a fool would endure it.

Then Paul was a fool, and there are ways in which we Christians must be plain fools for Christ's sake in the eyes of the world. One is our way of believing. Another is our way of living, and another is our way of dying.

I. OUR WAY OF BELIEVING

Christian truth is utter foolishness to the world. Christians believe in the sovereignty of God. And by this, we mean the absolute authority, rule, and government of God in the whole of reality, which exists apart from Himself in the realms of nature and grace. It implies that there is only one God to be worshiped. "The Lord he is God; there is none else beside him." "He is God in heaven above, and upon earth beneath: there is none else." This principle supposes the fact of creation. When anything independent of God is posited, we deny the Divine sovereignty. "By the word of the Lord were the heavens made; and all the host of them by the breath of his mouth." On this Creatorhood of God rests our piety in adoration, prayer, and praise. His sovereignty consists in the right of rule and dominion over all things of His universal possession. "The earth is the Lord's." "The Most High ruleth in the kingdom of men." His sovereignty is exercised in government in accordance with what He decrees. "Surely as I have thought, so shall it come to pass; and as I have purposed, so shall it stand." His power pervades all, efficiently bringing to pass His will by ordinary providence, by the dispossession of earthly authority, and by the free acts of men. This doctrine of Divine Sovereignty is repudiated by the world. Men either make God identical with the world or an abstraction of force. That one should believe that God has a plan which is being wrought out in the midst of the wrath of men is considered folly, yet the Christian believes that all things work together for good for the called.

The second foolish thing Christians believe, according to the world, is the fact of revelation. The believer accepts the fact that God has spoken, has revealed Himself, His will and His purpose. He believes that this revelation is given in the Bible, that the Bible is the Word of God. Many things testify to this, but God witnesseth to His Word. His revelation is infallibly inspired. Some are willing to admit that the Bible contains the Word of God, others that it witnesses to the Word of God, and others that revelation is the opposite side of human discovery. But those who accept the Bible and the Bible's claims and the Christian teaching about revelation as a means of knowing the things of God, otherwise closed from men, are called fools by the world.

Another foolish thing which Christians believe, according to the world, is the doctrine of the atonement. The Christian teaching believes in a substitutionary, satisfactory atonement for man's guilt, made by Christ to God, thereby reconciling God to men. This is declared to be a legal process of imputing man's guilt to Christ, and Christ's righteousness to men. "He hath made him to be sin for us, who knew no sin; that we might be made the righteousness of God in him." The world is willing to talk about the example of Christ, the nurture of the Christian faith, the governmental atonement, the love of God manifested on Calvary, the acceptation of the death of Christ as if it were the death of all, but it rebels at the vicarious satisfaction of Calvary. This is called by opprobrious terms, and that one should die for all is said to be an impossibility. This doctrine of the cross, which is our Gospel and our hope, is foolishness to the world, and it is even hated by some. In modern terms, people who accept Christianity in place of evolution, revelation instead of the authority of reason, and atonement instead of merit, are fools, yet there are men who so hold, namely, Christians.

There are many other things Christians believe which cause the world to dub them fools. Such is the supernatural nature of prayer, which changes things in the world, and is more than mere subjectiveism. Such is salvation by grace, not by works or character. Such is a future judgment for the deeds done in this world.

II. IN OUR WAY OF LIVING

The way Christians live is foolishness to the men of the world. Take a few examples. First, tithing. A believer brings the first-fruits of his earnings to God. He acknowledges God's corner in his field. He seeks first the kingdom of God and His righteousness. He tithes his income as a rule of Christian life. This portion of his substance he gives to missions, to evangelism, to Christian education at a great personal sacrifice. He could use this same money for a lovely vacation, for fine clothes, to buy automobiles, to own a better home. Yet he knows that this is God's will, and he loves to give because God wills it. The world cannot understand such action. It is not liberal in its giving, and it considers such a person a fool. The world, in contrast, gathers, seeks security in things, lays up for tomorrow, but God calls such people fools, and illustrates it with the parable of the rich man who filled his barns and took no thought for his soul.

Another illustration of the Christian way of living is the observance of the Lord's Day. The believer places the church, the worship of God, soul-winning, the spiritual things, first. He sets one day apart in seven as a day of spiritual invigoration. He fulfills the Biblical adage, which says:

"If thou turn away thy foot from the Sabbath, from doing thy pleasure on my holy day; and call the Sabbath a delight, the holy of the Lord, honorable; and shalt honor him, not doing thine own ways, nor finding thine own pleasure, nor speaking thine own words: Then shalt thou delight thyself in the Lord; and I will cause thee to ride upon the high places of the earth."

The world thinks the Lord's Day is a time for holiday, parades, carousal, patriotic display, vacation, and exercise. Those who do God's will on the Lord's Day are called Blue Noses and fools, and yet experience and history have proved that man and beast and machine need a day of rest.

Another illustration of the Christian way of living is the willingness to serve. Christians walk circumspectly, "not as fools, but as wise, Redeeming the time, because the days are evil." Christians practice love to God and to their neighbor. They believe, and literally accept, that this is the first law, and follow the illustration of the Good Samaritan, whether in the case of Florence Nightingale in the Crimea, or Frances Willard in redemption of fallen humanity, or Jane Addams in the slums. They follow the example given by Jesus Christ in humility and service. This Christian teaching has stimulated men in all walks of life, from those in public office to private employers, to live for public service. They remember the words, "Inasmuch as ye did it unto one of these, ye did it unto me." The world, on the other hand, formulates its philosophy in egoism, believing that selfishness is the prime moving factor in life. The philosophers call it utilitarianism; any one who doesn't take care of No. 1 first is a fool. The world may praise idealism, but it will not follow the Christian way of idealism. Those who do are fools.

Another illustration of the Christian way of living is the endurance of suffering. Christianity is a way of life glorifying suffering and infusing a meaning into it. Christ declared that Christians should rejoice if they were persecuted for righteousness' sake, for great is their reward in heaven. Peter proclaimed, "If any man suffer as a Christian . . . let him glorify God on this behalf." And Paul declared, "These light afflictions which are but for a moment work out for us a far more eternal and exceeding weight of glory." Christians often deliberately choose pain for the sake of Christ. Self-denial is a principle of Christianity. Thus Moses chose "rather to suffer affliction with the people of God, than to endure the pleasures of sin for a season." Thus the heroes of the faith have endured as seeing the invisible. Such lives are inexplicable to the world. They are mere folly. The world cannot understand the Early Church's willingness to suffer for its belief in Christ. The world has no appreciation for the victims of the inquisition or for the sufferers in the time of the Reformation. The world seeks pleasure, happiness, and that alone.

The Christian way is a way of obedience of God. The will of God to believers is supreme. There is an authority above the individual man, but with the world the will of man is autonomous and is supreme. It forever exalts man, and humanizes Deity. It doesn't understand.

III. IN OUR WAY OF DYING

The world considers that the Christian way of dying is foolishness. The Christian is fearless of death, not with bravado, but with simple faith. The Christian knows that to die is to go to be with the Lord, to be absent from the body, but present with the Lord. The believer knows it is better to go to be with Christ than to remain here. The believer sorrows not as they that have no hope, when death comes. The believer looks for the crown of righteousness which the Lord will give him in that day. For him the sting and victory of death are gone. Through the revelation of God, he has abounded in the knowledge of the future life and the resurrection body. He knows that One has tasted death for him and removed the power of death. The Christian knows how to die. This has been proved many times in the present war. The Christian can face bereavement in resignation and even in triumph, singing:

> "My Jesus, as Thou wilt,
> Oh, may my will be Thine,
> Into Thy hands of love
> I would my all resign.
> Through sorrow or through joy
> Conduct me as Thine own,
> And help me still to say,
> 'Thy will be done.' "

Profitable would it be to tarry upon the illustrations of how Christians die. When John Wesley was dying, his face lighted up, and he proclaimed, "Best of all is that God is with us." It became the watchword of Methodism. When Livingstone died, he was on his knees in prayer, and so was found by the natives of Africa. When

Tyndale died, outside the gate of Brussels by strangulation and burning, he prayed, "Oh, God, open the King of England's eyes."

Paul illustrated in his death the Christian way of dying. Without fear, with no cowering or shrinking, he waited until the Lord would take him. As he knew how to live, he knew how to die, without fear.

Let the world call me a fool. I still will stand on this rock, I will trust this God, and walk in this way. Think of the man God calls a fool. He who says there is no God, who trusts in riches, he who believes not the Scriptures, is a fool, according to God. Far better is it to play the fool in the eyes of men for a season, as Paul did, than to be pronounced a fool by God forever.

XXVIII

THORNS IN THE FLESH

TEXT: *"There was given to me a thorn in the flesh, the messenger of Satan to buffet me, lest I should be exalted above measure."*—II COR. 12:1-10.

OUR THEME COMES as a result of two glimpses into Paul's inner life which he granted only once in his writings. It is seldom that strong men permit others to look into the strictly private and personally precious regions of their lives. But if we are on the watch for these moments we may avail ourselves of rare opportunities for learning the secret of their triumph and their victory.

Recently the chancellor of a great university gave a small group of men the opportunity to see something of the spiritual idealism and of the motivating purposes of his life. In tender and self-revealing fashion he described the spiritual objectives of education and of his desire not only to prepare men to be doctors, lawyers, and merchants, but to give them an understanding of the spiritual values of life. Even the much criticized and commended but admittedly beautiful buildings of the new university were revealed to us as embodiments of the spiritual dream. This unusual opportunity to look into the inner recesses of a man's life brought a sense of reverence, a consciousness of widening horizons, and an awakening of sympathy for one's fellow men in this group of men, which they had not anticipated.

Here Paul shared with the Corinthians the great experience of his life. So reticent is he in telling it that he refers to himself in the third person, although there is no doubt that Paul was referring to himself. Only the necessity of vindicating his apostleship would ever have brought him to the point of speaking of it. He said that he knew a man in Christ, that is a believer, who fourteen years before was caught up into the third heaven. Paul says he does not know whether this man was in the body or out of the body, but that when he was caught up into the third heaven which is called paradise, he heard unspeakable words, that is, words which could never be completely comprehended, and which were not lawful for man to utter. Here is a description of an experience which is beyond the power of human words to make clear. Yet it had entered into the life of Paul. As near as we are able to understand, the third heaven is the place where God eminently manifests His glory. The Bible speaks of a heaven in which fowls fly, and a heaven which is adorned with stars, but the third heaven is the abode of the blessed. We are not capable of knowing very much of the particulars of that glorious place and state. At least, we know that it is called paradise and that there everything that man lost in his first estate will be restored. Paul heard words here, probably the language of angels, which it is not lawful to speak. As he wrote to the Corinthians, the tongue of angels would avail a man nothing had he not the love of Christ in his heart.

We are led to believe that this experience of Paul's was connected with the stoning which he endured at Lystra. There he and Barnabas had been taken for the gods Mercury and Jupiter and the populace went about to do sacrifice for them. With great effort did Paul restrain them. Later, the same multitude, led by reprobate Jews, dragged Paul outside of the city and stoned him. He was left for dead. Struck many times, so that he was taken for dead, it is evident that Paul was unconscious and badly bruised. Nevertheless, as the disciples stood round about him, he arose and walked back to the city. This seems to be the one experience when Paul could justly say that he did not know whether in the body or out of the body. God still had work for Paul to do and He miraculously restored Paul to health.

The second personal experience which Paul relates here was rarely shared because of the embarrassment which it caused him. He describes it as a thorn in the flesh. It came as a result of his first experience, his exaltation. He received it in order to keep him humble. It is a profound Christian truth that the higher we go in our spiritual exaltation, the deeper we must go in suffering in order to keep our balance. The larger a tree becomes, the deeper its roots must go. Paul's humiliation consisted of a thorn in the flesh. No figure could more aptly describe the irritation and trouble and inconvenience caused by this evil than that of a thorn. One must stop everything he is doing and remove the sliver or thorn before any measure of comfort will come to him. It is difficult to know what Paul's thorn was. Some think it was a physical malady, such as opthalmia, which resulted from the light above the brightness of the sun on the Damascus road, and again from the glory which Paul beheld when he was exalted to the third heaven. This theory is supported by his claim that the Galatians would have plucked out their eyes for him if this would have helped him. Others have advanced the claim, but without foundation, that Paul was subject to epilepsy. We do know that he kept a physician with him constantly. Another consideration is that Paul was buffeted by bodily temptations. He said, "I labor to keep my body under," and he advised others to "mortify the deeds of the body." According to Paul, the flesh was in a constant war against the spirit. Nothing is more distasteful, repulsive, and humiliating to a man of God than to be tempted in this fashion. Again his thorn may have been the opposition which came to him through false apostles, and through opposition which arose because of his contemptible speech. Perhaps he had an impediment in his speech.

Whatever this thorn in the flesh was, it constituted a source of great discouragement to Paul and a hindrance to his work. He confesses that three times he besought the Lord to remove it from him. Paul was mighty in prayer, and his prayers stand out as most moving and beautiful. Yet here is an illustration of one to whom God had committed the gift of healing, and who walked on the highest spiritual plane, whose prayer was refused. God answered the petitioner, but He did not grant the petition. Paul would never have earnestly set aside three seasons of prayer concerning this thorn had it not stood in the way of his effective work and caused him great inconvenience. But God did not remove it. Paul's explanation of this is that God permitted him to be buffeted lest he should be exalted above measure, lest pride and self-sufficiency spoil the high privileges which God had bestowed upon him. The two experiences entered into equilibrium and because of them Paul was kept in sympathy with his fellowmen, and yet could speak with authority concerning their spiritual lives. Let us remember that pride goeth before a fall. "Let him that thinketh he standeth take heed lest he fall." God's people should be very careful when they communicate their experiences to take notice of what God has done to keep them humble as well as what He has done to favor them and for their advancement.

I. Divinely Permitted Thorns That We Must Bear

Though Paul called his thorn a messenger of Satan, yet he recognized that God permitted it to afflict him. God never instigates human suffering or trial. He merely permits the enemy of our souls, who is constantly seeking an opportunity to accuse us before God and to overthrow us, to afflict us for a divine purpose. Hence, we see that even in Paul's permanent affliction, divine good was wrought. This is true of all divinely permitted affliction.

Burdens and trouble are inevitable in the life of man. Said Job, "Man is born unto trouble, as the sparks fly upward." Burden-bearing is universal. He who speaks on the subject of affliction never gets far from the dwelling place of human beings. Perhaps in these days more different kinds of suffering afflict men. In the Song of Solomon the Shunamite maiden invoked both the south and the north winds to bring fragrant aromas from the garden of the desert. She knew that it not only takes the soft south wind to produce the beauties of nature, but also the chill, brisk north wind. Time was when it seemed that only the south wind would blow over our country; prosperity and plenty were experienced by all. But now affliction has come, and in the Divine providence it is touching us that the better life may ensue.

No man's life is without a burden. Job's comrade had seen him succor and comfort others who had been afflicted and he was amazed at the discouragement which came over Job in his own affliction. Said he, "Thou hast strengthened the feeble knees. But now it has come upon thee, and thou faintest; it toucheth thee, and thou art troubled." Every man's life has something in it of the baptism of fire. It is easy to envy another who is seemingly free from trouble, burden and care. But were his experience known, no one would exchange his own burden for that of the seemingly care-free soul. Each man's burden is particularly and peculiarly suited to himself, and therefore it has a purpose.

The name of the thorn which afflicts us is legion, for the thorns are many. There is the insignificant thorn of frustrated hopes and ambitions. Many a man has hoped to reach a certain goal, to become a college graduate, to advance in his industry or office, to possess his own home, and has been frustrated in his desire. It has become a thorn in his flesh which irritates and disturbs his daily life. Insignificant as it seems to an outsider, it may fill the whole of his life and ruin the possibilities of contentment.

Another thorn is financial loss. Some have passed through straitened circumstances as a result of economic conditions and have permitted this thorn to overcome them. God permitted it to happen as a means of good to them as individuals, to their families, and to society as a whole, but they lost sight of all this and thought only of the thorn.

Personal illness is sometimes a thorn which destroys one's usefulness. I remember a companion of my boyhood who was stricken with infantile paralysis. He had been a very selfish, spoiled boy. Meeting him fifteen years later, still bearing the marks in his body of his suffering, one was impressed with the depth and sturdiness of his character, which was a blessing to all who knew him. It is said that a soldier of General Antigonus, who was suffering from a usually mortal affliction sought the point of extreme danger in every battle and fought with great fury, courting death. As a result, he performed great exploits, which were noticed by the general. In appreciation, Antigonus sought out a famous physician who was able to cure the man of his disease. Thenceforth, he was useless as a soldier. He feared to go into the hottest parts of battle, and protected his life at every turn. One's thorn sometimes contributes to one's character.

Bereavement drives some to permanent grief and despondency, whereas it may become, under the hand of God, a factor in the purification of one's soul and in the extension of his sympathy. In the story of Margaret Ogilvy we are told how she gained a kind, sweet look. Like most Scotch mothers, she was ambitious for the intellectual life of her son. At great sacrifice, he was put through the ordinary schools and sent off to college. One day came a telegram saying that he was very ill. The mother hurriedly departed to comfort her son. The train had no sooner gone from the station than a telegram arrived announcing the death of the boy. When she returned, the mother looked long at the christening robe, and turned her face to the wall. Later, when a neighbor would come in for sympathy in her bereavement, she would say, "Dunna greet, Janet." And with tears, the neighbor would say, "But you're greeting yourself." Bereavement is able to transform one's life to wide usefulness or to personal despondency.

In *Brothers Karamazov*, Dostoievsky puts this truth into the mouth of father Cosima. "At the dawn of my life, when I was a child, I had an elder brother, who died before my eyes at seventeen. And later on in the course of my life, I gradually became convinced that that brother had been for a guidance and a sign from on high for me. For had he not come into my life . . . I should never have entered on this precious path."

Paul became discouraged as the result of the thorn which he had to bear, and discouragement results universally from burdens, tribulations, and affliction. We remember that Elijah, who had performed great exploits in purifying Israel of the religion of Baal, later sat under the juniper tree and said, "It is enough. Take away my life." He was physically weary from his exertion. He was overpowered by a sense of loneliness, and he believed that his work was a failure. This is the result of burdens which are difficult to bear. Discouragement may easily lead one into sin. Recently, one who was guilty of gross sin accounted for it with the statement, "I was so lonely that I did not care what happened." Discouragement is the devil's strongest instrument to overpower a soul. Let not our burdens or afflictions turn us to discouragement.

II. THE DIVINE PURPOSE IN THESE THORNS

The thorn in one's life is a revealer of character. Until affliction comes, we never know what is in us. Only suffering and disappointment can make this known. The storms of life are necessary. I crossed the ocean one summer on the S.S. *Washington* when it made its second voyage. We were caught in the tail-end of a hurricane and the waves beat so high that the boat was compelled to stop its motors. In discussing the storm with one of the crew while physical uneasiness and fear held many of the passengers, he said, "I would like to see what this boat would do in a real storm." A great ship can never be tried in calm water. The north wind and the storm are necessary for the revelation of one's character. Said a certain person in speaking about a tragedy which had entered the life of another, "If that had happened to me I would have committed suicide." If, in reality, that had happened to this individual it might have revealed to him the latent powers of his own nature.

Affliction develops character. There can be no victory without conflict. It takes struggle to accomplish any great objective. During the Crusades the Damascus swords were famous for their keeness. It was a time when warriors were covered with coats of mail and it was necessary for an opponent not only to pierce but to cut into this armor. The Damascus blade could always cut the iron. Tradition has it that the Damascus steel was tempered in a fire made from charcoal of the desert thorn bush. Tribulation entered into the making of the sword.

The divine purpose of these thorns is to purify life. When Paul reached the city after his stoning, he preached to the disciples and exhorted them to continue in the faith, saying, "We must through much tribulation enter into the kingdom of God." Henry Ward Beecher suffered calumny and attack which brought great sorrow into his life, but through it he reached great heights of Christian ministry and said, "Man cannot enter the kingdom of God without strife." Gold is purified by fire, which consumes the dross and leaves the valuable metal. Says the Scripture, tribulation "yieldeth the peaceable fruits of righteousness unto them which are exercised thereby." Accept the thorn in your life with thanksgiving, and let it work out the Divine principle and purpose.

III. DIVINE PROVISION FOR THOSE BEARING THORNS

When God answered Paul's petition it was with the promise, "My grace is sufficient for thee: for my strength is made perfect in weakness." The Lord has made provision to sustain us in the midst of our afflictions and burdens. It is His Divine grace. Grace signifies two things: first, the good will of God towards us, which is enough to enlighten us and is sufficient to strengthen and comfort us, to support our souls and cheer our spirits in all afflictions and distresses. Second, it signifies the good work of God in us, the fullness that we receive from Christ which is suitable and seasonable for His followers. Christ understands our need and He supplies His strength and glory sufficient for our affliction. This Divine grace can be received only through prayer. We are not told to cast our burden away but to cast it upon the Lord, for He is able to sustain us.

It is true that God makes His strength known in weakness. This is a secret of Christian character. You know how to swim. The water sustains you when you rest in it and trust yourself to it. It is not necessary to struggle to keep yourself up. The man who struggles is soon worn out. Similiarly, God is omnipresent, is roundabout us on every hand. If we trust ourselves and our burdens to Him, He will sustain us and we may use our energy and strength to move forward. Human extremity is God's opportunity. The admission of weakness and inability in connection with prayer for Divine power is the source of spiritual success.

Paul's thorn was not removed, and he derived contentment and satisfaction from it. He said, "Therefore I take pleasure in infirmities, in reproaches, in necessities, in persecutions, in distresses for Christ's sake: For when I am weak, then am I strong." Paul did not seek these afflictions, nor is it right for us to do so. But when they came, he knew that they would result in greater spiritual power and accomplishment in the kingdom. Luther said that he never undertook any fresh work but he was visited either with a fit of sickness or some powerful temptation. It takes tribulation and affliction to make a man.

We cannot forget that the crown of our Savior was made of thorns. They brought unbearable pain and anguish to Him in the midst of His other sufferings. God permitted Him to bear them for a purpose. In the hour of His own darkness and discouragement Jesus cried, "Why?" Numerous others have not been able to understand the reason for their affliction. Without the thorns of Christ and what they represent, there would be no salvation for us who believe. God has a purpose in the thorns which He permits to come into the lives of all those who trust Him. His grace is sufficient for you.

XXIX

NOT YOURS, BUT YOU

TEXT: *"I seek not yours, but you: for the children ought not to lay up for the parents, but the parents for the children."*—II COR. 12:11-19.

THE GREAT APOSTLE Paul is speaking. Wherever Paul is revealed to us we stand amazed before his greatness. Here he is concluding his vindication of his apostolic position and authority. An attack on his apostleship by calumniators at Corinth had compelled him to boast like a fool. Now he was concluding that great boast. The Corinthians, instead of commending him and defending him before his calumniators, lent attentive ears to the criticisms of his character and his apostleship, as a result of which he was compelled to defend himself before them. And as he concludes it, he tells them that he is not trying to excuse himself, but is speaking before God in Christ, namely, at the great judgment seat of Christ. They would have to answer for the truths which he now was proclaiming. They, in turn, would be compelled to judge between the false apostles and the true Apostle Paul on the basis of the life which he lived.

The tremendous list of Paul's sufferings and trials presented in the eleventh chapter might be such in which the ordinary man would glory, for they outstripped that endured by almost any man of the apostolic group. Yet Paul immediately adds that he is "nothing." This awareness of the nothingness of himself was characteristic of St. Paul. His enemies had accused him of being nothing and he agreed. Christ is all. He is nothing. In Ephesians, when he is declaring his position as a minister of the grace of God to the heathen that he might make all men see what is the fellowship of the mystery, he declared that he was the least of all saints. Paul had an aversion to glorying, and since he was wise, he recognized that playing the part of a fool by boasting did not become him. It was not his natural rôle. Since, however, they compelled him to delineate the kind of life he had lived, he was compelled to act as a fool in telling them. No one had a better right to glory than St. Paul, yet because of all this he also reveals how God had kept him humble by giving him a thorn in the flesh. The value of that thorn and resultant humility was known by St. Paul, and only under the duress of criticism was he willing to narrate his achievements and his trials for their sake.

His apostolic position is plainly declared by him in the words, "In nothing am I behind the very chiefest apostles." It is true that Paul did not know the Lord Jesus Christ in the flesh. He refers in this epistle to having known Christ after the flesh, but he was speaking not of knowing Christ in the flesh, but of having a fleshly knowledge of the Lord Jesus Christ. He knew certain facts about the birth, life, death and teachings of the Lord Jesus Christ, but he held to this knowledge as a natural man or a fleshly man. The fact that Paul had not known Christ physically or in the flesh might make some men think him less an apostle than were Peter and James, but when St. Paul joined the great apostolic conference at Jerusalem the apostles added nothing to him. When they saw that the Gospel of the uncircumcision was committed to him, they extended to him the right hand of Christian fellowship. Do not make the mistake of thinking that Paul's teaching about the Lord Jesus Christ and the Gospel is not the heart of things. Some tell us that we must go back to Christ and not spend so much emphasis upon St. Paul's teaching, but St. Paul's gospel was the same gospel as that of Peter and that of John the beloved as well as of the other apostles. Paul was God's choice as the apostle to the Gentiles. He was added to the original apostolic band by the personal appearing of the Lord Jesus Christ to choose him to expound the gospel to the Gentiles. Hence, St. Paul is always recognized as one of the apostles.

Paul speaks of his apostolic credentials which were manifested during his stay in Corinth. Luke does not tell us in the Acts of the miracles wrought by St. Paul during his Corinthian sojourn, but there were many things in the apostolic history that were not mentioned by Luke. Here, however, Paul says, "Truly the signs of an apostle were wrought among you in all patience, in signs, and wonders, and mighty deeds." Just as many wonders and signs were done by the apostolic group following Pentecost, manifesting their credentials as the apostles of Christ, so St. Paul performed his great works and wonders in the midst of the heathen at Corinth. These signs were largely unique to the apostolic era. Christ had promised His disciples that they would do greater works than He did because He went to the Father. Immediately on the day of Pentecost they began to do those mighty works as the apostolic representatives of the Lord Jesus Christ. That was one of the four eras of miracles in the history of the world. Unless we expect the same apostolic authority which these men enjoyed, it is hardly right that we should expect a repetition of the apostolic power to do miracles. It would be easy for us to examine some of the occasions on which Paul exercised his credentials. One, of course, was the healing of the father of Publius on the isle of Malta. Another was his miraculous recovery after being stoned at Lystra, but for the most part the use of this power is not described by Luke or by Paul. The manner of using his apostolic power is described as being "among you in all patience." Even in this epistle St. Paul was exercising abundant and true love. He was not calling down fire from heaven upon his opponents, but he was pleading with men to accept the truth and do what was right. The exercise of apostolic power in patience could not be better illustrated than the relationship of St. Paul to the Christians of Corinth. He had no vindictiveness, no judgment, no punishment but only patience in the most provocative situation possible. The clue to this is given in the holy and heavenly passion which dominated the life of St. Paul in his seeking the souls of men rather than the things of men. Let us examine his reference to this in relation to the Corinthians.

I. PAUL'S LIFE OF SACRIFICE

Paul said, "I myself was not burdensome to you . . . and I will not be burdensome to you: for I seek not yours, but you." The truth had been clearly stated to the Corinthians that the laborer is worthy of his hire. This principle was expounded by St. Paul in his first epistle. He declared clearly and unmistakably that those who preach the Gospel are to live of the Gospel. Exactly as no one goeth to warfare at his own charges and as no one planteth a vineyard without eating the fruit thereof and no one tendeth a flock without drinking the milk thereof, so the preacher of the Gospel was to live by the things of the Gospel. Paul declared that it was altogether right if the apostles should sow spiritual things to these Gentiles to reap of their carnal things, for the Lord hath ordained that they who preach the Gospel should live of the Gospel. The tragedy is that so many Christians do not think that this is God's will and believe rather that a servant of the Lord should live on charity, that there should be no correct and honoroble relationship between those who receive the spiritual good from the servants of the Lord and those who minister of that good. Illustrations of such a mistaken viewpoint are legion in the history of the church. Many people have the mistaken idea that they should compel or contribute to the sacrifices which a servant of the Lord ought to bear. What folly! The sacrifices God's servants undergo ought to be voluntary and not compulsory. It is obvious that Christ has laid down the principle that disciples must be willing to leave all for His sake, whether father, mother, houses, lands, sister, brother or any other thing held dear to us, but Christ never compelled them to do such things. His followers are to live the life of sacrifice voluntarily, and not to be compelled to do it by those whom they serve.

In this connection Paul speaks satirically of the Corinthians' attitude. He himself had never utilized his right and privilege of living by the Gospel He had labored with his own hands to support himself in order not to be burdensome to the Christians, but now they held this very thing against him and criticized him for it.

So Paul said, "What is it wherein ye were inferior to other churches, except it be that I myself was not burdensome to you? forgive me this wrong." Others, no doubt, had received gifts and support from the Corinthian Church, but St. Paul had never accepted any. Some churches base their superiority on their income, on the salary they pay the minister or on other mundane considerations. We have often heard such things referred to in the introductions of prominent Christian workers at public gatherings and services. By this standard, naturally, the Corinthian Church would be inferior to other churches, for it had not paid St. Paul a salary at all, for he had worked with his hands. Yet what wonderful works have been done by men who have supported themselves by secular work while doing the Lord's work as an avocation. I think now of a medical man whom I recently met in Wshington, D.C., who spends his Sundays and spare time voluntarily laboring in decadent churches. As soon as one is thoroughly renovated and the congregation built up, he asks them to call a minister and he himself goes on to labor in some other field. Paul ironically asked the Corinthians to forgive him for such a wrong in that he did not charge them for his ministry. Yet he called to their attention that it was a labor of love and "the more abundantly I love you, the less I be loved." The wrong was really on the other side. They had owed him a great debt of gratitude, which they were not discharging. There will be some great accounts of injustice and fickleness to faithful, sacrificial servants of the Lord that will have to be settled by some Christians at the judgment bar. St. Paul did not escape that experience in his apostolic ministry.

But the aim of the true servant of God is not for the possessions of those whom he serves. Only a false apostle seeks the wool of the sheep rather than the sheep themselves. St. Paul stated once and for all the real aim of an under shepherd of the Lord. "I seek not yours, but you." The passion of a true shepherd as taught by the example of the Lord Jesus Christ is not to fleece the sheep but to give his life for the sheep. Thereby he proves that he is not a hireling but a true shepherd. Power rests upon a personality who is dedicated to redeeming men, to the winning of souls, to seeking souls, not worldly gain. Such a personality is irresistible in its persuasive power. Undoubtedly, the influence of the ministry and of the servants of God will depend upon the possession of this attitude, declared by St. Paul.

II. THE PRINCIPLE A LAW OF NATURE

St. Paul appealed to a law of nature in support of this attitude in his life. Said he, "For the children ought not to lay up for the parents, but the parents for the children." This is a truth evident to all. When babes make their advent into the world they are helpless, indigent and dependent, and so babes in Christ need the ministry of their parent. Even to advanced years children can hardly contribute much to the financial support of the family. Nature decrees that parents shall pass away before the children and that they shall have no need for hoarding wealth for themselves, whereas a legacy left to children is beneficial. Usually all that parents ask from their children is love, respect and obedience.

The analogy is applied by St. Paul to himself and the church. He was the spiritual father of the Corinthian Church. Through his labors, trials, sufferings and faithfulness that church had been born and he loved them in the Lord. Gladly, said he, he would spend and be spent for them. The last bit of strength of his was theirs for the asking. He was willing spiritually, physically and mentally to exhaust himself for the sake of that church because of the love he had for it. Regardless of their not requiting his love, he loved them just the same. Their attitude was one of disloyalty, ingratitude and disrespect. His was one of continuing love.

Everything Paul had in mind was for the edification of this church. His warnings, chastening, corrections and pleas were all for their good, for their upbuilding, their establishment in Christ. This was all that he wanted for those Corinthians. Judged by such a standard, how far short of a true spiritual ministry the service of many of us falls. Paul's desire was for them to be right with God, to be edified, to be true believers. He wanted them, nothing less. This is the measure by which to judge our ministry and service, our motive and aim as servants of the living God.

III. THE PERSONAL LOVE OF GOD

The application of this brief statement, "I seek not yours, but you," must not be left with men alone, for it may be lifted to the realm of the Divine heart and mind. Thus also God's dealings with us are aimed to win us entirely to Him. His is the position of a loving, pleading, heavenly Father. He is correctly illustrated by the forgiving father in the parable of the Prodigal Son. "Not yours, but you I want," says the Lord. His redemptive love was manifested in Christ, in whom He reconciled the world unto Himself. He asks nothing of men but believing faith revealing their gratitude to Him for what He has done. He manifests this love in His providential care over us through our experience. His recurrent mercy constantly declares that He seeks us and not ours. Hence, He exercises fatherly chastening, restraint, limitation, judgment and guidance, all because He is desirous of winning us entirely to Himself.

We ought to recognize the difference between giving what is ours and giving ourselves. Just as Paul held the example of the Macedonians up to the Corinthians, we ought to examine that illustration. They first gave themselves to the Lord and then they were willing to give of their material substance. Once we have given ourselves to Him, there is nothing else which we will withhold. Therefore, let there be no confusion in mind between the giving of things and the giving of self. God wants us. It is not sufficient to dedicate our children to Him, to present our tithes and offerings to Him, even to preserve the Lord's day holy unto Him, if we are reserving ourselves from Him. Only consecration of self in all of the departments of our life is what God seeks. He wishes to possess us entirely.

Does God possess you? Have you ever covenanted with God thus, telling him that you finally and unalterably turn the control of your life over to Him and that He possesses you? If you have done that, have you fulfilled your agreement with Him since, or have you violated that agreement, repudiated your word and continued to live for self? What is your state now? Perhaps you have never given yourself to God as His possession. Gladly has He spent for you, giving of Himself on the cross that you might be saved. Paul expresses it, "He that spared not his own Son, but delivered him up for us all, how shall he not with him also freely give us all things?" Yes, God was spent on Calvary and we may be sure that out of His great heart of love, ungrateful and unresponsive though we may have been, He has been seeking us, our souls, our lives, ourselves. Let us give them to Him.

XXX

EXAMINE YOURSELVES, WHETHER YE BE IN THE FAITH

TEXT: *"Examine yourselves, whether ye be in the faith; prove your own selves. Know ye not your own selves, how that Jesus Christ is in you, except ye be reprobates?"*—II COR. 12:20—13:1-10.

PAUL'S REFERENCE to his intention of coming again to Corinth raises a question of whether it was a third preparation for coming or a third visit. There are some things which favor each argument, and a decision upon the matter must be left to the scholars, but it seems more simple to us if we consider this to refer to his second visit, and that he was hindered from coming to them before this time. An interim visit during his residence at Ephesus is feasible, however. Conditions of sin and rebellion which developed in this church of which he was the spiritual father and which he dearly loved necessitated the visit. These sins included divisions, parties, strife, immorality, drunkenness, error, and resistance to his authority. The first epistle to the Corinthians deals with these aberrations, and the visit of Titus was intended to correct them. When Titus returned with the story of the repentance of the Corinthians, the discipline of the erring ones, and their obedience to him, Paul was greatly comforted.

This letter was written under the influence of the good news which Titus brought. Chapters 1 to 7 constitute an outpouring of Paul's soul concerning the Gospel and the ministry. Chapters 8 and 9 constitute an exhortation concerning the great collection. Chapters 10 to 13 constitute a final vindication of Paul against the attacks of false apostles, with a strict warning concerning his own coming.

The purpose of this projected coming of St. Paul to Corinth was formally to examine the condition of the congregation. It was his hope that he would not discover them in unrepented sin. He said, "I fear, lest, when I come, I shall not find you such as I would, and that I shall be found unto you such as ye would not: lest there be debates, envyings, wraths, strifes, backbitings, whisperings, swellings, tumults." He feared lest he must reveal himself in a capacity of apostolic authority which they would not desire. He had threatened in his first epistle to come with a rod and to discipline these sinning believers. He tells them now that he will not spare them, and for this cause he is writing with "sharpness," that he might produce a transformation in them before it is too late. Formal hearings of a church court would establish by two or three witnesses the guilt of those who needed discipline. A true judgment would prevail. At this coming, Paul did not intend to reveal weakness, but the power of God. He had ministered in weakness, in love, and in suffering. Now, he would exercise the powerful, apostolic prerogative of judgment. He was going to edify and establish the church in righteousness. He desired, as he stated, their perfection, and prayed that they would do no evil. His coming was intended to remove these imperfections by discipline and judgment. Their character was dearer to him than his reputation.

At the same time, this was a warning to the Christians to examine themselves by way of preparation. He urged them to ascertain whether they were in the faith, that is, saved, joined to Jesus Christ in the new life, or whether they were self-deceived. There was a grave possibility in the light of their sins that they had a spurious faith, and, being self-deceived, were holding a false hope. God expects holiness in those who profess to be in the faith.

He advised them to prove themselves. They were to put the test of Christian faith to themselves rather than to others. When something is awry in us, we have a tendency to criticize and condemn others. That is the time to look at ourselves. These Corinthians had indulged in criticism of St. Paul. They would have done better had they examined their own lives.

He advised them to learn if Christ was in them, or if they were reprobates, which meant lost, condemned, and set for judgment. We may know that Christ is in us by the fruits of His Spirit. Do not take this greatest of all decisions and matters for granted. You may be mistaken.

There is a spiritual analogy in this teaching for us, namely, the crisis of the Word of God coming to us today. That Word is not only historical, pertaining to the Corinthians, but is the living Word, and it faces us with a crisis.

I. Our Coming Lord

Christ came to the Corinthians in the word of Paul. Paul claimed that Christ was speaking in him, that the power of Christ was exercised in him towards them, and that Christ in him would not spare them in judgment. Through the apostolic manifestation, Christ, the

Gospel, and life and death as results of the reaction to the Gospel were present with the Corinthians in St. Paul's ministry. That is always true, that wherever the living Word of God faces men they are brought to a crisis. The two personal comings of St. Paul were almost symbolical. First he came in weakness and in humiliation. Next he promised to come in power and judgment. In the interim, his letters speak to them on his behalf.

Thus God's Word has come to us in Christ. Christ first came in weakness and humiliation. He is described as "crucified through weakness." Sin and sinful men did what they pleased to Christ in His offer to us of the Gospel and of salvation. They rejected Him and scorned His teachings. They blasphemed Him, buffeted and scourged Him, mocked and crucified Him. Evil seemed to triumph over Christ in His first coming into the world. Such weakness is often taken as the nature of Christianity. Men seem to think they have a right to persecute, calumniate, and reproach Christians and Christ, and then they resent it when they are resisted. This weakness is only half of the story. Thus Paul came in weakness, human insufficiency, and humility, but at the same time he possessed other power. But some people have received Christ when He came in His weakness, humiliation, simplicity, and pure truth. They became Christian believers and were saved. They received His dying for them, His meekness and admission as the means of their salvation and as the way of life. All such live now by the power of God. Thus St. Paul said, "Though he [Christ] was crucified through weakness, yet he liveth by the power of God. For we also are weak in him, but we shall live with him by the power of God toward you." Yes, Christ will come again in glory and power. He is absent now, but He speaks to us by the written Word, urging, inviting, and warning. We must give heed to that written Word. But He is coming to judge, and He will not spare. He also will establish righteousness. Great are Paul's passages on the holy awe in which the believer should anticipate that second coming of Christ. We are told that we must stand before the judgment seat to answer for the deeds done in the body, and we are warned that only the commendation of the Lord will count. When Christ comes again, it will be for judgment. And yet that very coming is the great hope of believers, for in that hour they shall be vindicated before the world. That coming has been prepared. It is imminent, and of it we are warned. It should be the source of our purification, for "He that hath this hope in him purifieth himself even as he is pure."

II. OUR CONDITION OF LIFE

It is time to try ourselves, whether we be in the faith. We may test ourselves by the truth which the saints believe. The Gospel is the truth, once and for all committed to the saints. Christ tarried on earth forty days after His death and preceding His resurrection in order to give instruction to His disciples concerning the Kingdom of God. The only way of accounting for the unity of the teaching of the apostles in a body of doctrine is because of this instruction given by the Lord Jesus Christ. Generally, that doctrine is summarized by the historical Church in the Apostles' Creed. The faith here means the objective set of truths making up the Christian religion and differentiating it from all others. It is folly to think that we can worship a different Christ or receive the communion from a Christ different from this Christ of history and Scripture. Examine yourselves, whether you believe these truths. Is this Christ, who was God incarnate, dying on the cross and living again, the object of your confidence? This is the first step you must take—to lend assent to the truth.

Examine yourself, whether you have made a committal to Christ, whether He be in you. The essence of a committal is the step of trust, acting on the truth or the Word of God. Paul said, "We can do nothing against the truth, but for the truth." This is a mere committal. Salvation necessitates a trust in the truth in Christ, that is, a hearty reliance on Him for salvation. Nothing else constitutes a committal. Intellectual assent is insufficient. Baptismal position cannot substitute for it, and church acceptance is not enough. Our committal must be to Christ. He must be our Lord, Christianity our way, and holiness our life. This is evidence of a committal.

We should examine ourselves, whether our works reveal themselves as the fruit of righteousness. Righteousness inevitably follows such a committal to Christ. The mind of Christ ought to be in us. The Spirit of Christ ought to be in us. The will of Christ ought to be in us, all of which will produce the fruit of the Christian life. If the opposite is true, your profession is incredible. Everything the Corinthians did is repeated in the life of some professing Christian today. Low moral and spiritual standards give a false impression of the Church. God desires our perfection, our cleansing from sin, our maturity in life. If we do not cleanse ourselves, but continue in sin, there is grave doubt of our being in the faith.

III. THE CRISIS OF FAITH

Paul said "Jesus Christ is in you, except ye be reprobates." The Word is coming to you now, just as if you were face to face with Christ in His weakness, His humiliation, and His dying. The sacrament of the Lord's Supper is the parabolic and symbolic Word. As Christ is the eternal, the incarnate, the living, the prophetic Word, He is also the parabolic Word. Hence, when you take the communion, you are meeting and facing Christ exactly as you face Him in the Bible. This act of receiving the communion is your crisis. Are you submissive, obedient, worshipful, receptive? If so, there is life and blessing for you from Him.

There are two alternatives held before us. The first is Christ in you. Christ in you means the condition of forgiveness, salvation, deliverance, life, and glory. Paul preached "Christ in you the hope of glory." This is a great mystery, namely, the mystery of the new birth, but you may know that He is in you by the witness of the Spirit given unto you. "In Christ" and "Christ in you" describe the Christian's new standing before God. "If any man be in Christ Jesus he is a new creature." He has a new existence before God. Christ in you is synonymous with having eternal life. John says, "He that hath the Son hath life eternal." This is victory, perfection, and sanctification.

The other alternative is that of being reprobate. Such an individual is lost, regardless of his profession. If Christ is not in him, death will be the gate of hell for him, and the punishment of judgment awaits him. Being without God, he is without hope. For such a one to partake of the Lord's Supper is to eat and to drink damnation. The Word coming to him in a crisis is for his eternal loss. Therefore, let not a true believer act as a reprobate, appearing to be one before the world. It is a disgrace to permit sin in a believer's life. Paul said, examine yourself, not examine another. If never before you have received Christ crucified for you, for your salvation, and for your life, receive Him now, that you may live by the power of God, delivered. When we have looked to self and repudiated our sin, we may look to Him for cleansing.

This is your crisis, and on it your heavenly status depends. Are you in the faith, or are you reprobate?

XXXI

PEACE, THE GIFT OF GOD'S LOVE

TEXT: *"Be perfect, be of good comfort, be of one mind, live in peace; and the God of love and peace shall be with you."*—II COR. 13:11-14.

THIS IS PAUL'S valedictory to the Corinthians. It begins with the word "farewell." It is the end of a long course of instruction which we have followed in detail. Paul speaks at various times as a father, a teacher, a friend, an authoritative apostle, and a judge. The two epistles to the Corinthians take children in the faith and lead them through great truth into sanctification and perfection. This was no small task. His farewell to that church will be our farewell to this epistle. We are happy that he sums up his advice and message in a final statement, for it is replete with meaning.

A memorable address was made at Dartmouth College at a recent graduation before seniors and their fathers by a lawyer who was a trustee of the college. Said he:

"My generation forgot some things and overlooked others which you can neither forget nor overlook if there is to be an ultimate, satisfactory result. . . . We completely misconceive the nature of peace. Peace is not merely the cessation of violence for the maintenance of material comfort. . . . What is peace? In olden times the salutation, 'Peace be with you,' indicated the estimation in which you were held. The Lord Jesus Christ said, 'My peace be with you. My peace I give unto you.' What did He mean? At the very time He made that statement, men were slaughtering each other all over the world just as they are today. We know that the best thing we can wish for any one who has died is, 'May he rest in peace.' The clue may be found in His statement that He gave not as this world gives. I think He meant that interior peace, based on conviction and faith, which armed a man against the things of this world, and made him impervious to famine, wars, cataclysms, and even death."

This is the kind of peace about which Paul was talking. There never was a greater need for it than in this present disturbed world.

Thus we see how appropriate is Paul's valedictory to the Corinthians. We have little interest in the early Christian custom of greeting one another with a holy kiss which designated the family unity, but we have much interest in the source and the possession of this peace. In our age, if we do not have an interior peace, we will have no peace at all. We live in a time of strife, tumult, and confusion of a revolutionary era. This thought of Paul's, repeated elsewhere in Holy Scripture, that God is the God of peace, is very precious.

I. THE SOURCE OF PEACE—THE TRIUNE GOD

Paul clearly states the doctrine of the Trinity in this apostolic benediction used universally in the Christian Church, "The grace of the Lord Jesus Christ, and the love of God, and the communion of the Holy Ghost, be with you all." It is not a statement of the relation of the persons of the Trinity to each other, but is a statement which, along with many others, brings out the doctrine of the Trinity. A dogmatic statement of the doctrine of the Trinity must be founded on many Scriptures. Here, the Trinitarian doctrine is taking form in the Church in the revelation of God in Christ and by the experience of the Divine life which the Church had through the Spirit. How any one can read the New Testament without seeing the foundations of this truth is difficult to know. Well does this benediction of the apostle forever raise a barrier between Christian and Unitarian Churches.

The Bible presents God as a triunity—Father, Son, and Holy Spirit. The Greek Church describes this triunity with the words "same" and "being." The three centers of consciousness of Deity were of the same being, that is, eternal, coexistent, and equal in love, knowledge, and power. The Latin Church speaks of one substance, but three persons. We do not believe in a triad of deities, or in three manifestations of Deity, but in a Triunity. The Bible truth explains this by presenting the Son as eternal, pre-existent, incarnate God, with glorified humanity. The Spirit is described as proceeding from the Father and from the Son, equal in attributes. The Bible does not speak of successive manifestations of God in three persons, but simultaneous manifestations. Philip Schaff says, "It has been looked upon in all ages as the sacred symbol and fundamental doctrine of the Christian Church, with the denial of which the Divinity of Christ and of the Holy Spirit, and the Divine character of redemption and sanctification fall to the ground." The ignorance of this doctrine in the Church is alarming. All that some people know about the Trinity is this apostolic benediction. The Spirit of God has been reduced to a mere influence or attitude. Christ has been humanized so that He is only a man in whom God manifested Himself, as He may in us. Many people believe that Unitarianism is Christianity, but the Bible presents conversation between the Father and the Son, in which there is mutual address. The Father said, "Thou art my Son." The

Son said, "Father, glorify thou me." Nevertheless, it is true that by the work of redemption we may become sons of God, so that we may partake of this Divine, eternal life of the Trinity.

The activity of the Trinity is revealed in this benediction. First is mentioned "The grace of the Lord Jesus Christ." Why does Christ come first? Because Divine favor and grace can come only through Christ. This is an absolute rule, due to the Divine righteousness. Sinful man cannot stand before a holy God without the mediatorship of Christ. Some think that they may approach God in a substitute way, but this is not the Gospel. God's justice must be satisfied before He can receive us. This implies that Christians alone are being addressed, for only they have known the wonders of Divine grace. On unmerited grace the believer depends until the end. The cleansing blood of Christ and mercy of God enable him to enter heaven.

The love of God comes second because this benediction is pronounced upon persons who already are Christians. It is the love of God for His own, making possible many gifts which cannot be bestowed upon the unregenerate. Grace is really love toward the undeserving, emanating from God in Christ, and grace and love toward believers involve communion. These cannot be separated. The grace is properly first.

The love of God is the outgoing love of the Eternal for the unsaved, as evidenced in the gift of Christ. By this He commends His love toward us that while we were sinners Christ died for us. Having expressed that love which made us His own, we now come to know the love from which nothing can separate us, which is the source of every blessing bountifully bestowed upon us. God loves His own, and, as seen in Christ, He loves them unto the end. It is this God of love Who is with us. Therefore, the sinner who bows at the cross, overwhelmed by amazing grace, shall rise to live in the sunshine of Divine love.

The communion of the Spirit demands a person, for a person alone can establish communion. Such a person the Spirit is. Jesus attributed to Him the powers of personality, and applied the personal pronoun to Him many times in His address to the disciples in the upper room. Here the Spirit is placed beside the other two persons of the Trinity. In the Divine economy, He is the agent Who makes grace and love effective. He alone regenerates, quickens, and works God's will. A Christianity without the person and work of the Spirit is impotent and false, imparting no salvation or present experience.

Do you know this Triune God? Do you know the Lord Jesus

Christ as the God of grace, removing your sin, reconciling you to the Father, procuring Divine favor and blessing in your life? Or is He merely a name? To know His grace, you must meet Him at Calvary, bow at His pierced feet, weep out your repentance, and follow Him. Do you know the love of God, the Father, or the God of love, the God who so loved the world that He gave His only begotten Son. If so, He must be loved in return. Do you know the Holy Spirit, convicting, comforting, delivering, guiding, helping, and bestowing fellowship with the Triune God? If so, you can sing

> "Holy, Holy, Holy! Lord God Almighty!
> All Thy works shall praise Thy name,
> In earth, in sky, in sea;
> Holy, Holy, Holy! Lord God Almighty!
> God in three persons, Blessed Trinity."

II. THE PRINCIPLE OF PEACE

How shall we assure ourselves of the presence of this Triune God of love and peace? Paul says, "Be perfect . . . and the God of love and peace shall be with you."

To be perfect means to be adjusted to God's will. The word is *katartizo*. The word is used nine times in the New Testament as a medical term, signifying the replacing of a joint after dislocation. The meaning is never sinless, though holiness must be an inevitable result of such adjustment of man to the Divine will. Paul used the word in the beginning of his first epistle to Corinth, saying, "I beseech you . . . that ye be perfectly joined together in the same mind and in the same judgment." He wanted no divisions. Only under such conditions can the body of Christ, which is the Church, function properly. It cannot function with dislocated joints. In Hebrews, the word is used, "The God of peace make you perfect to do his will." Here again it means adjustment to the will of God. This time it is individual. Your problem in perfection is whether you will adjust yourself to the will of God. Then and then only can He keep you from falling and from sin. With dislocated joints, one cannot run. He would stumble and fall. There are no prizes for such a one. Hence, if we would overcome and be victorious, we must be perfect or adjusted to God's will. In the life of Jacob, this necessitated a great wrestling with God. Before his struggle, he was out of adjustment spiritually. His mind was not adjusted to God's will, but his body was perfect. After the struggle with God, he limped physically, but he was in harmony, at peace, perfect with God. Let Jacob's struggle be yours, and, as he did, say, "I will not let thee go, except thou bless me." Sad to say, there are many in Jacob's class who must be beaten bodily before they will adjust their minds—away from silly things—to the will of God. Sanctification has exactly this meaning. Paul says, "The very God of peace sanctify you wholly." He means that we shall be separated from things sinful, as from weights which hinder us in running a race. If you would win the race, you must be separated to God. This means practical holiness. Hence, Paul quoted the Lord as saying, "Come ye out from among them . . . and be ye holy." "Let us cleanse ourselves from all filthiness of the flesh and spirit, perfecting holiness in the fear of God." In all these, peace is connected with our relation with the God of peace. Once we bring ourselves into harmony with Him, the interior peace of God, which passeth all understanding, will keep our hearts and minds in Christ. Moreover, it is this inner peace which enables us to live in peace. This is most practical. Christian perfection means living in peace with one another.

Paul says, "Be of good comfort . . . and the God of love and peace shall be with you." This returns us to the introduction to the epistle where he calls on God as the God who comforteth us in all our tribulation. That comfort is wrought by the Holy Spirit. Jesus called Him the Comforter, and His presence constitutes the Divine help in all our tribulations and trials. Peace is also connected with the Comforter. Jesus said, "Peace I leave with you, my peace I give unto you. . . . Let not your heart be troubled, neither let it be afraid." The Spirit is God with us now, and our yielding to Him is necessary for the spiritual rest and comfort of the Divine presence. One cannot comfort himself. He must be comforted of God. All is provided for us by the Triune God, so that our lack is our fault rather the Lord's. "Be ye comforted." Put yourself in a place of adjustment to His will that the Spirit may fill and comfort you.

Lastly, Paul says, "Be of one mind . . . and the God of love and peace shall be with you." Translated, this is: Mind the same thing. This speaks of unity among the believers, like the unity of the Church at Pentecost. Such unity can come only by seeking God's will. This is what the entire epistle was written for. Only peace can result for those that are of one mind, and that, the mind of Christ. When an individual is single-minded, he is an integrated personality. When a home is single-minded, there is peace. When a Church is single-minded, it has unity.

III. THE FRUITFULNESS OF PEACE

The result of such peace is that the God of love and peace shall be with you. Think of what the presence of the Triune God in your individual life means. In comparison with this, nothing else matters; health, prosperity, home, war, whatever you may mention, all are inconsequential in comparison with the presence of God. If God is with us, that is best of all. That is why Moses declared in the Word of Truth, "If thy presence go not with me, carry us not up hence." But when God is present, this is the source of all other things bestowed in His great love. We know that we can trust Him.

Have you the consciousness of His presence? What a wonderful thing it was for the disciples to walk with Jesus. They enjoyed His teaching, His assistance, His kindness, His direction. What despair they had in His absence after the crucifixion. That brought disillusionment and discouragement, but how their joy returned when they realized God's presence and power in the baptism of the Holy Spirit. They received new life, undertook greater labors, and had wonderful blessings.

You, too, may have the blessing of His presence. You may have the peace of God, enjoy the comfort of God, be adjusted to the will of God, experience the holiness of God, and be comforted in His service. All this the God of peace and love brings to us. If you have not the presence of this God of peace and love, if you do not enjoy His peace, begin that adjustment to His will now: confess, commit, surrender, and obey Him, and you will enjoy His peace and love.

What greater wish could we have for you than that which Paul had for these Corinthians in his valedictory message? "Finally, brethren, farewell. Be perfect, be of good comfort, be of one mind, live in peace; and the God of love and peace shall be with you."

www.ingramcontent.com/pod-product-compliance
Lightning Source LLC
Chambersburg PA
CBHW050340230426
43663CB00010B/1929